PRAISE FOR

Hindsights

The WISDOM and BREAKTHROUGHS of REMARKABLE PEOPLE

"HINDSIGHTS offers messages of hope, spirituality, and the universality of the human experience."
—*Bookshelf*

"You'll want to buy ten copies to give to your closest friends."
—*Mactalk*

"Thirty-three illuminating interviews with a prismatic spectrum of contemporary heroes."
—*Seattle Times*

"An offbeat, unsettling, at times inspiring, and insightful book by one of the most uncommon business thinkers in America today."
—*Industry Week*

"An intelligent, warm, lively, thoughtful, and genuinely insightful book [that's] fun to read."
—BELLERUTH NAPARSTEK,
author of *Staying Well with Guided Imagery*

"A fabulous collection of candid interviews. The hindsights of these individuals are personal yet strike a common chord of humanity."
—*Dallas Morning News*

"A beautifully presented collection of interviews with a thoughtfully diverse group of individuals."
—*Willamette Week* (CA)

"Engaging....The interviews are dynamite. HINDSIGHTS is a book people will want to share with others."
—*California Computer News*

W9-AFF-801

Hindsights

The WISDOM and BREAKTHROUGHS of REMARKABLE PEOPLE

GUY KAWASAKI

WARNER BOOKS

A Time Warner Company

Warner Books Edition

This Warner Books edition is published by arrangement with
Beyond Words Publishing, Inc.,
13950 NW Pumpkin Ridge Road, Hillsboro, OR 97124.

Warner Books, Inc., 1271 Avenue of the Americas, New York, NY 10020

 A Time Warner Company

Printed in the United States of America

First Warner Books Printing: September 1995

10   9   8   7   6   5   4   3   2   1

Library of Congress Cataloging-in-Publication Data
Kawasaki, Guy
    Hindsights : the wisdom and breakthroughs of remarkable people /
Guy Kawasaki : illustration, Qiana Rickabaugh.
        p. cm.
    Originally published: Hillsboro, Ore. : Beyond Words Publishing,
c1993.
    Includes Index.
    ISBN 0-446-67115-0 (trade)
    1. Conduct of life. 2. Interviews—United States. I. Title.
[BJ1581.2.K36 1995]
170'.44—dc20   95-11978
                                                                CIP

Cover design and photography by Julia Kushnirsky

To my wife, Beth,

without whom all hindsights

would be regrets

CONTENTS

. . .

ACKNOWLEDGMENTS

· · ·

The first draft of anything is shit.

ERNEST HEMINGWAY

You may think that creating a book involves an author sitting on a veranda and gazing over a sun-bleached seashore as prose traces an idyllic path through his consciousness and onto a page. Guess again. Creating a book is work. It is also a team effort. This is the *Hindsights* team:

Thirty-three people appear in this book. They gave generously of their time to allow me to interview them. More importantly, they gave generously of their souls.

Julie Livingston, my editor at Beyond Words Publishing, Inc., and John Michel, friend, editor, and computer wimp, had the most influence on *Hindsights.* Without them, I might not have finished the book—and it certainly would not have been as good.

Jean Mickelson and Richard Theriault were subjected to the most painful tasks: reading early, numerous, and repeated drafts of interviews. They were judges, devil's advocates, and coaches.

I interviewed many more people than those who appear in *Hindsights.* They merit acknowledgment because everyone I interviewed contributed to the book.

Neil Abercrombie, Robert Alvarado, Jonathan Arnold, Bill Ashby, Joel Belz, Mike Bessie, Jim Bouton, Nathaniel Brandon, Peggy Cartwright, Lanice Coleman, David Coon, LaDoris Cordell, Jonathan Crane, Stan Dale, Donald Dell, Peter Deuben, Indra Devi, Ed Dwight, Doug Engelbart, Margie Erickson, Dorothy Fadiman, Jackie Finnerty, Lazlo Fono, Scott Gilbert, Mimi Gina, William Goldberg, Doug Hall, Susan Hancock, Wendy Hoag, Cynthia Hoffman, Richie Horowitz, Rika Hoshizaki, William Hudnut III, Sandra Kurtzig, Gaelyn Larrick, Karyn Mashima, Thomas McInerney, John McMillan, Joyce Meskis, Joe Moglia, Gordon Moore, Gordon Nakagawa, James Opfer, Cleo Parker-Robinson, Michail Perelman, Sam Reeves, Anne Robinson, Bob Rogers, SARK, Lee Sarokin, Nicki Scully, Eric Sollee,

Eric Stanton, Bob Stupack, Heng Sure, Y. A. Tittle, Norman Vaughan, Ken Veit, Marianne Weidlein, Hans Winiger, Hazel Wolf, Gordon Wright, Carl Yanagawa, and Carla Zizo.

Behind the scenes, dozens of people provided assistance including arranging for interviews, furnishing background information, and providing feedback. I apologize to anyone who I've left out.

Tim Basham, Cliff Bernath, Richard Bolles, Greg Carlson, Dan Chun, Pam Chun, Mary Core, Joe Cosby, Marie D'Amico, Michael Daughtery, Bert Decker, Jan Deprim, Julie Duffy, Paul Edwards, Ted Ewanciw, Rob Falk, Mike Franco, Dave Grabel, Karen Gustin, Bill Harkins, Kathryn Henkens, Lee Hinde, Craig Hirai, Joe Holiday, Ruth Holt, Linda Illsley, Leor Jacob, Bill James, Jennifer Johnston, Beth Kawasaki, Aaron Kirshner, Barry Landis, John Lanyi, Joe Marsella, Marty Mazner, Dale Minami, Jeff Mori, Sandy Mori, Norman Nason, Genny Nelson, Mark Neuenschwander, Paul O'Brien, Randall Oxford, Nick Roberts, Adam Robinson, David Romm, Audrey Rust, Jack Schachtebeck, Dan Shafer, Alma Shepherd, Gerry Smedinghoff, Dwight Smith, Bob Soltis, Tassia Soodi, Will Spens, Linda Taft, Rick Taft, Laura Tucker, Stephanie Vardavas, Jane Walsh, Karen Whitehouse, and Jon Winokur.

Kim Alfano, John Fox, and Regina Lau transcribed inaudible tapes and made them into text. Inez Templeton provided research assistance. Jacqueline Kan, copyediting goddess, made things right *and* better. Marvin Moore provided the final touches.

Jon Olsen, Heidi Rickabaugh, Qiana Rickabaugh, and Robin Rickabaugh (the "Flying Rickabaughs") of Principia Graphica designed and illustrated this book, and Barry Smith of Blue Sky Research set the type. Together, they produced a book that exceeded my expectations—and my expectations were very high.

Finally, my thanks to Cindy Black and Richard Cohn at Beyond Words Publishing, Inc., for believing in me and my vision for *Hindsights*. (We'll show New York!)

That's the *Hindsights* team. If you like this book, give them the credit. If you don't, it's my fault. In either case, in hindsight, no author has worked with a finer group of people.

$\mathcal{F}$OREWORD

. . .

I have a friend whose favorite criticism of a movie is: "I didn't like it. The characters never grew, never learned anything from their mistakes, just kept repeating the same old behavior. They were the same at the end of the movie as they were at the beginning."

In the movie called "life," the same criticism may be made. Some people never grow, never learn from their mistakes, just keep repeating the same old behavior. While others, to the contrary, continue to grow—not outwardly, but inwardly—as long as they draw mortal breath. In our best moments, we want to emulate them. We want to be people who grow, personally, all our lives.

The key is *action* and *reflection*. Action, reflection, action, reflection. That is the rhythm of those lives which continue always to grow. As the philosopher has said, "The unexamined life is not worth living." Live your daily life, live it to its fullest, live it in the most impulsive way and richest way you can; but then find regular times to sit down and meditate upon what you have done. See what you can learn. I know a man who every night sits down opposite a blank white wall in his house and mentally replays the day, as though he were watching a movie of his life—to see what he did right, what he did wrong, and what he can learn from his mistakes.

"Hindsights" is an alternative word to describe the fruits of such reflection. We look back. We tell our story. We see what we can learn from our story, what we can do differently in the future, how we can be more wise. That is our hindsight, which we then carry forward with us into the future.

The people my friend Guy has interviewed in this book are primarily people committed to personal growth. Here, in their conversations with Guy, they look back. They tell their story. And they summarize their learnings, their hindsights. Where they do not summarize their learnings, you are left to your own deduction as to what they were and are.

Guy, as interviewer, has done his work well. Now you, as reader, must do yours. Here you will be helped if, as you read each story, you reflect upon what there is in your life that is similar to the experiences they are recounting. For, no other man's story, no other woman's story is ever boring so long as you can find some way to relate it to your own life. I hope that by the end of this book you will not be the same, but will have learned and will have grown, in this wonderful, fascinating movie called "life."

Richard N. Bolles
author of *What Color Is Your Parachute?*

$\mathcal{I}$NTRODUCTION

. . .

When you sell a man a book you don't sell him just twelve ounces of paper and ink and glue—you sell him a whole new life.

CHRISTOPHER MORLEY

This book was born of pain. I began writing it as my wife and I reached a moment of truth in our marriage: Should we get divorced? When you face this kind of decision, you become enormously retrospective and contemplative. What could I have done to make a better marriage? Where did I go wrong? Why did this happen to us? These kinds of questions dominate your thinking.

Eventually I extended my reflective thinking beyond my marriage to my life. I realized that I had not spent enough time with my family and friends. I wondered why I hadn't broadened my interests beyond my work. My success seemed unimportant faced with the prospect of not having a life partner to share it with.

Over the course of several months of counseling and intense conversations with my wife, I recognized that many other people have gone through emotional and difficult experiences before me. I wondered what advice they would have. What did they value? What did they regret? What would they do differently? What were their hindsights?

I could not find a book that provided the answers I was looking for, although I found plenty of books filled with platitudes. I also found plenty of interview books, but none of them came right out and said, "This is what happened to me, and this is what I learned." So, I wrote the book I was trying to find.

I asked people—not necessarily rich, famous, or powerful, but people who'd had significant life experiences—to share their insights, revelations, and regrets with me. In many cases, they unveiled painful and traumatic moments so that others might benefit from their experience.

The most important lesson I learned from listening to these people talk about their hindsights is that people are more alike than they are different.

Although no two interviewees ever said the same thing the same way, four conclusions appeared again and again:

· We are what we are because of what we've done and what's been done to us. We cannot change our past; we can only learn from it.

· Happiness is a function of family, friends, and spirituality. Not money. Not power. Not social status.

· Great things are accomplished because we didn't know how hard they would be up front.

· Every person has the ability to change and improve the life of another person.

This book is optimistic. It is about hope, progress, and change. Interviewing these people changed my life. I hope that reading this book will change yours.

Guy Kawasaki
September 1993
San Francisco, California

Defying Gravity

. . .

Brenda Reed

. . .

PEACEMAKER

$\mathscr{P}$ERSEVERING AGAINST THE SYSTEM

. . .

There is in every woman's heart a spark of heavenly fire, which lies dormant in the broad daylight of prosperity; but which kindles up, and beams and blazes in the dark hour of adversity.

WASHINGTON IRVING

On February 1, 1968, Captain James Eddie Reed was killed in the Tet Offensive in Vietnam when a mortar round exploded near him. In July 1987 his wife, Brenda Reed (age forty-six), reviewed her husband's service records and reconstructed the events of his death. Based on what she found, she believed her husband acted with gallantry and deserved a Silver Star. She was determined that he would get this honor, so in July 1988 she submitted an application to the Army Board for the Correction of Military Records.

In his final battle, Captain Reed and his men were outnumbered ten to one. The mortar round killed him and three lieutenants while he was saving the rest of his infantry company by directing gunfire from a parapet. Captain Reed had already been awarded two Bronze Stars for valor and meritorious service, an Army Commendation Medal for valor, a Purple Heart for being wounded in a previous battle, and a Purple Heart posthumously. However, he was not awarded a Silver Star—a medal given for "gallantry in action against an opposing armed force"—for his bravery in the battle that took his life.

The Army Board for the Correction of Military Records stonewalled Brenda for two years, so she started circulating a petition and telling her story to the press. Finally, in November 1990, the Army agreed to give Captain Reed a Bronze Star, but Brenda would be satisfied with nothing less than a Silver Star. Finally, in June 1991, twenty-three years after his death, the Army awarded a Silver Star to Captain Reed. Brenda's successful quest shows that a person can challenge the establishment and win. Her story is about perseverance.

Reed invited me to her temporary home in Oakland, California, for this interview. She was living there because her house burned down in the Oakland fire in 1991. There are few Army mementos around the house because, as Reed explains, the fire purged her memories of the Vietnam War.

Healing the Wounds of War

———

REED ASSERTS THAT THE ARMY REFUSED TO AWARD HER HUSBAND THE SILVER STAR BECAUSE IT DIDN'T WANT TO ENCOURAGE A FLOOD OF DECEASED VIETNAM VETERANS' FAMILIES TO TAKE SIMILAR ACTIONS. REED DIDN'T CARE WHAT THE ARMY'S RATIONALE WAS; SHE WANTED RECOGNITION FOR HER HUSBAND'S VALOR.

• • •

The primary reason I took on this challenge was to unify my family and to heal my family from the wounds of war, so that we could live our lives more fully, more richly, and have a sense of peace. Our political leaders have a serious attitude problem where the Vietnam issue is concerned. It is a consciousness that has prevailed for far too long, directly related to the Vietnam era and to those people who served in that country.

In my dealings with the military establishment per se, I found — for the most part — that the individuals who were officers or military personnel were extremely cooperative, helpful, and understood my situation. Once it got into the hands of a civilian board, the Army Board for the Correction of Military Records, the prevalent attitude was: It hasn't been done before; therefore, we cannot do it. The attitude was one of limitation and an unwillingness to create a precedent — this would be the first Silver Star to go to a Vietnam vet since 1975.

The men and women who went to Vietnam did their duty, and they served their country honorably. I became the symbol of what went wrong and of the unwillingness to deal with this in a forthright manner. Most people give up when the Army says no. I'm of a different ilk. When people say to me, "Sit down and shut up," I stand up and shout. I shouted, "No, you will not see me in hell.

I will have this award for my husband. I will have the truth. And you will deal with me with integrity."

Truth Conquers All

REED HAD ALMOST GIVEN UP WHEN SHE CALLED TO FIND OUT THE RESULT OF THE INQUIRY BY THE ARMY BOARD FOR THE CORRECTION OF MILITARY RECORDS. BUT WHEN A SECRETARY SARCASTICALLY TOLD HER, "HONEY, YOU LOST," HER DETERMINATION REDOUBLED, AND SHE CONTINUED HER EFFORTS.

• • •

When I made it very loud and plain and clear that I was not going to go away, even if I did have to go to federal court, then I got to the right man, Mr. Bill Clark, who is truly a man of integrity, a man who was willing to look at the truth, a man who said, "For this person to have gone this far, there's more to this than meets the eye. We have to look at this."

We have placed in positions of prominence in this country men who have no vision. Men who are not willing to take a chance and say, "Wait a minute, there is something not exactly right here." At that point in time, I had spent my entire life savings to take this on, my home was about to go into foreclosure, the Gulf War was heating up, and I was wondering how far I could really go. And this woman laughed at me.

I said to myself, No, I've come too far; I have too much support all over the country from people I don't even know; I cannot let one woman laugh at my husband or at my commitment. Finally I said, "Look, I'm not going away. You have screwed around with my family, my husband, and me for the last time."

When you come from a place of truth, and if you align yourself with that which is right, and true, and good—that which you know will serve to help other people—then nothing can stop you. No one can stand in your way. No one can say to you, "Sit down and shut up," and get away with it. No one.

Facing Your Enemy

———

REED WENT TO VIETNAM IN 1987 AS PART OF HER QUEST FOR THE TRUTH ABOUT HER HUSBAND'S DEATH. SHE LEARNED ABOUT WAR, DEATH, AND THE LINKS BETWEEN PEOPLE IN WARRING COUNTRIES.

. . .

The trip to Vietnam was the turning point in my life. It was incredible—the most wonderful place for me. It's where this alchemical process of healing really began. I found myself in the home of a village chief southwest of Hanoi. I sat down on this woven mat on the floor; and his wife, a beautiful peasant woman in her black pajamas and a long braid, brought tea; and the chief poured the tea for us.

This man was responsible for capturing twelve American pilots. I had mixed feelings about this: How could I sit down with a man who symbolized everything that I had hated my whole life? I wanted to blame this man, or men like him, for all my unhappiness and all my sorrow.

I looked up, and on the wall there were photographs of two men in uniform with citations for heroism, and I was deeply moved. I asked about them. He said that those were his two brothers who had been sent to the south to fight and had never come home. He looked at me very thoughtfully and said, "We have to put the past behind us."

My village-chief friend in Vietnam—he's just like me. He's just like you. He has the same hopes and dreams and aspirations. He's not my enemy. He never was. From that point on, my mission was to get beyond my story. The essence of my being was not being a war widow. I had to look deep inside my own consciousness and say, All right, Brenda, are you going to go through the rest of your life playing at being a victim? Or are you going to take another tack here? How is this going to serve other people? What are you made of?

———

ONE OF REED'S HINDSIGHTS IS THAT SHE SHOULD HAVE SPOKEN OUT AGAINST THE VIETNAM WAR. IRONICALLY, SHE LEARNED ABOUT FREEDOM OF SPEECH WHEN SHE WAS ON THIS TRIP TO VIETNAM.

. . .

I met a woman who was a tour guide in Nha Trang near the Cam Ranh Bay, and going through the market, we encountered a soldier who had no arms or legs. He was lying in the midst of some rotten food, and he was filthy.

I was just devastated by this. I arranged to take a picture because I am a photographer and pictures can say a lot. The tour guide grabbed my camera and wouldn't let me take this picture.

Later we had a lengthy discussion about the freedom of speech. She was frightened that maybe I would get a photograph and carry that truth out, and that this would haunt her in some way. She was absolutely terrified.

She was deeply concerned about what I would say—whether I would misrepresent her in any way. She was not at liberty to exercise her freedom of speech. I saw firsthand the absence of the freedom of religion, the freedom of assembly, and the freedom to express your point of view.

I have these freedoms. They are my birthright. They are the birthright of each and every person in this country. When you have a birthright, you should never squander it. It's something to be valued and celebrated, respected and honored every day.

I lied to our family [about the Vietnam War while it was going on]. I lied to my children. I lied to myself. Not in a malicious way, but in a way to protect us. But when you lie, the universe lies back, so consequently I had walked along my entire adult life with half-truths like maybe the Vietnam War was a good thing.

I supported the war by my silence. That was a lie. When I saw the evidence of how it was ruining people's lives, firsthand evidence of what was going on, I did not have the courage to take a stand.

I didn't act. I was insular.

I should have stood up and spoken my truth then. I should have demanded the truth about what happened to Eddie Reed in 1968. I was twenty-one years old, and I bought into what the people in power said to me.

I will be asking questions every day of my life from now on. I will not accept a half-truth from anybody in a position of power in this country ever again. None of us should. Never sit down and shut up. Never.

Healing Your Pain

WHEN THE SILVER STAR WAS FINALLY PRESENTED TO REED, IT WAS THE CULMI-NATION OF THE HEALING PROCESS—FOR HER AND MANY OTHERS.

. . .

The day of the presentation was very symbolic. My husband's family are good and simple people; they live on a farm in Tennessee. My mother-in-law has been very reclusive since Eddie died. She does not travel. She doesn't go places. She's not a worldly woman. But she came to Washington, D.C.

She and my father-in-law and Eddie's brothers—they all came. Their wives came. Cousins. Aunts. Uncles. People who had demonstrated against the Gulf War were there. Members and leaders of the Vietnam veterans and the disabled-veterans groups—virtually every veterans' organization in the country was represented there. Senators, congressmen, the Department of the Army, the men who had served with my husband, his commanding officer, and the press corps who had participated in Vietnam were all present.

The symbol of healing was that there were people in vast opposition in that room, and every single person was unified and moved. We were there under the guise of acknowledging my husband's heroism, but what we were truly doing was honoring the heroes within ourselves. We were honoring that ability to put down this story, to put the story behind us.

It was a historic thing to have this award presented in the House Armed Services Committee hearing room, because that's where the Vietnam War began. The money was appropriated, and all sorts of decisions that changed the lives of every person in the room that day happened in that very room. We had come full circle.

The Blessing of the Oakland Fire

———

THE SAME YEAR THE ARMY PRESENTED REED WITH HER HUSBAND'S SILVER STAR, HER HOME BURNED DOWN IN THE OAKLAND FIRE. SURPRISINGLY, THIS FIRE RELEASED REED FROM THE PAIN OF HER HUSBAND'S DEATH AND HER STRUGGLE TO GET THE SILVER STAR.

• • •

I could see that the fire was moving very quickly, so I got into my car and went back to my house. I went to the top floor, where Eddie's picture was still on the wall. I stood there and stared at the picture for a long time. Finally I said, "You know, Eddie, this is really hard. This is the day I truly let go. I'm not going to take you with me. I'm not taking the past with me."

Rather than to go frantically through my house grabbing things, I chose to go into every room in my home and call up a happy memory. I remembered the good. I blessed the rooms, and I thanked the house. As I was going through this process, the windows began to break and the house began to fill with smoke, but I knew I was safe. I knew that what I was doing there was absolutely right.

I didn't have to be a victim anymore. I knew that I was a winner. I took the Army on. A naive little girl from east Tennessee who grew up on a tobacco farm could take on the establishment and win. I wasn't anybody's victim anymore.

———

REED HAS LOST A HUSBAND IN A WAR, FOUGHT THE MILITARY ESTABLISHMENT, AND WATCHED HER HOME BURN DOWN. SHE IS A PERSON WHO KNOWS HOW TO COPE WITH GRIEF.

. . .

Eddie Reed would not want me to wallow in a pit of sorrow for my entire life. Know in your heart—and I believe deeply in God—that wherever your loved one is, this person is living a full, happy, and wonderful life.

Honor your grief. Say to yourself, I am releasing the pain of this event in my life; I am moving forward, and there's good here. Sometimes it's hard to see the good when you're in the dark places. You have a choice. Choose life and expect the best.

Absolutely have faith that the very best can happen, and it soon will. What happened to me with Vietnam, with the medal, with the fire storm, is that when I got to the very end, I was so much more than I ever dreamed I could be. Life looks so much better than I ever imagined.

———

Ethel Grodzins Romm

. . .

CEO AND MAVEN

$\mathcal{C}$ONTROLLING YOUR MENTAL STATE

• • •

Observe things as they are and don't pay attention to other people.

HUANG PO

Ethel Romm (age sixty-seven) looks like Dr. Ruth and talks like Tom Peters. She is the president and chief executive officer of Niton Corporation, a company that builds lead detectors and radon detectors [radon is a radioactive gas]. It's appropriate that she builds gas detectors, because she *is* a gas.

Romm started her career in 1942, in the middle of World War II, immediately after high school. She became a draftsman in the engineering department of Bausch Machine Tool Company in Massachusetts. Three months later, the Air Force hired her to check engineering drawings for accuracy and feasibility. When she left two and a half years later, she was the head of the drafting department. After the war, she went to Associated Engineers and ran crews that designed large power transformers for General Electric.

In addition to having been an engineer, Romm has been a construction manager, an interior designer, a newspaper and magazine columnist, and an author. (She wrote the best-selling children's spelling book *Throw Out Wednesday*.) She also raised three sons. Five-feet-one-inch tall and beaming with energy, Romm is proof of a person's ability to defy and ignore the limitations imposed by society.

Romm and I met in the dining room of my hotel in Boston, Massachusetts—she came to my hotel instead of making me find her office outside the city. Were I not Japanese and she Jewish, we would have looked like a mother and son meeting for breakfast.

Coming of Age During World War II

———

ROMM IS A SECOND-GENERATION AMERICAN. IN 1924, HER MOTHER ARRIVED AT ELLIS ISLAND ALONG WITH THOUSANDS OF OTHER IMMIGRANTS FROM EASTERN EUROPE.

. . .

It's an accident of history that I'm here, because my mother nearly married somebody in Lithuania. I could have ended up a lamp shade. That's luck. Many successful people have the odd idea: "I did it myself. All by myself. I'm so smart, so talented."

———

ROMM ENTERED THE WORK FORCE DURING WORLD WAR II. BECAUSE MOST MEN WERE AWAY FIGHTING, WOMEN COULD GET MANY JOBS THAT OTHERWISE WOULD HAVE BEEN CLOSED TO THEM.

. . .

It was 1942 when I graduated from Manchester Central High in New Hampshire. I was fit for nothing productive — I had no work skills, but every defense plant in New England wanted me. Bosses didn't say, "Ethel, you have no training." "No useful education." "You're a girl — what can you know about engineering or manufacturing?"

Instead, it was, "Am I glad you're here!" The boys were far away in planes and tanks, and factories couldn't hire chimpanzees, so they had to try women. We turned out fine. Why do we need a war to learn such things?

The war gave me the chance to apprentice. The choices were endless. You discovered what welders do, what riveters do, and what drafters do. I learned what kind of work there was and what I was suited for. We hardly provide such opportunities now.

Two hundred years ago, if you were a girl and your mother was a duchess, you knew you'd be a duchess. If you were a boy and your father was a cobbler, you'd be a cobbler. Their job — and your future job — was right in front of you. Now we don't know what work is. If your dad is an accountant, would you know what he does all day?

———

ROMM IS EVIDENCE THAT A FORMAL COLLEGE EDUCATION ISN'T ALWAYS NECESSARY FOR A SUCCESSFUL BUSINESS CAREER. YET SHE DISAGREES WITH THIS LINE OF THINKING.

Young people sometimes say to me, "You don't have an education. You made it. Why do I have to stay in school?" My answer is always the same: I came of age in a different time—everybody needed you and wanted you and was ready to train you.

Times aren't like that anymore. I learned everything I know by apprenticing to very smart people. You don't have that entrée anymore unless you start with a formal degree.

The Role of Management

MANY CEOS CONSIDER THEIR FUNCTION TO BE OVERSEEING THEIR COMPANY'S FUNCTIONAL AREAS, SUCH AS RESEARCH, PRODUCTION, MARKETING, AND FINANCE. ROMM VIEWS HER ROLE DIFFERENTLY.

. . .

I don't do much "work" in my company—I run it. It's like running a construction site: I don't have a hammer in my hand, but I'm walking around the job all day. A CEO has two main jobs: to live in the future and to pick good people. If I don't live in the future, the enterprise won't have a future.

The people who do the work have to be the very best I can find. No one else is likely to last around me. It's the single most important thing I do for my company, and the next most important is keeping us all happy. First-rate people hire people who are smarter than they are. That is the best yardstick you can find for measuring your own middle managers—or the president of our country, for that matter. Anybody who chooses second-rate people is third-rate. Get rid of them.

ROMM ALSO BELIEVES THAT MANAGERS SHOULD BUILD CONSENSUS INSTEAD OF ENFORCING THEIR WILL.

. . .

Business is a garden of forked paths, and when we can't agree on which one to take, then I make the call. There are occasions when you have to say, "I'm the president, and it's got to go this way," but that's the weakest appeal of all.

If it's everybody's decision—if everyone has helped to make it, or talked you out of something—then we're all rowing together. Bosses say, "Go!"; leaders say, "Let's go!" In America we don't teach kids much about cooperation—it's always rugged individualism and competition: me against you. That self-centeredness is one of the things you must melt away when you're building a team.

One problem with the bullying style of American management is that it's hard for that type of manager—both men and women—to see why or how they are inefficient. They believe that they are succeeding—after all, nobody mutinies. They fail to understand that when you are the boss, everyone salutes you and follows your orders, regardless of your personality.

Thus, they are misled into believing that their meanness or callousness is keeping everyone in line. They can easily get the idea that if they don't command, control, and coerce, the place will fall apart. The feedback is all wrong.

Emotions in the Workplace

MANY PEOPLE HAVE ARGUED THAT WOMEN ARE TOO EMOTIONAL AT WORK. ROMM BELIEVES THIS IS AN ADVANTAGE.

. . .

We raise our sons to be too stiff-upper-lipped. I remember one engineer back in the fifties because he was so competent. Suddenly, he was taking twice as long as he should have to design a power transformer, and he couldn't add two and two.

I learned that his wife had left him. He had told no one. With men, it can take a while to get to know that sort of thing. Women, on the other hand, might burst out crying. The first time somebody asked me, "Don't you hate hysterical women?" I smiled and said, "Have you ever worked with stoic men?"

Until the late eighties, I had never worked around a lot of women. I like it when someone starts to cry, because you know at once you've got a problem, and the two of you can tackle it. Without tears, it can take days to know. We don't hire machines, we hire people, but we often act as if we are supposed to be machines.

In fifty years of working around men, no one in my workplace has ever made a pass at me or a lewd remark. Those fellows would have to be six kinds of an idiot to try it. Why? 'Cause I'm the chief. On a construction site, it might not be obvious for the first twelve minutes who is running it. But when you find out, disrespect is not going to be on your mind.

Picture, for instance, tens of thousands of troops at Westover Army Air Base about to go overseas, and a handful of civilians, mostly young women. When I walked along a road and a platoon marched by, the sergeant always ordered, "Eyes left!" The fellows would grin, stare, and usually whistle. I'd smile and maybe curtsy—fun.

But when I got back to the balcony at Base Hangar, the door I walked through had my name on it: Ethel Grodzins, Drafting Supervisor. Who's going to mess with that? Just as rape has nothing to do with love or even sex, so bullying harassment—sexual or otherwise—is all about power.

Controlling Your Mental State

———

IF ROMM KNOWS A SECRET TO DEFYING GRAVITY, IT'S CONTROLLING YOUR MIND-SET.

· · ·

Franklin D. Roosevelt caught polio at the height of his career. It looked like the end of his world. He once described how he spent a whole year trying to get his big toe to move. After that, what kind of problem could be too difficult?

We all have a big toe to move. For most of us, it's much easier than overcoming polio. In my case it was my remarkable, loving mother: brilliant and depressed. After my mother, like Roosevelt's big toe, everyone has been easy to deal with.

She was not an easy person. I think that's why her three kids are so cheerful without trying. Everyone is a pleasure for me. I know a thousand ways to lift your heart — I'm programmed to counter gloom.

Running a business, or even a crisis-every-hour construction site, is a lead-pipe cinch compared to raising a family. In your family the worst that can happen is dreadful — a terrifying and eternal nightmare. In business, what's the worst that can happen — you lose some money?

Unhappily, the West has the ancient Greek patrician idea of work: work is beneath you and fit only for slaves. So, instead of everyone pitching in to make workplaces the greatest places to be, our people say "Thank God it's Friday" and look forward to retirement.

The other day on an airplane, the man seated next to me — noting my age — asked why I hadn't retired, and I chewed him out properly. Would he have asked Picasso that? Churchill? Get a job you love, and you never *work* a day in your life.

———

Rick Smolan

. . .

CHALLENGING THE STATUS QUO

. . .

Keep away from people who try to belittle your ambitions. Small people always do that, but the really great make you feel that you, too, can become great.

MARK TWAIN

Rick Smolan (age forty-two) was sitting in a bar in Bangkok in 1979 when he got the idea for an unusual book about Australia. It would be composed of pictures that photographers would shoot during a twenty-four-hour period, and later, collectively, the photographers would decide which pictures were to be used. The project would be by photographers and for photographers.

This idea became *A Day in the Life of Australia,* and the project led to a series of *Day in the Life* books about other places, including Ireland, Japan, Hawaii, China, the U.S.S.R., and America. In total, four million copies of the *Day in the Life* books have been sold to date. Previously, a coffee-table book that sold more than 15,000 copies was considered a runaway best-seller. In this chapter Smolan explains how he successfully challenged the status-quo mentality of the photojournalism industry, but his interview is applicable to anyone who's been told that their projects are doomed.

Smolan is currently running a new company called Against All Odds Productions. I drove over to Smolan's house in Mill Valley, California, for this interview, and we talked in his studio next door. It's a nerd's and photographer's heaven: computers, cameras, books, and photographs are scattered everywhere in hip disarray.

The phone rang every five minutes or so. His assistant, Denise, was working while we talked. She tried to ignore what we were saying—except when Rick cracked a joke. Then she laughed, and we knew we had an audience. Smolan is best when he has an audience.

A Day in the Life of a Photojournalist

THE *DAY IN THE LIFE* SERIES WAS BORN OUT OF A SENSE OF CAMARADERIE AMONG PHOTOJOURNALISTS AND A SHARED SENSE OF FRUSTRATION WITH HOW PHOTO-JOURNALISM WORKED.

. . .

There are about two hundred men and women in the world who are photojournalists. They are of all different nationalities, different racial groups, and different ages. The one thing they all have in common is a childlike curiosity about the world. They're born storytellers — except the way they tell their stories is not with words, but with pictures. In many ways they serve as the world's eyes.

These people tend to be loners by nature, and most live in hotels eleven months out of the year. After a while — and I was one of these people for five or six years — you start to realize the only family you have in the world is other photojournalists, because they show up where you show up. It's the only continuity you have in your life.

One of the frustrations all these photojournalists share is the fact that they're out there looking at the world, and somebody back in New York, who didn't have the experience, looks through the photographer's film and, more often than not, picks something that reminds him of something he's seen before.

These editors look for a picture that feels familiar and comfortable — one they think their audience will understand instantly. Very often it's a cliché. They don't like pictures that ask questions. They like pictures that give answers. The irony is that often the most interesting pictures are the ones that are slightly enigmatic — that are slightly open to interpretation.

All of us would sit around the bars complaining about the editors we worked for. We'd sweat blood and bullets and put our lives on the line, and then we'd pick up the newsmagazine a week later, and it would have this little, stupid picture which meant nothing to anybody.

Because of this I came up with an idea to invite my heroes and my peers and some of the new, young photographers to come to Australia to take extraordinary pictures of an ordinary day.

Persisting Against Conventional Wisdom

SMOLAN'S SUCCESS WITH THE *DAY IN THE LIFE* SERIES ILLUSTRATES WHAT CAN HAPPEN WHEN YOU BUCK THE SYSTEM AND DO WHAT YOU THINK IS RIGHT.

• • •

The way most publishers would do a book like this is to make up a list of things that have to be in the book—kangaroos, the Opera House, wallabies, and guys wearing hats with corks bobbing off them—and then go out and send photographers to illustrate those things.

When I went out to publishers looking for someone to publish this *Day in the Life* book, they basically laughed me out of their offices. The fact that I wanted to do it on a day when nothing happened, that I wanted to photograph ordinary people, that I didn't want to include all the tourist attractions and all the things that had to be in a book about Australia, meant that it was a doomed idea from the beginning.

In addition, the fact that I wanted to hire a hundred photographers and fly them all to Australia, house them, feed them, transport them around, and get them cars, hotels, and film was such ridiculous overkill. The reaction they all had was, "Go buy stock pictures and call it *A Day in the Life*. Who cares if you actually did it in one day? The public would never know—what would be the difference?"

I went out anyway and was basically turned down by everybody. They said nobody would be interested in a book of photographs of complete strangers, taken on a day when nothing happened in some godforsaken country like Australia. Out of desperation, I went to private companies like Apple, Kodak, and Hertz, and asked if they would give me film or computers or hotel rooms or airfares.

In return, I told them I'd give them a private edition of the book, which they could give away as Christmas gifts. Many of these companies had excess airplane seats or film or whatever. I convinced them to turn something that was basically valueless to them into something they could use.

I didn't know anything about business at all. If I'd known more, I wouldn't have done it. My ignorance got me so far in a hole that I couldn't back out. I owed too much money, and I'd gotten too many people involved. I would have gladly called it off if I could have crawled away and pretended I'd never started it, but there was no way to crawl back out of the hole.

All I could do was keep digging—hoping I would pop out the other side.

———

SMOLAN'S EXPERIENCE SHOWS THAT SOMETIMES, TO QUOTE THE POET THOMAS GRAY, "IGNORANCE IS BLISS."

. . .

Sometimes you're protected by your ignorance. There's no such thing as a right and wrong way to do anything. I think the more you become an expert in something, you almost limit other ways of doing it. You probably get very good at one way of doing it, but you start assuming that's the only way to do it.

Your idea is not a good one if everybody says, "What a great idea!" When everyone is telling you this is going to be the next big thing, I always figure you should head in the opposite direction. The opportunities for a big win are, by definition, in the place most other people are not looking.

Also—maybe it's a way of rationalizing rejection, but if it was obvious, somebody else would be doing it. So you have to start figuring out how to trust that little voice inside of you that tells you when something's a good idea despite the fact that the whole world is telling you it's not.

Ninety percent of it is just being stubborn and obstinate and pig-headed. My father used to accuse me of having tunnel vision when I was a kid. When I was focused on something, you could talk to me or hit me, and I wouldn't notice. I would be totally fixated on something, and the rest of the world would disappear.

Empowering People

SMOLAN ATTRIBUTES MUCH OF THE SUCCESS OF THE *DAY IN THE LIFE* BOOKS TO THE SPONTANEOUS QUALITY OF THE PHOTOGRAPHS. EMPOWERING PHOTOGRAPHERS TO TAKE THE SHOTS THEY WANTED WAS ONE OF THE BEST DECISIONS HE MADE.

• • •

My idea was to make up assignments for the photographers, make sure they were geographically spread out, make sure the assignments didn't overlap too much, and then say, "If you don't like what we've set up for you, if you think it is boring and not a good assignment, then come up with your own ideas. You're the person on the spot. If you're staying with a family and they say their six-year-old daughter is doing an elementary-school play tomorrow night, and you think that's more interesting than going to the coal mine we assigned you to, great."

Probably 50 percent of the pictures in the book come from a photographer's own initiative and spontaneity. That's why the books are fun: they have that sense of discovery instead of illustration. So much of journalism and publishing today is illustrating someone else's idea.

As a photographer, I found, at least toward the end of my career, there was this unspoken rule that said, "If you come back without pictures, it's your fault, and we won't hire you again, so you make it happen. We don't want to know how you made it happen.

Just don't come back without something we can use." That means you're supposed to illustrate, and it got to be very frustrating.

Getting Back to What You Love

IN 1986 SMOLAN SOLD THE *DAY IN THE LIFE* SERIES TO COLLINS PUBLISHERS BECAUSE IT HAD BECOME A SYSTEMATIZED BUSINESS THAT TOOK SMOLAN AWAY FROM THE THINGS HE LOVED TO DO.

• • •

I watched what was an antiestablishment, antipublishing, fuck-the-publishers-we're-gonna-go-out-there-and-do-this-book-anyway-if-there's-no-market-if-there's-no-money-we-don't-care-it's-not-a-business-it's-just-going-to-be-a-book-by-photographers-for-photographers venture turn into an institution that now takes six months of planning to give cameras to schoolchildren.

We had eighteen people, and I spent all of my time resolving battles between people, or calming people down, or firing people, or hiring them, or dealing with all the mechanisms of interpersonal relations instead of working on what I love: photographs and books.

I was delegating all of the things I loved. I wasn't taking pictures. I wasn't editing pictures. I wasn't working with designers. I was hiring people to do all those things so I could make more money. There's a simplicity to life when you're *doing* the creative side of it instead of *managing* the creative side.

It's like looking at an empty field of tall grass. No one's walked across it, and you're the first. You walk across it, and you don't fall into any potholes or break your leg. It's very hard for anyone else, or even you, not to take that same path again, because you know it's safe, and it got you there.

BEING A LONER AND A THINKER PARTIALLY EXPLAINS SMOLAN'S DESIRE TO GET BACK TO A SMALLER ORGANIZATION, AND IT EVEN EXPLAINS HIS ATTRACTION TO PHOTOGRAPHY.

When I was a kid, I was very shy. I didn't know how to get along with people, so I spent most of my time by myself. My hobbies were amateur radio, where I'd sit in the basement and talk to people by Morse code; and photography, where I could watch people without having to actually engage them.

I always felt that people were given a tool to relate with other people when they were born, and that tool had been left out of my kit. I figured if I watched people enough, I'd figure it out.

I'm actually quite social now, but I like my own thoughts. I like spending days by myself walking and thinking. There's a rhythm and a momentum and a focus and a concentration that I don't have when I'm around people too much.

That's a common theme with a lot of people I've met who are risktakers. At a certain point either you don't trust people or you've spoken to yourself so often that there are several of you who converse. They become your counsel, father figure, and older brother.

Conquering Your Fears

AS HE LOOKS BACK, SMOLAN RECOGNIZES THAT CONQUERING THE THINGS THAT SCARED HIM MADE HIM STRONG.

. . .

Make it as difficult as you can for yourself. The very thing that you are the most terrified of is where your power is. If it's easy, you didn't earn it. Don't think: I can never write a book, I can never make a movie, I can never ski down that mountain. Head toward the terror, not away from it.

It's not like I know this now and do it automatically. It's one of those lessons you go through your whole life, remembering over and over and over again and relearning: do the opposite of what your instincts say. One of the voices inside is a frightened little kid who says, "Mommy, Mommy, take care of me."

There's still a little kid inside me who gets awkward and embarrassed. There's also a practical voice — that I hate — reminding me that life's getting shorter and that says, "If I spend the month doing this, I'm not spending the month doing these twenty other things."

I ignore it and try to do the opposite. It's like jumping off a cliff and trying to figure out how you're going to build your parachute on the way down. The trouble is, until you jump off the cliff, you don't have the motivation to figure it out. You never end up getting the confidence in yourself if all you do are safe, predictable, and secure things.

———

Mary Kay Ash

. . .

ENTREPRENEUR

*B*REAKING THE GLASS CEILING

• • •

Whatever women do they must do twice as well as men to be thought half as good. Luckily, this is not difficult.

CHARLOTTE WHITTON

Friday the 13th is a lucky day for Mary Kay Ash because she opened the doors of her cosmetics company on Friday, September 13, 1963. After working for twenty-five years in direct sales, she had retired earlier that year and intended to write a book about sales to help younger women. She had been frustrated in her own career because she had hit the glass ceiling—the artificial limits placed on a woman's career in the male-dominated world of business.

Mary Kay started her business in a 500-square-foot store in Dallas, Texas. She stocked nine beauty products that were displayed on a shelf purchased from Sears Roebuck and Company. Her first eleven employees were her twenty-year-old son, Richard, nine beauty consultants, and a secretary. Mary Kay's initial assets were her life savings of $5,000, her dream of building a company that was run by the Golden Rule, and her years of sales experience.

In 1991 the retail value of the company's sales topped $1 billion. How did the retired saleswoman with a little store become a cosmetics giant? She tapped into an enormous resource: housewives and other women who were never let through the door of corporate America. She made them into sales consultants who bought products from the company and sold them to other women. Today there are approximately 300,000 Mary Kay Cosmetics sales consultants in nineteen countries on five continents. Remember her accomplishments when artificial barriers are placed on you.

I interviewed Mary Kay in Dallas, Texas, during a meeting for Mary Kay Cosmetics sales consultants and managers called Awards Seminar '93. While many people think a sales meeting with 500 people is a big deal, a Mary Kay Cosmetics Seminar means that 40,000 people—mostly perfectly coiffed women dressed in pink or red business suits—take over a city in four waves of 10,000 each. It was a scene that would warm the heart of any red-blooded capitalist.

If you've been reading this book carefully, you'll notice that Mary Kay is the only person who declined to list her age. Actually, she wanted me to list it as "thirty through." Also, with the exception of "Victoria," everyone is called by their last name. Somehow, using Mary Kay's last name, Ash, didn't seem right. She can only be Mary Kay.

Women in the Sixties

IF YOU KNOW ANYTHING ABOUT MARY KAY COSMETICS, YOU WON'T BE SUR-PRISED TO FIND OUT THAT A SALES CONSULTANT'S EARNING POTENTIAL OR POSITION IS NOT LIMITED BY GENDER. THIS POLICY IS A DIRECT RESULT OF MARY KAY'S EXPERIENCE IN THE BUSINESS WORLD.

• • •

I worked in the corporate world for twenty-five years. In my last position I was the only person on the road for my company, doing the recruiting and training. I needed an assistant in the worst possible way—if you divide forty-three states into fifty-two weeks, you see that I didn't get to a state but once a year.

I took a man, an ex-tablecloth-salesman, out on the road with me, who I thought was going to be my assistant, and I spent nine months teaching him everything. When I went back to the headquarters in Dallas, I found out that the president of the company had hired a firm from Chicago to find out why we weren't growing faster.

Here is what they came up with: Mary Kay was so powerful that she could take the company away because customers didn't know who the president of the company was. Then I found out that the man I had been training for nine months was going to be my boss at twice my pay. That was the straw that broke the camel's back.

I went home and cried all night—which is strictly a female thing to do [*sarcastically*]. It was probably one of the saddest days of my life, because I had worked for that company for eleven years—

sometimes eighteen to twenty hours a day. If the owner had called the next day, I would have gone back. Being told that I could leave the company and take all its customers with me hurt my feelings because nobody was more loyal than I was.

For several weeks I sat at the dining room table trying to clear my heart of the bitterness I felt. To do that I took a legal-sized pad and wrote down everything good the companies I had been with had done. After two weeks of writing down everything good, I had cleared my heart of the bitterness. Then I took another legal pad and wrote down all the problems the companies had.

For example, when I asked the question, How do I get from here to there? the answer was, You are in the wrong body. In the early sixties women were not even considered for executive positions — people assumed that because you were a female, you could not do it. They never gave any consideration to your ability, your talent, or anything like that.

Then I thought, If you are so smart, what would you do if you had the opportunity and the responsibility to solve these problems? I wrote what I would have done, and then I read both pads in preparation for writing a book that would help women overcome the obstacles I had encountered.

When I read the pads, I realized that I had written a marketing plan that would give women an open-ended opportunity. One day I thought, Wouldn't it be great if somebody did something with this instead of just writing about it? So the book didn't get written for twenty years.

Starting Mary Kay Cosmetics

MARY KAY INTENDED TO START HER COMPANY WITH THE HELP OF HER HUSBAND. SHE WAS GOING TO HANDLE PRODUCT DEVELOPMENT, RECRUITMENT, TRAINING, AND SALES. HE WAS GOING TO HANDLE ACCOUNTING AND ADMINISTRATION. UNFORTU-

NATELY, IT DIDN'T WORK OUT THAT WAY.

. . .

One month to the day before we would start, my husband died of a heart attack at the breakfast table. We had spent or committed every penny to the business, so on the afternoon of the funeral, I met with my two sons and daughter and sought their advice. My son Richard, who was twenty at the time, said, "Mother, I'll move to Dallas tomorrow to help you." He had a brand-new bride of two months, and she screamed all the way from Houston when he quit his job to do this stupid thing with his mother.

How would you like to turn your life savings over to your twenty-year-old? I saw Richard as a kid fresh out of school. I thought he could pick up the boxes I couldn't. I wasn't sure he would even be able to fill an order, but he was the only thing I had. My other son, Ben, was the kind of kid you couldn't get up in the morning, and if you got him up, you couldn't get him dressed. If you got him dressed, you couldn't get his breakfast down him. If you got his breakfast down him and sent him to school, the school would send him home.

He heard Richard say he'd move to Dallas to help me, and he said, "I'd like to come and help you and Richard one of these days when you need me." I thought, Heaven forbid! In the meantime, he reached in his breast pocket and pulled out a savings passbook with $4,500 in it and said, "Mom, I think you can do anything in the world that you want to do. Whatever you want to do with this, you can have it"—this is from a child who has been put down all of his life because of his antics. That's the day I forgave him for all that stuff. [*Laughs.*]

My attorneys sent for a pamphlet to tell me how many cosmetics companies went broke, to discourage me. My accountant told me that I could not give the commissions I was proposing—50 percent instead of the usual 30 percent—and that we'd go broke in six weeks. I handed my daughter a sample case and said, "You start in Houston—do something with this." People told me, in no uncertain terms, that I didn't have a chance.

So Richard, myself, and a secretary and nine consultants — well, they were just friends of mine who didn't have the heart to say no — started the business in 500 square feet of space in Exchange Park. I don't think the consultants intended to stay around. That was our crazy start.

———

MARY KAY HAS A LOT TO SAY ABOUT SELF-CONFIDENCE, MAKING IT FROM SCRATCH, THE GLASS CEILING, AND OTHER PROFESSIONAL ISSUES. SHE'S ALSO ONE OF THE NATION'S TOP BUSINESSWOMEN. HERE ARE SOME WORDS OF WISDOM FOR WOULD-BE ENTREPRENEURS.

. . .

If you want to build a company, go work for somebody who is already doing what you want to do, and learn from their successes and their failures before you invest your money. As I drive to work I see signs along the highway: Grand Opening September 10th or something. Sure enough, they open after they spent $100,000 on the decor. Three months later, they're out of business. Why? Because they didn't thoroughly investigate where they were putting their business.

My ace in the hole was that I had twenty-five years of experience in direct sales. I knew how to sell, how to train, and how to do everything except the administrative end — that is where Richard came in. What do you have to have to start a really good direct-sales company? First of all, you have to have a product that is so good that people will hunt you up to buy it, because in direct sales, people can't buy it in a department store or drugstore.

Secondly, you have to have something that your salespeople can believe in so much that they can sell it. At the time we started, our saleswomen did not believe in their own God-given ability. They would say, "If I can…I hope…Maybe…."

Cosmetics was an ideal product for me to start with for two reasons. First, it is something that women all feel they are experts in at age twenty. Second, I had been using a local woman's cosmetics products for ten years, and I thought they were the best thing I had ever had on my face. People I met would say, Mary Kay, what are you doing to your face? Did you have a face lift? What's happened?

The woman who made them never really got the thing off the ground because she sold them out of her little home beauty shop at the wrong end of town, and, as we say in Texas, "That dog won't hunt." So I went out and bought the formulations from her heirs after she died. I took the formulations to a man here in Dallas who had forty years of experience in producing cosmetics. He thought so much of my idea that he turned it over to his young son and said, "Make this stuff for this woman. We'll never see her again."

Praising People to Success

MARY KAY TRIES TO RUN HER COMPANY LIKE A FAMILY. SHE ATTRIBUTES MUCH OF HER SUCCESS TO USING PRAISE AND UNDERSTANDING TO MOTIVATE HER EMPLOYEES.

• • •

Mary Kay Cosmetics stands for an opportunity to give women an equal chance. The lesson I learned is that if you establish your philosophy as God first, family second, career third, you can succeed. Women understand that. They want to be a good mother and a good wife, but they want to have some success in their lives. They want a career.

It's been estimated that more women have cumulatively earned over one million dollars from Mary Kay Cosmetics than from any other career. Our top national sales director will probably earn over one million dollars in commissions this year alone. The eighty national sales directors average commissions well into six figures a year, and we have hundreds of other sales consultants earning over $50,000 a year.

We have done this by giving women confidence and self-esteem.

Sometimes women come to my office, and I'll say, "Tell me your name." They go *whhh* [*mumbling*]. They have such a lack of confidence that they can't even tell you who they are. Three to six months later, the same person comes back, and she'll say, "Mary Kay, I'm so and so." I think to myself, Could this be the same woman I met three months ago?

This is accomplished by praising people to success. We give them a ribbon after they attain their first sales goal. They pin it on, and they probably wear it to bed! Then we give them another ribbon when they meet a second, higher goal. We applaud them. We applaud everything they do right.

We call our meetings success meetings—not sales meetings. The directors are taught to applaud their people to success. This is like giving encouragement to a baby as it learns to walk. We develop self-esteem. We teach them to sell. In the meantime we are teaching them to be experts at makeup. All these things added together give them confidence.

When I have to criticize somebody—which is seldom—I never do it behind a desk. Instead, I sit with her or with him on the couch. First I tell them something they did that was just terrific, and then I say, "By the way, would it be better if we did such and such in another way?" Then I praise them for something else, and the woman or the man walks out of there—not with their feathers all melted down, but with a good feeling—thinking that it might be a good idea and maybe they should do that. And like it was their idea.

———

MARY KAY IS ARGUABLY ONE OF THE BEST SALESPEOPLE IN AMERICA. WHAT ARE HER SECRETS?

. . .

First of all, if you can gain the trust of the person you are selling to, your sale is half made, and you have to know your product to be able to gain the trust of the buyer. If you know your product well enough, you can present it correctly and with integrity.

Second, you need to be able to express yourself, so take a Dale Carnegie course or something like that. Learn how to express yourself in front of people. We start off with people having a training week in which they book five of their close friends so they are not so inhibited. They hold these sessions to get confidence so that when they book somebody who is not a friend, they'll have the confidence to stand up in front of them.

Juggling Spouse, Children, and Career

MOST MARY KAY COSMETICS SALES CONSULTANTS ARE WOMEN WHO ARE FILLING MULTIPLE ROLES AS MOTHER, WIFE, AND BUSINESSWOMAN. MARY KAY TEACHES THEM HOW TO AVOID BEING STRETCHED TOO THIN.

. . .

Men don't spend dollar time on penny jobs. They don't stay home and iron the shirts and vacuum the floor and all that foolishness. They have enough sense to let somebody else do that, but women have a terrible time doing this. It doesn't matter who scrubs the floor as long as it gets scrubbed, right? So I try to encourage them to hire somebody to do all those things so they have time to spend on their career.

We try very hard to get our consultants to organize themselves. The best way I have found is a little pad of paper we issue called "The Six Most Important Things." I teach consultants to write down the six most important things they have to do the next day every night before they go to bed. I suggest that people organize things by priority. First, put the thing they most don't want to do at the top. Then write down the six most important things—not sixteen, because this is frustrating, but six.

Most sales consultants hold one class [a meeting with potential customers in one of their homes to learn how to use Mary Kay products] a day at most, and it takes two hours to put the class on. If you have the class at ten o'clock in the morning, you are home before the first child gets out of school. I encourage sales consultants not to run themselves into the ground by working on weekends. This time belongs to their family, so they should try to cut Mary Kay business off until Monday and give their time to their family over the weekends.

Besides, papa gets really interested when lots of money starts coming in. You'd be surprised how his attitude changes when she starts making five, six, seven hundred dollars a week even in the beginning. I even had a man write me recently to thank me for the fact that he had been able to get to know his children—since his wife has been holding her Mary Kay classes at night, he's come to know his children. It sounds crazy, but these things happen.

The Pink Cadillac

AN INTERVIEW WITH MARY KAY WOULD BE INCOMPLETE WITHOUT HER HINDSIGHTS ON THE USE OF PINK CADILLACS AS A SALES INCENTIVE.

. . .

The pink Cadillac has probably become the best advertising gimmick that anybody has ever thought of. If you live in Kalamazoo and you don't know a thing about Mary Kay Cosmetics, when that pink Cadillac drives by, you say, "That's a successful Mary Kay person!"

We now have more than 6,000 cars worth more than $90 million on the road, and pink Cadillacs have become a Mary Kay trademark. It began about three or four years after we started the company. I needed a new car, and by that time I could afford to buy a Cadillac, so I went down to the dealer and told him I wanted a new Cadillac, and I wanted it painted pink—the color of our lip and eye palette.

He looked at me like I was crazy and said, "Oh, Mary Kay! You don't want to do this. Let me tell you how much it is going to cost you to get this thing repainted when it gets here and you don't like it." I said, "Please, I want it painted pink." He said, "OK, I'll paint it pink, but don't forget I warned you!"

Needless to say, when the car arrived, I loved it! I had been driving my husband's black Lincoln; you could sit at an intersection until death do us part, and nothing would happen. When I drove up to an intersection in that pink Cadillac, people let me go! That is still true today. If I let you borrow a pink Cadillac, you would not believe how the world changes.

———

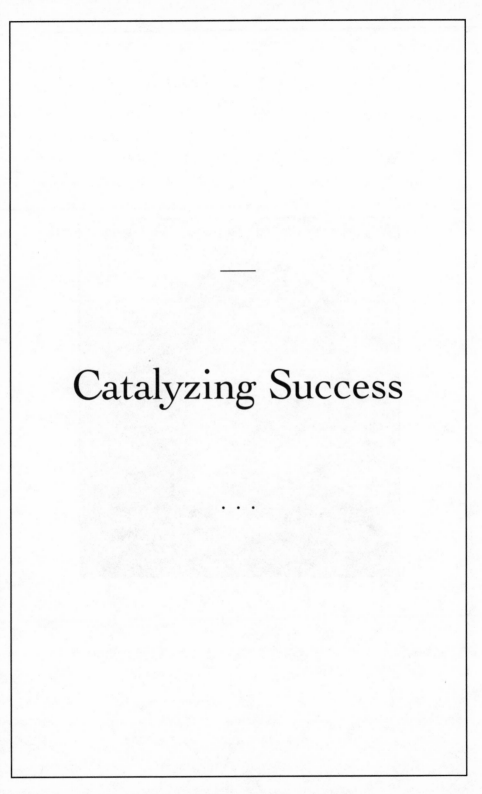

Catalyzing Success

. . .

Tom Peters

· · ·

MANAGEMENT GURU

CREATING AND MAINTAINING EXCELLENCE

. . .

If you don't do it excellently, don't do it at all. Because if it's not excellent, it won't be profitable or fun, and if you're not in business for fun or profit, what the hell are you doing there?

ROBERT TOWNSEND

Tom Peters (age fifty) forever changed the meaning of the word *excellence* when his book *In Search of Excellence* was published in 1982. Peters and his co-author, Robert Waterman, Jr., made the word stand for action, innovation, and customer service. Later Peters wrote *Thriving on Chaos* and *Liberation Management* and co-wrote *A Passion for Excellence* with Nancy Austin.

Peters was the most influential management guru of the eighties: thousands of companies and people embraced his business philosophy. In addition to writing, he is a motivational speaker (at the rate of $75,000 per appearance) and runs a consulting firm called The Tom Peters Group. In this interview Peters explains the success of *In Search of Excellence* and the process of achieving excellence, the difficulty of maintaining it, and the desirability of getting fired.

Our interview took place on a Sunday morning—excellence knows no rest—in The Tom Peters Group office building in Palo Alto, California. The building is decorated with his business tenets; for example, "We love our customers" is scrawled on the third-floor elevator door. We sat around a simple, handcrafted conference table that probably bears no similarity to the built-to-impress conference tables in the companies Peters examines.

The building was quiet because Peters and I were the only people there, yet he boomed his answers as if he were making a speech. Peters is very animated when he talks about excellence and the successes and failures of American businesses.

The Success of *In Search of Excellence*

PETERS AND WATERMAN WERE MANAGEMENT CONSULTANTS AT MCKINSEY AND COMPANY, ONE OF THE MOST PRESTIGIOUS MANAGEMENT-CONSULTING FIRMS IN THE WORLD, WHEN THEY WROTE *IN SEARCH OF EXCELLENCE*. THE BOOK STARTED AS A PRESENTATION FOR CLIENTS AND BECAME A BEST-SELLER. EVEN PETERS'S PUBLISHER WAS SURPRISED.

. . .

My memory tells me that the first printing of *In Search of Excellence* was 12,000, but it certainly wasn't over 15,000. It was a given that business books don't sell. Moreover, it was not a silly given, because when Harper & Row shopped the book around to bookstores, the bookstores said they didn't want it.

This ended up putting lots of money in Bob's and my bank account because, after Harper & Row discovered nobody wanted it, they decided to raise the price. With the McKinsey imprimatur, they thought it would sell to corporate folks, so they could price it out of sight.

We gave it away to all kinds of people, like Sam Armacost [chairman of Bank of America], who got turned on by it. A lot of McKinsey clients got turned on, too. It was absolutely a word-of-mouth takeoff.

PETERS BELIEVES THAT MANY ELEMENTS ALIGNED TO MAKE *IN SEARCH OF EXCELLENCE* SUCCEED.

. . .

It was a not-bad product with phenomenal timing, so the first answer is "a million factors." The second answer is "a half-dozen key reasons," but this misses the point because there really were, if not a million, certainly hundreds or thousands of reasons.

First, in the week or month *In Search of Excellence* was published, unemployment in the U.S. hit 10 percent for the first time since the Great Depression, so people were phenomenally hungry for answers.

Second, in a way, people didn't really read the book. People's sense of the book was that it was a story about great American businesses and an exoneration of American management practices — at a time when all the news was about great Japanese companies.

My hypothesis was exactly the opposite. The book is an attack on conventional management followed by some business practices that seem to work. If anybody read the damn thing it wouldn't have sold, because the first 100 pages was a flat-out attack on American management.

Third, people say that in the middle of recessions the two things that sell well are cosmetics and Disney movies because people are trying to put on a happy face. *In Search of Excellence* turned out to be — this is ludicrous in my mind, but I certainly understand it — a happy-face book.

Fourth, Allan Kennedy and Terry Deal [co-authors of *Corporate Cultures: The Rites & Rituals of Corporate Life*], Bill Ouchi [author of *Theory Z: How American Business Can Meet the Japanese Challenge*], and Richard Pascale and Tony Althos [co-authors of *The Art of Japanese Management*] got into the market a year ahead of us. In retrospect, it was a blessing because people became royally pissed off with the thinking that only Japanese management practices were worth a damn.

Fifth, Bob and I wrote about real companies and named names. If you go back and read the work of people like Peter Drucker — which is not to criticize the conclusions he reaches — I would be surprised if you could find the mention of a specific company in his first ten books. [Drucker is the godfather of management gurus. He wrote, among many other books, *The Effective Executive*.]

Finally, this book criticizing management came from McKinsey, the bastion of conservative management practice, and we were smart

enough — in retrospect, although it wasn't our intention at the time —
to put the book in a black cover. It was a very sober book from a very
sober institution that said some very unsober things about managing.

——

ONE OF THE APOCRYPHAL STORIES ABOUT *IN SEARCH OF EXCELLENCE* IS THAT
HARPER & ROW PAID WARNER BOOKS $500,000 TO DELAY THE RELEASE OF THE PAPER-
BACK VERSION WHEN THE HARDBACK BECAME A BEST-SELLER. WARNER HAD BOUGHT
THE PAPERBACK RIGHTS FOR $50,000, SO IT MADE $450,000 WITHOUT DOING A THING.

• • •

Harper my ass. You're looking at who bought it back. The
whole thing needs to be put in the context of the time. I never thought
I would write a book, and I knew if I did, it would be for friends and
family, so I never imagined that it would mean even small change.

I was so shocked Harper & Row sent me a book contract that
I signed the thing — we never looked at the contract. So I signed the
contract, and somewhere in there was a clause that about six months
after the thing came out, the paperback would hit.

It turned out that Warner picked up the paperback for a song,
and then the book hit number one on the best-seller list. I don't
remember the number, but we paid Warner something like a half-
million bucks to keep it out of paperback for another six months.
I think Harper and I split it. Waterman was still at McKinsey, so he
couldn't do anything like this.

Maintaining Excellence

——

IN THE YEARS FOLLOWING THE HEYDAY OF *IN SEARCH OF EXCELLENCE*, CRIT-
ICS HAVE ATTACKED IT BECAUSE MANY OF THE BOOK'S "EXCELLENT" COMPANIES LOST
THEIR LUSTER AT THE END OF THE EIGHTIES. IS THE DECLINE OF THESE COMPANIES
EVIDENCE THAT PETERS WAS WRONG, OR PROOF THAT IT IS EXTREMELY DIFFICULT TO
MAINTAIN EXCELLENCE?

• • •

Bob and I were McKinsey guys. We worked with big companies, so the book was about big companies. McKinsey gets called in when a company is sick, so my most significant consulting experiences were with Xerox in the mid-seventies and British Telecom, which at that point was still part of the British Post Office. By definition, in selecting so-called "excellent" companies, we selected them at their peak. There was no way in hell that forty-three of those companies could have continued to perform that way.

The much more significant point is that the book absolutely blew understanding the pace of change. For example, even though IBM, Wang, and Hewlett-Packard are in the book, if you can find "information technology" in the index to the book, I would be shocked out of my wits. If you can find anything that refers to global in that book, I would be shocked out of my wits. So the two biggest trends that have changed the world in the last ten years just weren't there.

The first of the eight basics in *In Search of Excellence* is "a bias for action" [the idea that excellent companies make decisions and try things rather than endlessly analyze problems]. To look at those forty-three companies today and say they have a bias for action makes me sick to my stomach. However, compared to what Bob and I had been working with, some of the "excellent" companies did have an action bias.

IBM WAS ONE OF PETERS'S "EXCELLENT" COMPANIES. SINCE THE BOOK'S PUBLICATION, IBM HAS SUFFERED HUGE FINANCIAL LOSSES AND HAS TERMINATED ITS CHIEF EXECUTIVE OFFICER.

. . .

IBM's problem was that they were too damn good, too damn early. The essence of their success was the slavish devotion to the customer that we talked about in *In Search of Excellence*. "Close to the customer." Great. But "close to the customer" meant a certain kind of IBM salesperson close to a certain kind of customer in a certain fashion.

My father worked for forty-plus years at the Baltimore Gas & Electric Company and was involved with it starting to slowly computerize little applications in finance and personnel. Who was running computer departments? An accountant—because that is where companies started automating. There was no such thing as a computer person, so you had an accountant who was scared to death of the machine.

IBM had exactly the right answers. Their machines weren't great—neither were anybody else's—but they were phenomenally good at taking care of this scared-to-death, noncomputer-professional person. That led to the IBM that we all came to know and love.

I attended an IBM "buggy-whip manufacturers" convention around 1984. It was a two-day meeting for the National Accounts Division. Honest to God—I swear this is barely an exaggeration—the 150 somewhat-overweight white males in that room absolutely looked like they had all come out of a Model-T production line. They wore the same black vest with the same black suit. They were the ones who were dealing with the guys in the glass houses at Bank of America and General Motors.

———

HEWLETT-PACKARD, ANOTHER ONE OF PETERS'S "EXCELLENT" COMPANIES, HAS REMAINED SUCCESSFUL INTO THE NINETIES—THOUGH NOT WITHOUT TAKING SOME LUMPS ALONG THE WAY.

. . .

HP is such a perfect story that I am not sure you learn anything from it. Here was this company that was good at independent boxes called instruments. They were fanatics about quality but disorganized enough so that division X and division Y and division Z were going their own way.

They had these wonderful nuggets called divisions, with phenomenal engineering skills and a shocking orientation toward quality, and, in their own fashion, a great customer reputation. So they proceeded to destroy all that. They made a central computation lab. They tried to learn marketing and strategy and centralize that in Palo Alto.

Whether it was David Packard [co-founder of the company] coming in and laying down the law to John Young [the CEO at the time] or not, somehow at the right moment they reversed the tide. Once they learned to do computers and to do marketing, they let an awful lot of the power go back out to the field and retained a lot of what I thought, and what my Hewlett-Packard informants were telling me, they were losing. That's the miracle.

Creating an Excellent Company

PETERS HAS STUDIED MANY ORGANIZATIONS AND HAS HOBNOBBED WITH THE CEOS OF SOME OF THE MOST SUCCESSFUL COMPANIES IN THE WORLD. HE BELIEVES THAT ACHIEVING EXCELLENCE CREATES A PARADOX.

· · ·

To get good, you have to be consistent; to be consistent is to be vulnerable to being blindsided by somebody. That is the ultimate managerial paradox. The reason Apple is an $8 billion company today instead of a $1 billion company is largely because Steve Jobs was fired.

As Apple started to grow, and guys came from DEC and IBM and slightly more polite cultures than Cupertino, Steve acted like an asshole and alienated most of them within nanoseconds. But to go from Apple II to Apple III to Lisa to the first moments of Macintosh to what is happening today required some stability—but at a cost.

I can't imagine a scenario where Apple is a leader twenty years from now. Maybe it will be ten times bigger—like IBM's size today. It's hard to kill these suckers at that size! But setting the agenda? It's an insane thought. Microsoft will be the same way.

. . .

The essence of success is failure. Nobody does anything right the first time. The essence of the gymnast who makes it to the Olympics is that when she or he achieves relative perfection at the age of eight in comparison with other eight-year-olds, they keep pushing themselves until they fall off. There is no success without having the nerve to push not to the limit, but beyond your limits, and the definition of "beyond your limits" is "failing."

It was the ability of Federal Express to do something as stupid as Zap Mail and blow a billion bucks on it when they were only a $2 billion company. Among other things, they proved they could embarrass themselves phenomenally in public and live to tell the tale. The reason that most companies start well and don't continue to repeat the magic is that they are a lot more embarrassed to have that kind of a fiasco.

Achieving Job Satisfaction

PETERS HAS COME TO DEFINE JOB SATISFACTION IN VERY SIMPLE TERMS THAT HAVE LITTLE TO DO WITH MONETARY COMPENSATION.

. . .

You've got to get a kick out of whatever you are doing. I'd rather see you as a happy UPS driver enjoying your customers than a miserable senior accountant at a Fortune 500 company making $75,000 a year. You only get one trip around, so you've got to enjoy what you do and who you do it with.

I remember a young man came up to me after a speech I gave at Cornell and asked what he should specialize in his second year. I told him if he had to ask, he didn't get it. If none of this stuff turns you on — if you are not compelled to go in this direction or that — then you are wasting your time at the business school except to get a certificate.

This doesn't mean there isn't a lot of bullshit in life. There are a lot of envelopes still to be licked, but fundamentally, is the company a place where you enjoy the people you work with? Are you turned on by the sorts of things you are pursuing?

My hypothesis is — and this does not speak to people who were born in the ghetto and have handicaps — the world is loaded with smart people, the world is loaded with energetic people, and there is even a large subset called smart, energetic people. But unless you are smart, energetic, and turned on, you haven't got a snowball's chance in hell.

———

IN CONCLUDING OUR INTERVIEW, I ASKED PETERS FOR HIS ADVICE TO STUDENTS WHO ARE ABOUT TO ENTER THE WORK FORCE.

• • •

First, never start your career working for a company with more than 250 people, because in a small company you can figure out every part of what the company does.

Second, if you are not turned on by the person — even from the personnel department — interviewing you, forget it. You are not necessarily going to fall in love and marry the person who is on the other side of the table, but if you can't imagine hanging out with this person, then you've got a problem.

If you are not turned on, do not assume that this person is the one exception to the rule and the other 23,999 people in this institution are raging, inexorable thunder lizards. If you are confronted with a stiff, assume there is a statistically significant outcropping of stiffism.

My other smart-aleck comment is, by definition, do not interview with anybody who sends interviewers to your school. If they have enough fat to send interviewers to your school, that suggests they are not the company you want to be associated with.

Students—and endangered middle managers—should desperately pursue getting fired. In these environments where staffs of a thousand are getting reduced to a hundred, unfortunately and understandably, people try to hunker down. They assume if people can't see 'em, maybe they'll avoid the next set of cuts.

At least do something interesting. If you get fired, you will be more valuable in the marketplace because you've tried something. I tell MBAs I get a fair chunk of change when I give speeches, and I am doing this one for free. My repayment is that they've got to promise me that a third of them will have been fired by the age of thirty-two.

Al Attles

. . .

PRO BASKETBALL PLAYER

$\mathscr{S}$EIZING THE DAY

. . .

Champions aren't made in gyms. Champions are made from something they have deep inside them—a desire, a dream, a vision. They have to have last-minute stamina, they have to be a little faster, they have to have the skill and the will. But the will must be stronger than the skill.

MUHAMMAD ALI

Al Attles (age fifty-seven) is proof that first impressions can be misleading. When I met him, the first two things that struck me were that he's not very tall for a man who played professional basketball, and his voice sounds as though it could grind you up. After the interview, however, I concluded that he stands very tall and that I would like to be his buddy.

Attles started playing basketball for the Philadelphia Warriors in 1960. He played with other basketball greats such as Wilt Chamberlain, Rick Barry, Jeff Mullins, and Nate Thurmond. Attles earned the nickname "The Destroyer" because of his intense, hustling style of play.

After retiring as a player in 1971, Attles coached the Warriors for twelve years. Under his direction, the Warriors won the NBA championship in 1975 by defeating the Washington Bullets in four straight games. He is now vice president and general manager of the Warriors, and the twelfth winningest coach in NBA history. His story is about seizing opportunities and maximizing them.

Attles's office at the Warriors' home court in the Oakland Coliseum was too small for us to meet in, so we talked in the arena itself. An empty arena designed to hold 20,000 people is a strange place for two people to talk. We sat in the cheap seats and went one-on-one.

Making Your Own Success

PEOPLE TOLD ATTLES THAT HE WOULDN'T SUCCEED IN COLLEGE OR IN PRO BAS-KETBALL. HE WAS NOT CONVINCED. HE SET HIS PRIORITIES, FOLLOWED HIS INSTINCTS,

• • •

I wasn't going to go to college at one time. I stayed out a year working in a department store. That department store probably had more to do with me being here than anything else, because it showed me something I couldn't see myself doing the rest of my life. In effect, it pushed me into going to school.

I ended up going to a school in an area of the country where I didn't ever think I would go—the South. It was a very enjoyable experience. My priorities changed so the number one goal on my mind was graduating college.

I was told by a guidance counselor in high school that I couldn't do college work and I wouldn't play professional basketball because I was too small. There's a motivational speaker by the name of Les Brown who says, "Never let someone else's opinion of you determine your reality."

That's basically what happened to me. I didn't allow myself to be led into the trap of what others were saying about me. I was able to go to college. I was able to make the honor roll, I was able to graduate college, and I was able to make a professional basketball team.

Creating Options

ATTLES PLAYED PROFESSIONAL BASKETBALL AND WENT ON TO COACHING AND MANAGEMENT. EVEN IF HE HADN'T PLAYED, HE WAS A REALIST, SO HE HAD A SAFETY NET.

• • •

When I got an opportunity to try out for a professional basketball team, I never thought I was going to make it. But if I hadn't gotten drafted to play for the Warriors, I could have taught school. We're not always able to take our number one option and succeed at it, so if you don't have any other options, you get very frustrated.

I don't think you should give up, but you need options in your life. Maybe college isn't for everybody, but thinking that is a big mistake a lot of people make. The rules in basketball say five people can play on the floor at one time. Business has rules too. When the requirement of a job was a grammar school education, anyone with anything less than a grammar school education was eliminated. As you moved up the ladder, if you didn't have a high school education you couldn't go on.

I played with a good friend in New Jersey. He was an outstanding basketball player and an outstanding baseball player. He chose baseball. He was a good player, but there are a lot of good players. Instead of going to college he went to play baseball, and he was doing very well.

However, as you move up the ladder the competition is stiffer. Finally, he ended up not quite making it, and it became a fixation with him. I heard that for ten or fifteen years he worked doing something he didn't want to do, and every spring he'd get his glove, his bat, and his spikes and go down to Florida and try to make a team.

———

ATTLES BELIEVES THAT HARD WORK IS NECESSARY TO ACHIEVE SUCCESS, BUT HE IS NOT SO NAIVE AS TO BELIEVE THAT EVERYONE WHO WORKS HARD WILL GET WHAT THEY WANT—ESPECIALLY IF THEY WANT TO BE A PROFESSIONAL ATHLETE.

• • •

We've all been led to believe that if you work hard, most of the time the right thing will happen eventually. It doesn't always happen this way—particularly in sports—because only half a percent of all the people who want to, get an opportunity to play professional sports.

It's very difficult to look at that in the beginning, because we all believe that if half a percent of the people are going to make it, then we will be in that half-percent. That's why athletes get where they are: they believe they're going to be that one.

Try to get as many options as you can, but never take the

position that the odds are stacked against you, because statistics can be made to mean anything. However, they are a barometer that lets you know some averages and measurements — where you fall within the map. There's always gonna be someone who defies that, but you feel a lot more comfortable about yourself if you're qualified to do other things.

Timing and Opportunity

——

ATTLES EMPHASIZES THAT TIMING AND BEING IN THE RIGHT PLACE AT THE RIGHT TIME WERE BIG FACTORS IN HIS SUCCESS. HE MAY NOT HAVE CREATED THE OPPORTUNITIES, BUT HE WAS PREPARED TO TAKE ADVANTAGE OF THEM.

• • •

The biggest mistake many people make is that they think they create the opportunity. You can go to every school in this country and get every degree possible, but if somebody doesn't create that opportunity for you, then you've got to take something else.

I don't care how good I was, if somebody didn't come to me and say, "Al Attles, we want you to try out for the Warriors," then I don't try out for the Warriors. And if I didn't try out for the Warriors, there's no telling if I would have tried out for anybody else. There's no telling if I would have ever played basketball.

When I got the tryout, things shifted to me. Now I've got to do something to make the people who gave me the opportunity say, "This guy may be able to help us." Someone else creates the opportunity, and you have to be prepared if you get the opportunity.

I've kept the perspective that someone else planned for me to get here. I'm not going to get into too much of the religion thing, because I don't want to put that on people, but I know that I'm here because of a lot of other people and a lot of things that have happened to me.

The Role of Money

ATTLES PLAYED IN THE NBA BEFORE THE DAYS OF MEGABUCK SALARIES, BUT HE HAS BEEN FINANCIALLY SUCCESSFUL AS A PLAYER, COACH, AND GENERAL MANAGER. STILL, FOR ATTLES, MONEY PLAYS AN IMPORTANT ROLE ONLY IN ITS ABSENCE.

. . .

The only time money's important is when you don't have it. If you want to go to the supermarket and you have money, you never think about it. But if you go there and you don't have the money, now it's important.

Peace of mind is something you can't buy. Some people say, "You give me millions of dollars and I'll have peace of mind"—well, it's easy to say that. I think if you can do what you want and go where you want, then you're successful financially.

I've seen too many people who are so busy trying to accumulate money that when it comes time to spend it, they're frustrated: somebody else is making more, so they've got to make more. Then you hear people who are so concerned about making money, they don't get the chance to enjoy it.

A friend of mine who was working with senior citizens told me about this gentleman. This gentleman said when he was young, he was going to save all his money, and when he got to a certain age, he was going to travel and do all these things. Now he's got his money, but he can't go anywhere.

Adjusting to Retirement

AT SOME POINT, INJURY OR AGE FORCES PROFESSIONAL ATHLETES TO STOP PLAYING THEIR SPORT. MANY ATHLETES WHO BECOME CELEBRITIES HAVE DIFFICULTY COPING WITH RETIREMENT.

. . .

There are two common denominators: aging and death. Regardless of how good you are, at some point you won't be able to do the same things. You can't run as fast. You can't jump as high. Your reflexes aren't the same. You have to be prepared for when people stop singing your praises and you stop making all kinds of money.

You see a marvelous player in Michael Jordan, but I can remember a marvelous Wilt Chamberlain, Jerry West, Bob Pettit, Oscar Robertson, and Bill Russell. None of them plays now, but basketball is still here. Each generation has somebody who does things that defy description.

When you finish, it's a very frustrating thing to some people. It's not always about the money—it's the life-style, the accolades. I've heard people say they would have been better off if they had not played professional sports. My advice is not to wait until you're about to retire to make your determination about what you're going to do next.

Also, understand that when it's over, it's over. When I was coaching I had to cut two good players. Both of them started crying, and they asked me what they were going to do. The thing I was most saddened by was that I didn't have an answer for them. Enjoy it and understand you're only here for a short time doing it. And there's life after professional sports.

Sports and Society

FOR ATTLES, THE ROLE OF SPORTS IN SOCIETY IS SIMPLE: THEY ARE A WAY TO MAKE A LIVING.

• • •

We've taken sports out of the context of what they really are and made them a fantasy. People don't look at it as a job where you make money to provide for your responsibilities, but that's basically what it is. People have put it on a pedestal above where it should be.

We've excused some people from certain things and allowed them to do things. What happens if you excuse people enough is eventually they think they can do almost anything they want to because they're special.

If you do something and you're not a celebrity, you get in trouble for it. Athletes get away with it. Pretty soon they start thinking they can do anything they want, and people start making excuses for them. They think they don't have to toe the line, and the more they don't toe the line, the more difficult it is when it comes time to toe the line.

———

ATTLES RECALLS THAT HIS FATHER TAUGHT HIM THE IMPORTANCE OF KNOWING RIGHT FROM WRONG EARLY IN LIFE.

· · ·

When you do something wrong, you have to suffer the consequences of it. I remember something my father did to me when I was in the fifth grade. I was playing with a classmate and something happened. The teacher didn't see the beginning of it. I told her this, and she said something, and I said something back. My father said that even if she was in the wrong, she was the teacher.

It wasn't just a talking to I got that night. [*Laughs*.] I think that was the only time my father ever really gave me a beating. But I honestly believe it had something to do with changing my whole perspective on things.

I remember the day I graduated college, we went in a room together—just he and I—and I asked him if he remembered the day this happened in the fifth grade. He said he did, and he thought that if he had not done this, I wouldn't be graduating that day.

———

Phillip Moffitt

. . .

$\mathscr{P}$ROVING NAYSAYERS WRONG

. . .

Nana korobi ya oki. (Fall down seven times, get up eight.)

JAPANESE PROVERB

When Phillip Moffitt (age forty-six) was a sophomore at the University of Tennessee, he, Chris Whittle, David White, and Brient Mayfield published a student guide called *Knoxville in a Nutshell*. This publication led to their creating campus guides for over a hundred colleges around the United States, and, later, national magazines such as *Parenting* and *Successful Business*. They named their company 13-30, for the age range of its target market.

In 1979, 13-30 bought *Esquire* magazine. At the time, *Esquire* was fading financially and editorially, but the entrepreneurial Moffitt and Whittle believed they could turn it around. Moffitt became the editor-in-chief—the person who made *Esquire*'s content appeal to affluent baby boomers—and chief executive officer.

Esquire became the publication that defined hipness and political correctness—before "politically correct" became a negative expression. Moffitt and Whittle showed the naysayers who thought *Esquire* couldn't be a success what a revitalized product and hard work can do. Think of his experiences when the odds against your success seem insurmountable.

This interview took place in Moffitt's office in Belvedere, California, an affluent community across the Golden Gate Bridge from San Francisco. He was the Southern gentleman: calm, relaxed, and confident—the kind of person who, having achieved success, wants to help others.

Learning from Failure

———

AFTER ACHIEVING SUCCESS WITH 13-30, MOFFITT WANTED TO MOVE ON TO GREATER CHALLENGES. THE FIRST TIME HE TRIED TO BUY *ESQUIRE*, ANOTHER COMPANY BEAT HIM TO IT. ABOUT TWO AND A HALF YEARS LATER, MOFFITT GOT A SECOND CHANCE.

・・・

At the press conference the day we took over the magazine, I said that *Esquire* was a great institution, that it had gotten a bit shabby, and my job was to refurbish it. I viewed myself as just a caretaker of an institution that belonged to everyone in journalism. Arnold Gangridge [the founder of *Esquire*] had a wonderful vision when he first created the magazine, and my task was to implement his vision for the baby-boomer audience.

It was a miracle that we were able to revive it, and it only happened because I didn't realize how hopeless the business conditions were. I was blinded to discouragement because I was in love with the magazine. It's not that I ever thought we were going to make that much money with *Esquire* — it was just that I need to be doing something meaningful, and the chance to save *Esquire* was a dream come true.

There was major-league naysaying in New York publishing circles: "Who are these guys from Tennessee? Why does this guy Moffitt think he can be editor of one of the great literary institutions?"

You tend to think the naysayers are much more important than they are. What matters are the people who will believe in you. If you've got a group of one hundred people, and ninety say, This is never going to work, but you've got ten who say, You might be able to do it, that's enough. I have discovered this is a rule in all business activity: focus on the people who believe in what you're doing and forget the others until you've achieved survival, and then start broadening out.

———

MOFFITT HAS COME TO BELIEVE THAT ONE CRITERION FOR SUCCESS IS BEING ABLE TO TOLERATE A LOT OF FAILURE ALONG THE WAY.

・・・

Our first business, 13-30, tottered on the edge of bankruptcy for three and a half years. Many times defeats are critical steps toward victory. People think success is made up of successes, but success is really made up of a series of failures.

I see an opportunity, I try, and I miss it. I see what I did wrong, and I try again, and again I miss. By the third time, I am sure I've really got it, but all I do is get closer. So I try again, and it works extraordinarily well, and people say, "What a success! This guy never fails"—not really understanding all the misses before the hit.

You've got to embrace failure as part of success. One hidden benefit of failure is that, although it may be horrible, it happens and it's over, while success goes on and on into the future. Failure is like a clean sword strike by a samurai and should not be such a shameful thing. It's the denial of honest failure—denying your role in it and therefore being unable to learn from it—that is crippling.

If you cannot embrace failure, you cannot succeed as an entrepreneur, because you do not incorporate what was to be learned from failure, and therefore your next attempt will not be more likely to succeed than the one before it.

Product Is King

ON THE SURFACE, *ESQUIRE*'S PROBLEM WAS A DECLINE IN ADVERTISING REVENUE. THIS DECLINE, HOWEVER, WAS MERELY A SYMPTOM OF A DEEPER PROBLEM WITH THE PRODUCT.

. . .

The instant diagnosis was to get more ad pages, but that wasn't realistic. We had to start with fundamentals: a magazine succeeds because of its readers, and then loyal readers attract advertisers. A magazine needs great writers because it's the writers who generate the magic appeal that brings in loyal readers.

What we did took a great deal of belief, patience, and perseverance. It was a fundamental rebuilding of *Esquire*'s franchise. One of the confusing ideas that arose during the eighties is that marketing is everything—that selling to the market is absolute. Wrong.

The product is what's absolute. The insidious thing about overemphasis on marketing is that it can create temporary, promotion-driven success without genuinely building a lasting franchise. All franchises are based on a product that converts samplers to loyal customers. Product is the beginning. It is the essence.

———

MOFFITT SAW THAT THE ONLY WAY TO FIX *ESQUIRE*'S EDITORIAL CONTENT WAS TO RECRUIT TOP-NOTCH WRITERS. MOFFITT EVANGELIZED THEM ONE AT A TIME.

. . .

I had to go to each writer and explain my ideas for the magazine, and let each of them experience my dedication to seeing that *Esquire* regain its luster. Then I would ask them to take an assignment based on trusting that I would get it all to come together. People will operate on faith if you make real contact with them. This is something we forget in business—that the personal approach often works best.

After a year, writers began saying, "This guy is doing a good job," and the momentum built. It took about three years before it was clear we were going to succeed, and during those years it often looked hopeless. During the worst period we were losing $25,000 a day, and I used to joke that we loved weeks with holidays because we had fewer days to lose money.

Moving On

———

MOFFITT SOLD *ESQUIRE* ON DECEMBER 31, 1986, SEVEN YEARS AFTER PURCHASING IT. HE HAD BEEN THRILLED WITH THE CHALLENGE OF REBUILDING *ESQUIRE*, BUT WHEN HIS JOB WAS DONE HE WANTED TO MOVE ON TO OTHER INTERESTS.

. . .

I was at a board meeting of the Magazine Publishers Association, really enjoying myself, when an alarm went off in my head and I thought, I will be attending meetings just like this and doing the same thing for the next ten years if I don't stop right now.

I excused myself, went upstairs, and called an investment banker who was a friend of mine. Six weeks later the magazine was sold. Most of the experts said such a transaction would require six months.

I had many reasons for selling *Esquire*, one of which was the very success the magazine had achieved. In business the more successful you are, the harder it is to get your hands on the product and day-to-day operations. Instead you end up managing the people who manage the people who do the work. Worse still, you spend almost all your time dealing with problems rather than opportunities. I like creating new media and building something from scratch. I don't find it much fun presiding over empires—fortunately, there's no lack of people who want that job.

The resistance to change one's life when you're successful is incredible. It means giving up something known, to take the chance of achieving something unknown that will provide greater satisfaction. This resistance is why most people only change their life as a result of failure. That's really unfortunate. Life is so short and offers such diversity that repeating anything for a lifetime, no matter how successful, is ultimately a failure in imagination.

———

Bill Walsh

. . .

FOOTBALL COACH

$\mathcal{B}$UILDING A CHAMPIONSHIP TEAM

. . .

This is the day of instant genius. Everybody starts at the top, and then has the problem of staying there. Lasting accomplishment, however, is still achieved through a long, slow climb and self-discipline.

HELEN HAYES

Bill Walsh (age sixty-two) is one of the most successful coaches in the history of professional football. He's mentioned in the same breath as Vince Lombardi and Paul Brown. During his ten-year coaching career with the San Francisco 49ers from 1979 to 1988, he led the team to three world championships—Super Bowls XVI, XIX, and XXIII.

Every coach has a style. Vince Lombardi was a disciplinarian. Paul Brown was an innovator. Walsh was an analyst. He planned every minute of every practice. He scripted the first twenty-five plays of each game in advance. He evaluated potential players not on the basis of physical standards such as height, weight, or speed in the forty-yard dash but on their ability to contribute to the overall improvement of the team.

His system worked. It shows in his win-loss record of 102-63 in professional football. It shows in his development of four outstanding quarterbacks: Dan Fouts, Ken Anderson, Joe Montana, and Steve Young. If you're still not convinced, it shows in his record of 49ers' assistant coaches becoming head coaches at Tampa Bay, Minnesota, Green Bay, New York, and San Francisco. There aren't many people more qualified to talk about building a championship team than Walsh.

Two years after he retired from his job with the 49ers, Walsh returned to coaching—this time at the collegiate level, at Stanford University, where he had coached from 1977 to 1978. While his assistants conducted a staff meeting in a nearby conference room, we met in his corner office at the Stanford Athletic Department. His office was simply furnished in early wood-grain laminate, and it was almost devoid of football memorabilia. Most people who have won three Super Bowls would probably be a lot more ostentatious about it.

Moving Up Slowly

———

AFTER WORKING AS AN ASSISTANT COACH FOR THE LEGENDARY PAUL BROWN AT CINCINNATI FOR EIGHT YEARS, WALSH WAS EAGER FOR A CHANCE TO BE A HEAD COACH. HE REALIZES IN RETROSPECT THAT HE WASN'T READY TO HANDLE THE RESPONSIBILITIES OF A HEAD-COACH POSITION, AND HE NOW UNDERSTANDS THE IMPORTANCE OF TEMPERING AMBITION WITH PATIENCE AND SELF-AWARENESS.

. . .

It's never soon enough for the aggressive and ambitious person — you feel you are falling short of your goals unless you have your successes early. I fell into that category for a period of time. I felt my special uniqueness warranted that I should be one of those coaches that becomes a head coach in their thirties or even early thirties.

People can become very anxious in their late twenties and early thirties. They like to think of their life in terms of making history rather than thriving on what they are doing. They get distracted when they should be growing, learning, improving, developing, and thriving on what they are doing. I struggled for a while because I was hoping to move more quickly in my career. That reduced the amount of enjoyment and gratification I might have had.

I am not sure that you ever really know when you're ready, unless you are in some kind of a job where you pass a written or an oral test. Other people can see it, but the candidate can't. But I do know that unless you are completely ready when you do have the opportunity for advancement, you fall short. Also, the person that reaches their goals later hangs on to those goals longer.

Winning the First Championship

———

WALSH FINALLY GOT HIS HEAD-COACH POSITION WHEN HE WAS HIRED BY THE

. . .

There was a certain amount of good fortune, but the 49ers are a good example of *not* having high-sounding goals as you go about the day-to-day development of an organization. I had hoped we would become a championship team, but when you come from ground zero, it's awfully hard to talk about going into orbit. The key was to get better and better, and for our standard of performance to improve and improve on a broad front, not necessarily in a single category.

At some point we'd break through, but I didn't have a timetable. Our improvement didn't show immediately, but when it did hit—when we were fully in sync—we were very, very good. It was a matter of a lot of hard work, a lot of detail work, and being willing to make decisions to improve our squad by degrees.

I always tried to improve our team by degrees rather than by some masterstroke that would change everything. The 49ers had made their "masterstroke" in trading for O. J. Simpson, and it was disastrous. I was doing it step by step, degree by degree. If a player was 20 percent better than the one I currently had, I would replace the present player. A lot of people asked, "Why bother?" But our squad got better and better—collectively rather than individually.

We also concentrated heavily on skills. With that in mind, we made a big turnaround. Our choices of personnel turned out to be very, very good, and when we made a mistake, we never allowed it to sustain itself or to perpetuate itself because we had too much pride to admit it.

After the Championship

AFTER WINNING THE WORLD CHAMPIONSHIP IN 1981, WALSH HAD TO DEAL WITH A NEW CHALLENGE: KEEPING HIS TEAM COMPETITIVE AND HUNGRY.

. . .

Complacency is going to be there. You have to live with it, but what you do is minimize it. The self-satisfied person is going to be self-satisfied, and it is your job to account for that, to minimize how it affects others, and to bring everyone through that mode as quickly as you can.

I did everything I could by demanding hard work and by making some changes in the personnel, and yet it still happened to us. You have to acknowledge that there is going to be a letdown after a lot of success, and you minimize it. You don't try to smooth it over, and you don't try to act as though it doesn't exist, because it does.

It is up to the coach to be willing to change key personnel. A good example was when I acquired Russ Francis when I still had Charley Young, because I felt Russ would be better than Charley by degrees. Another move was acquiring Steve Young with Joe Montana on the team. Those decisions were somewhat disruptive, but they tended to spur the team on to bigger and better things.

ANOTHER RESULT OF WINNING THE CHAMPIONSHIP WAS THE ELEVATION OF WALSH'S STATUS IN THE PRESS. SOME SPORTSWRITERS, FOR EXAMPLE, STARTED CALLING HIM A GENIUS. WALSH NEVER REALLY BELIEVED IT, BUT IT WAS TEMPTING TO GET CAUGHT UP IN THE HYPE.

. . .

Being called a genius was so outlandish that I couldn't take it seriously. No matter what people call me, the bottom line in sports is winning or losing. The only way I'd be measured is by how our team had done over a period of time. The labels are flashy and give you some visibility for a very brief moment, but then you get right back down to work.

On occasion, being called a genius was embarrassing because it has been used by competition to inspire their own team or motivate them. There was resentment among people who could see right through my being called a genius or were envious of it. The advice I give is don't turn your head toward them. Just keep going, because the bottom line is very simple: you win or you lose.

———

BEING CALLED A GENIUS WAS THE GOOD NEWS. FEELING BURNED OUT WAS THE BAD NEWS.

. . .

There is emotional fatigue that turns into physical and mental fatigue when you have sustained your efforts for long periods of time. Before you know it, you become exhausted, and that is what happened to me in 1982. [In 1982, the season after winning the world championship, the 49ers' record was a dismal three wins and six losses in a strike-shortened season.]

A good part of it was related to the previous three years in which we expended so much time and effort. My first year was two wins and fourteen losses. The second year was six wins and ten losses. There were eight straight losses in the second year.

We did win the championship in the third year, but by that time I was emotionally exhausted from the three years. Then when we struggled in 1983, I became cynical and embittered and had to look at leaving coaching because I was totally spent.

———

WHEN TWO OF WALSH'S FRIENDS TOLD HIM TO STOP FEELING SORRY FOR HIM-SELF, WALSH GOT A GLIMPSE OF HOW HE APPEARED TO OTHER PEOPLE.

. . .

If a stranger had said those things, I wouldn't have paid any attention, but people I was really close to and fond of were honest with me. That is probably what did it finally. I was at the lowest point, and I realized how I was being perceived. That straightened me out in a hurry.

You can turn inward and continually reflect on your own feelings to the point where you lose track of the perception other people have about you. All I really needed was a rest. Fortunately, in the process of indicating that I might not return, there were three or four weeks when I was able to regain my composure.

Focusing on the Right People

DURING THE EIGHTIES, RECREATIONAL DRUGS SUCH AS COCAINE BECAME A GREATER AND GREATER PROBLEM IN PROFESSIONAL FOOTBALL. WALSH, LIKE MANY OTHERS, HAD LIMITED EXPOSURE TO THE ISSUE. SUPERSTAR LINEBACKER THOMAS "HOLLYWOOD" HENDERSON CHANGED THAT AND TAUGHT WALSH A VALUABLE LESSON ABOUT FOCUSING ON THE PEOPLE YOU CAN HELP.

• • •

I came through an era when some people were into drugs and some people were absolutely ignorant of them. In the case of Hollywood Henderson, drug abuse was right there in front of me, and I just couldn't understand it because he was overwhelming me as a person. He was a very, very charming man, and it took me some time to see through that. I kept trying to give him every break, and I tried to understand everything he was doing.

I figured that slowly but surely I would pull him out of it. In reality his drug dependency was so severe that the only way to pull him out was total withdrawal or rejection by other people. As long as he could get anyone to listen to him, he could make it. He could continue his drug habit and somehow sustain himself.

Conversations often won't make a difference—all they'll do is temporarily soothe it. You have to be willing to take action. Action begins with therapy and counseling but can end up with someone actually being lost, so you turn your energies toward those who can be saved.

In Hollywood's case, there wasn't any way I was ever going to change him—that would come later in his life. The key for me was not to be distracted by it, but it affected my relationship with the other people I worked with.

Retiring and Returning

In his last year with the 49ers, Walsh won Super Bowl XXIII and decided to retire. Retirement is one of the most difficult issues for successful people like Walsh.

. . .

When you retire, you are celebrating and grieving at the same time. Grieving can turn into resentment because people fail to acknowledge you. It is very, very common for a person to have sacrificed and built something, then leave it and not be acknowledged by those who replaced him. It's a very empty feeling. The only advice I have is that people should be alert and aware of these dynamics so they can deal with them better.

It takes courage to retire, because you are letting go of something that has been your entire life. For some people this is very, very difficult. You have knowledge, you have expertise, sometimes you have power, and you are letting go of them.

In 1992 Walsh shocked the sports world by returning to coaching at the college level.

. . .

I came back at a different level of intensity — I would not have come back at the same level of intensity. Taking a professional football job wasn't even a consideration. This opportunity at Stanford was unique because I am familiar with the environment and can deal with it. I can be an educator here. If I had gone to some other university, my job would have been more of a procurer of athletes. This is the only job I would have taken, or else I would have remained in television.

My guess is that at some point I will be an assistant football coach for an NFL team. Hopefully I can still be of value. One of the toughest things is to downgrade your role. Some people do it gracefully, but a lot of people can't. The only way to deal with it is to consciously account for it, look at other people's experiences, and condition yourself to do it.

———

ALTHOUGH WALSH TOOK A COLLEGE-LEVEL COACHING POSITION, IT WAS STILL A DEMANDING JOB. WALSH UNDERSTANDS THE DANGERS AND TRADE-OFFS THAT HAVE TO BE MADE AT THIS LEVEL OF COACHING—OR IN ANY PROFESSION.

• • •

When you are driven to accomplish something, you are not always going to do everything correctly, and sometimes your family is shortchanged. The only hope you have is that they understand and that you are open to each other's feelings. You can't have everything.

The Joy of Coaching

———

WALSH WAS NAMED PROFESSIONAL FOOTBALL'S COACH OF THE DECADE FOR HIS PERFORMANCE IN THE EIGHTIES. YET HE MAKES THE SUBTLE BUT IMPORTANT DISTINCTION BETWEEN WINNING GAMES AND BUILDING A TEAM.

• • •

I have to relate my greatest joy to success. It would be contrived if I were to say it was to help my fellow man. I could try to be gracious, but my greatest joy was being successful—building and molding something that was better than the competition. I could point to individual games or seasons or programs, but it was really building and developing something.

Probably the most satisfaction in a relationship I got in coaching was when I could sit back and watch the 49ers perform without me—when the team could take the field, and it was resourceful and together enough to function well on its own. I could almost become a bystander watching something I'd molded. I knew that I had transferred my drive, my motivation, and my philosophy to them.

The next thing that became very important was producing people who became successful coaches. At different stages of your life, there is different gratification. There is a time when you just want to accomplish things personally, independently of anyone. In my age group, we are helping others with their careers—you just go through stages.

———

Overcoming Adversity

. . .

Lang Ngan

. . .

$\mathcal{M}$AKING IT IN AMERICA

. . .

Once I thought to write a history of the immigrants in America. Then I discovered that the immigrants were America.

OSCAR HANDLIN

Do you know the difference between an immigrant and a refugee? I'll give you a hint: most immigrants' first steps on American soil are in New York, Miami, Los Angeles, or San Francisco; Lang Ngan's (age forty-six) first steps were on a military tarmac in Fort Chaffee, Arkansas.

Ngan is a refugee from South Vietnam. In April 1975 she and her mother, father, and six younger brothers and sisters were evacuated from Saigon a few days before the communists took over the city. She worked for the American embassy, so had she stayed, she probably would have been persecuted by the North Vietnamese government.

Several months after their arrival in the United States, Ngan and her family moved to New York City, where she got a job working as a translator for the International Rescue Committee (IRC). Today, seventeen years later, she and her siblings have college educations and are part of the work force. Ngan's interview is about starting with nothing and making it in a strange place called America.

Ngan and I met in a co-worker's office at the IRC in Manhattan. It's a plain facility—plain as in "we use every penny we have to service our clients, not to buy nice furniture." There, Ngan, in broken English, teaches refugees how to survive in the land of opportunity.

Coming to America

NGAN BEGAN THE INTERVIEW BY EXPLAINING HOW SHE CAME TO THE UNITED STATES.

. . .

My grandparents migrated from China to Vietnam, and I was born in Vietnam. I used to work for the U.S. Embassy as a clerk in the consular section. On April 25, 1975, a few days before Vietnam fell to the communists, I was told by my boss about an evacuation plan for U.S. government employees. He realized that if I don't leave, I would be persecuted by the new government.

At that time I was single. I was twenty-nine years old, and therefore I was allowed to bring my parents and my younger siblings. I was told just the night before. We finished work at 6:00 p.m., and then I was told that my family have to go to some place. They planned to send us from that place to the airport the next morning at 9:00 a.m.

We didn't have a plan. Many people don't understand the difference between refugee and immigrant. They think, "Oh, you are like immigrant. You come here because you want to come here." The refugee is different because they have fled. No plan. Because my employment background, I was forced to leave.

My parents didn't want to go, because we left everything. Even the money in the bank, we couldn't go to get it because we were on such short notice. We were told that you are only allowed to carry a small luggage that didn't cause attention on the street. We only able to take a few clothes.

Opportunity and Hard Work

—

AFTER GETTING TO THE UNITED STATES, NGAN WAS DETERMINED TO FIND A WAY TO SUPPORT HERSELF AND KEEP HER FAMILY TOGETHER.

. . .

Most refugees don't know about America or Western society at all. My situation is a little better because I worked for the embassy. I don't—like most of people—think America is a golden mountain! I know life here is not easy. I know there is opportunities, but you have to work very, very hard to get it.

I start worrying the moment the plane took off. I am the only one who can speak some English. The rest of my family, nobody can speak a word of English. My father was blind. My mother, because she gave birth nine times, was very weak. [Two of Ngan's siblings died prior to her family's evacuation from South Vietnam.]

I am willing to take any kind of a job after I arrive here. I have a twenty-three-year-old brother and nineteen-year-old sister. I figure out that maybe three of us can take any kind of job and that might enable us to support our parents, but I have the four other brother and sisters: thirteen, twelve, nine, and eight. I told them that life in America is very hard and that I was afraid that we might not be able to support the whole family, so I might have to put them up for adoption. That was my plan on the flight.

———

NGAN MET THE MAN WHO RAN THE INTERNATIONAL RESCUE COMMITTEE OFFICE AT FORT CHAFFEE. HE GOT HER A JOB AS A TRANSLATOR, BUT THIS MEANT MOVING TO NEW YORK. SHE WAS AFRAID THAT IT WOULD BE HARD FOR HER FAMILY TO ADJUST, BUT AT LEAST THEY WOULD BE TOGETHER.

· · ·

I worry about the weather because we come from the tropical climate. That is the first concern—especially for my parents. They are not too healthy, and I am thinking, Are they able to suffer the cold weather here? But I have no choice. I was very happy that I am able to get a job, and it is a job that is related to the skill I have from Vietnam.

I asked the IRC person, "Do you think that with one person's salary, I am able to support a family of nine?" He thought a little bit, and he said, "No, I don't think so." My sister who was nineteen, she had studied English for two years before she left. She couldn't speak English, but at least she understand, and she can read some English.

Then he told me, "Maybe I'll hire two of you! [*Laughs*.] Probably with two persons' salary you are able to support the whole family." I told him, "Do I need to put my brother and sister up for adoption?" and he say, "No, we will help you. We will keep your family together." That is a big relief.

From that time I know that my family will not be split. We were so excited and appreciative. IRC helped one of my brothers to get a job in an electronic factory in Manhattan. With the salary for three of us, we are able to keep our family together even when we have to rent only two-room apartment, but we were happy—especially my younger brothers and sisters. They so happy that they don't need to be sent away.

Everything is so different because our life in Vietnam is very simple. In New York the first thing we have to learn is to ride on the subway! [*Laughs.*] I got lost the first day in the subway for a few hours because I didn't know how to get transfer. I don't know there is a subway map.

That is why I want to work in IRC, because I know the experience I have. When I start working as the case worker for the new arrival refugee, I know the first thing is the subway map. You have to teach them how because there is no subway in Saigon!

Looking Back on the Vietnam War

———

SEVENTEEN YEARS AFTER ARRIVING HERE, NGAN'S SIBLINGS HAVE ALL GRADUATED FROM COLLEGE. NGAN HAS MARRIED, AND SHE HAS ADVANCED FROM BEING A TRANSLATOR TO A COUNSELOR AT THE IRC. NOW SHE CAN PAUSE AND LOOK BACK AT THE VIETNAM WAR OBJECTIVELY.

. . .

It's very sad. When I talk to a lot of Americans in this country, if I tell them what happened in Vietnam, people think I am making a story. The Vietnamese have an idiom: living as a dog is better than living through a war. Our life was worse than a dog's.

When you have experience to survive the war, I don't care who is right, who is wrong. I just wish there is no war. It is unfair for somebody that just want to have the power to make so many people to suffer. It destroys people and destroys their futures.

Our life had no guarantee. We were living in the Chinatown of Saigon, and I have to go to work by Honda motorcycle every day. There was a bombing in front; if I left my home two minutes earlier, then I would be dead.

There can be bombing in the theater, in the restaurant, everywhere. We don't have any future at all. For the male is more problem because when they reach eighteen — the golden age [*laughs nervously*] — they have to be drafted. Most of my male classmates were killed during the war.

We have no plan for the future at all. Many of the family, the son has been drafted and is in the military. The salary from the military is not good enough to cover their living. Therefore, in many families the girl have to become a breadwinner. If she didn't have education or skills, she might have to become a prostitute.

They didn't want to be a prostitute or beggar, but they have no choice because you want to survive, and you want to help your family. Especially Asian people — female, if you are the oldest one, you think about the whole family. You don't care about what happens to yourself.

———

HAVE THE WOUNDS HEALED ENOUGH THAT NGAN WOULD RETURN TO VIETNAM?

. . .

Not yet, not yet. I have a nightmare that I went back and couldn't catch the plane back. I told myself that I was stupid to go back, and therefore I won't take a chance.

The Generation Gap

———

IN HER WORK WITH REFUGEES, NGAN HAS SEEN A GAP DEVELOP BETWEEN GENERATIONS. IT EVEN HAPPENED TO HER FAMILY.

. . .

One day I walk in Chinatown, and I met four different families. They told me all the same things: Now we are OK—some of them even running small business, and most of them got jobs and able to maintain their expenses of living—but it is so difficult to teach your children in this country.

We have Confucian philosophy: at home the children have to obey the oldest, even if they are not your parents; in school you have to obey your teachers, and also the teachers have the right to teach them not only academics but also character and behavior. But here it is different.

In the Vietnamese culture you don't look in people's eyes. Especially for the female, because the man always represent the family, and man is the speaker for the family. Many of the women have no social life. When a guest comes to visit you, many of the women hide in the kitchen or the bedrooms.

I have to explain to my parents that they grew up in a different society. They shouldn't expect their kids to be like them anymore, because if they act that way, their classmates will think they are crazy. My sisters say, "You tell me when I am talking to people to look down. 'Don't look at people's face and at people's eyes.' People will think I am crazy!"

When my youngest sister started junior high, suddenly she started using makeup, and she wanted to try my high-heel shoes. She come home and said that she was not happy at home because we forgot her birthday. We have so much other things to worry about, how can I remember her birthday?

She brought a shirt that she got from her friend's mother, and she told us, "How can you people forget my birthday? You see I got a shirt from friend's mother. Somebody who is not related to me remembered my birthday. My friend has a room by herself. She can decorate it whatever way she wants to. Her house has swimming pool. I have to sleep with my mother and my other sister. Four of us have to stay in one bedroom."

This is after we were first able to rent a two-bedroom apartment. I told her that you cannot compare to the children that grow up in this country. I said, "I try my best. This is my only way to be able to support the family at this point." We try very hard. I didn't even think about new clothes for me. I was still wearing the clothes I got donated from IRC.

The Grass Is Sometimes Browner

NGAN HAS BEEN THROUGH A WAR, AN EVACUATION, AND RESETTLEMENT, YET IT WAS DOING VOLUNTEER WORK IN AN ORPHANAGE IN VIETNAM THAT TAUGHT HER ONE OF THE MOST VALUABLE LESSONS SHE'S EVER LEARNED.

. . .

My volunteer job was I held the children that needs somebody to feed them. The first few days I cannot keep from crying because I saw children with flies on their face, and nobody have time to clean them. I am sure this group of children had the worst experience of the war.

Because I grew up in the war, I used to complain: I am also a human being like the other people in the other parts of the world. Why was I so unlucky to grow up in the war? There is no future because our life can be destroyed suddenly by not our fault—just because the war.

But that experience helping the orphans, I find myself I am so lucky compared to them. I grow up in a family, have parents and brothers and sisters, but these children grow up in an environment that the people around them are only able to just keep them surviving. Without love. Without care. Eventually you will find other people have worse than your experience and can educate you to keep surviving.

People grow up in this country are lucky. They can get everything that they want. They don't need to suffer hunger. They should learn more about the other corners of the world and that other people are also human beings. Those people are surviving in a way that is worse than an animal in this country.

In this society some people are very competitive, and they don't think about other people's feelings. They just want to get whatever they want. They want to be a hero. They want to be famous. A lot of people want to be successful. They don't care. They forget that they should have love. That is why somebody created the war—because they have so much hate.

———

Victoria

⋅ ⋅ ⋅

VICTIM OF ABUSE

BUILDING A LIFE

· · ·

And when you're alone, there's a very good chance
you'll meet things that scare you right out of your pants.
There are some, down the road between hither and yon,
that can scare you so much you won't want to go on.

DR. SEUSS

Think about your childhood as you read about Victoria's (age thirty-four). (Victoria is not her real name.) She comes from a family of six. Of the four children she is the only girl. Her father molested, raped, and emotionally abused her as far back as she can remember. When Victoria was in grade school, he was arrested for murdering one of her classmates. Although he was later acquitted, Victoria believes that he was guilty. She was also raped and molested by one of her brothers.

As if all this weren't bad enough, Victoria's mother was also abusive. She once locked Victoria, bound and gagged, in a closet for five days. She tried to drown her in a bathtub and sometimes prostituted her to male friends. Continuing the cycle of abuse that had, for her, become the norm, Victoria married a man who also abused her.

Victoria is now in recovery, but the effects of years of abuse still linger. On the phone before our interview, she told me that she suffers from post-traumatic stress that manifests itself in severe depression. Post-traumatic stress is often associated with combat veterans—and, in a sense, Victoria is a combat veteran. This interview is for people who are trying to recover from childhood trauma and build a life—or who know someone who is.

I met Victoria in an airport coffee shop in New England. She wasn't a trembling, empty shell of a person—you'd never be able to pick her out in a crowd. Between bites of apple pie and sips of coffee, we talked about her past and about her future while people around us ate dinner and waited for their planes.

What's Normal and What's Not

———

VICTORIA KNOWS SHE SHOULD HAVE SPOKEN OUT EARLIER, BUT SHE DIDN'T BE-CAUSE SHE WAS TOO SCARED AND BECAUSE SHE DIDN'T KNOW THAT HER EXPERIENCES WERE ABNORMAL.

• • •

My father went to a psychiatric hospital for thirty days and to jail for molesting me when I was five and for doing it to my aunt who's three months older than me. My mother was—back then they said she was—a paranoid schizophrenic. Later on in life they labeled her manic-depressive.

She was crazier than hell. You could see it in her eyes. One day she took the cord off the television set and wrapped the television set in a woolen blanket, tied a rope around it, and put it in the front closet. She was sure my father was spying on her through the television.

I was afraid for my brothers. I felt personally responsible—like I was their guardian angel. I was scared. I was scared because I saw a little girl I went to school with killed, and I knew that could happen to me. My mother said that it was supposed to be me who got killed.

I think I did the only thing I could have done in that situation: I blanked it out. I should have gotten help. I should have talked and talked until somebody listened. Know what my brothers did? My brothers ran away—one at a time, they ran away.

It never even occurred to me to run away. When something happens to you over and over and over again as a kid, and you don't know anything else because you're not really exposed to anybody else's family, you think it's normal. I thought sex with your brother and your father was all very normal.

———

VICTORIA WAS BAFFLED BY THE MIXED MESSAGES SHE WAS RECEIVING FROM HER PARENTS. WHILE THEY WERE ABUSING HER, THEY TOLD HER THAT THEY LOVED HER AND

• • •

Words don't mean shit. What counts is what people do. While I was growing up, my parents said all these incredible things to me like "I love you" while they were holding me underwater.

"I love you. This is for your own good." "I love you. I'm going to let my friends play with you for a while." "I love you, but you're responsible for the breakup of our marriage, so I'm going to belt you."

So I grew up with confusion, because as a kid you're taught that when a grown-up tells you something, you should believe it. Words don't mean anything. I think about this a lot of times. We really ought to be careful with that because we're all gullible — because we all trust words.

Choosing to Survive

AS A RESULT OF HER ABUSE, VICTORIA BATTLES DEPRESSION, UNCONTROLLABLE CRYING, AND SHORTNESS OF BREATH. SHE'S NOT OK, BUT SHE'S TRYING.

• • •

There's some damage that can't be undone. I don't consider myself OK. I can make it sound like I'm OK, but I'm a great bullshit artist because I've had to fudge my way through everything in life. I'm really a depressed son of a bitch.

A few weeks ago, there was a whole week I didn't sleep because every time I closed my eyes, I'd see these babies. I just started shaking and crying. It was too much. They took me to the hospital. What do they do? They give me this megadose of Thorazine. It takes two hours for this stuff to affect my system — normally it takes like fifteen minutes, they tell me.

Should I just feel sorry for myself and say, "Poor Victoria, this is just the end of the world now," and give up? No. You take what you got, and you make the best of it. I'm not complaining about my life. I'm complaining about my insides. I wish I felt better. At this point in time I haven't gotten there yet, but I know I'm not going to give that bad feeling to my kids.

I don't want people to think that I'm incompetent. I want people to see me as strong. I want them to see me as a survivor. It probably comes from the fact that I felt so bad as a kid that I have to feel good now.

———

AFTER BEING ABUSED THROUGHOUT HER CHILDHOOD, VICTORIA GOT MARRIED IN HER TEENS, GOING FROM ABUSIVE PARENTS TO AN ABUSIVE HUSBAND. IN ORDER TO CONTINUE HER RECOVERY, SHE HAD TO LEAVE HER HUSBAND.

. . .

I did a lot of talking prior to getting married. I talked a lot about sexual things. So did he. Him being normal, me making it up as I went along—because I really didn't have any sense of sexuality, despite my past, because I didn't have any remembrance of the sexual abuse [at the point in time when she was getting married].

My husband tied me up, and he inserted things in me and stuff. We were Jehovah's Witnesses. It's a pretty fundamental religion: husband's in charge, wife's submissive. That was probably the only kind of religion I could get into after the kind of life I had. It gave me boundaries.

He's telling me pray to Jehovah, and I'm praying my guts out—day in and day out—and it's not happening [sexual satisfaction]. He gets the idea that I want him to take me. You know that macho thing.

Obviously [*sarcastically*] the message I'm giving to him is, If you take me, it'll be pleasurable. Somewhere in there I had some pleasure, and because of that he decided that violence associated with taking me and having sex was the answer to the problem.

I did talk to a counselor who told me to get the hell out of there, but I had this religion banging me over my head that said, There's no way—you made a commitment to God and to the world, and you guys are stuck together forever.

I grew up in fear, and I sure as hell was afraid of this thing called God. I listened to the counselor and I kept saying, "Yeah, yeah, yeah. I'm going to try." But I was scared to death, not of my husband at that point, but of God.

I never realized I had choices. I never realized I had power. I learned early that I didn't have power and what I wanted didn't matter. What everybody else wanted, especially if they were a male, they got, and if I was in a position to give it to them, that was it.

It took me a long time to get out of my marriage, although I don't know that I could have done anything sooner. I should have talked to somebody and listened to some supportive advice.

I believe in a higher power, but I mostly believe in me. When I was a Witness I was told pray to Jehovah, pray to Jehovah. Everything gets worked out. The fact of the matter is if you're out of a job and you pray to Jehovah, he's not going to give you a job. You've still got to get up off your ass.

———

VICTORIA BEGAN TO TURN HER LIFE AROUND WHEN SHE LEARNED THAT SHE WAS IN CONTROL.

. . .

When I finally decided to make a decision, suddenly my life changed. That is the biggest thing that we can teach our children: we all have choices. As a child you're helpless—you've got these big people over you doing these things to you. You don't have any choice. As adults, we all have choices.

Getting Help

———

VICTORIA HAS COME CLOSE TO STRIKING HER CHILDREN—CLOSE TO CONTINUING THE CYCLE OF ABUSE IN HER FAMILY—BUT SHE KNOWS SHE CAN GET HELP, AND SHE RECOMMENDS THAT PEOPLE IN SIMILAR SITUATIONS GET HELP, TOO.

If parents are abusing their children and know they're abusing them, I hope with all my heart they'll do something to help themselves. It's really tough, but there are a lot of places you can go today where you don't get punished for admitting that you need help.

They've got all these really neat commercials on television. You know: count to ten and all this stuff. I use them. However, there have been a few times when I've picked Richard [her son] up by the front of his shirt and held him against the wall. I try to go for a walk. I try to go in my room and blast the music to escape.

There are a lot of agencies that want to help keep families together and not break them up. The court systems don't hold it against you like they did at one time. Suppose you're in therapy. They don't say, "You're a bad person because you're in therapy." They say, "Great, you recognized you needed help, and you got it."

———

SOMETIMES VICTORIA'S SONS TRY TO MANIPULATE HER BY MENTIONING THE ABUSE IN HER PAST, BUT SHE'S TOO SMART TO FALL FOR THAT.

. . .

When they get really pissed off at me, they throw it back at me. They say, "You're going to abuse us now, right? Just like you were abused." I get really angry when they say that sort of thing, but bright kids are very manipulative. I've got to make sure that I don't lose it at that point. I've got to realize that they're just trying to pull a punch here to get what they want.

One Person Can Make a Difference

———

VICTORIA HAD A MIDDLE-SCHOOL TEACHER WHOM SHE CREDITS AS A BIG FACTOR IN HELPING HER ACHIEVE A BETTER LIFE. SOMETIMES IT TAKES JUST ONE PERSON TO TURN A LIFE AROUND.

. . .

Jane's an eighth-grade teacher I met when I had just been raped by my brother and thought I was pregnant. I wrote her a note and told her this. We were becoming friends—I was helping her with labs and stuff. She teaches science.

Anyway, she got involved in my life, and she basically gave me this ultimatum: You tell your father that you think you're pregnant and what happened, or I'm going to. I did tell my father. That was a bad situation, too. But I wasn't pregnant. That helped.

I ended up coming up to New Hampshire with Jane and her husband that year in November. It was the first time I remember being away from Vermont and all the craziness. I fell in love with it. I talked to my first cow. I saw these rocks and went to a beautiful pool. Went up to two lakes and everything.

Jane was the first person I remember who listened to me, and because of that I was able to make some changes. She said things like "You're good people," "I care about you," "You're worth something," "Not only are you smart, you can do this."

I had absolutely no confidence. For the very first time in my life, I developed confidence. Not a lot, but a spark—enough to keep me going. Sometimes teachers, when parents don't do it, can do it. We as adults can do it for kids, even if it's not our kids, by saying positive things.

I see Jane as the reason that my life turned around. "So you believe, so it will happen." It's all about choices. If you believe it to be, it can be.

———

Charlie Wedemeyer

. . .

HUSBAND, FATHER, AND ALS PATIENT

$\mathscr{B}$REAKING DOWN BARRIERS

. . .

Character cannot be developed in ease and quiet. Only through experience of trial and suffering can the soul be strengthened, vision cleared, ambition inspired, and success achieved.

HELEN KELLER

Unlike most people his age, Charlie Wedemeyer (age forty-seven) looks forward to getting another year older, because he's supposed be dead. Seventeen years ago his doctor told him that he had only one year to live. Wedemeyer has amyotrophic lateral sclerosis, or ALS—also known as Lou Gehrig's disease because it killed the famous New York Yankees' slugger.

ALS attacks the nerve cells that transmit impulses to muscles and destroys muscular control. Most ALS patients die within a few years of contracting the disease. A few, like Stephen Hawking, the British physicist, and Wedemeyer, live for years. They are, however, prisoners of their bodies and require care twenty-four hours a day.

Wedemeyer grew up in Honolulu. He won all-state honors in football, baseball, and basketball and was named Hawaii's Prep Athlete of the Decade in the 1960s. He went on to be a football star at Michigan State University and played in the East-West Shrine Game and the Hula Bowl. At the time of his diagnosis, Wedemeyer was a high school football coach in northern California. Wedemeyer's story is about having courage, accepting support, and doing God's work.

I interviewed Wedemeyer in the ten-by-fifteen-foot den of his home in Los Gatos, California. Wedemeyer lives in this room with a tube in his throat so he can breathe and a tube in his stomach so he can eat. But it is far from the depressing atmosphere of a hospital room. There are bright, flowery sheets, shelves filled with books, a thirty-two-inch Sony XBR Trinitron television, and windows with a view of a garden. Because Wedemeyer cannot speak, Lucy, his wife, and Linda Peevyhouse, his nurse, read his lips and spoke for him.

The Diagnosis

At first Wedemeyer attributed the symptoms of ALS to past football injuries. However, the doctor for the football team he coached told him to get more tests because of the severity and progression of his loss of muscular control.

. . .

Lucy: On the way home, after the tests, he was flat on his back in the station wagon because he'd had a myelogram [an X-ray of the spinal column involving a painful injection of dye]. As we rounded a corner, he could hear the cheers from one of the rival high schools, so he wanted to pull over and scout the game!

Later, Charlie and I watched a television movie about Lou Gehrig, and we saw symptoms that were the same as Charlie's — dropping the steak-sauce bottle, dropping the fork, and shuffling the feet. When Lou Gehrig died at the end of the movie, we figured, "That's Hollywood. They got to make 'em die." The next morning, I went to the library to look up ALS, and I could only find one paragraph in a medical book. It didn't say that ALS was terminal.

I called the team doctor to let him know we saw the movie about Lou Gehrig. To underplay the situation, he said that was nice, and asked Charlie to drop by. I told him not to tell Charlie anything unless I was there. Well, he told Charlie the tragic diagnosis and that he had one year to live. That was seventeen years ago.

Being Used by God

Wedemeyer lives in defiance of his doctor's prognosis. Although it requires a two- to three-hour procedure to leave the house, Wedemeyer, his wife, and his nurse make speeches to prisons, youth organizations, and church meetings all around the United States.

Charlie: It was very difficult at first to see my body wither away. I had to come to the point where I had to accept it and make the best of my situation. There is only one reason I'm alive seventeen years later, and that is because God has work for me to do. I believe God has a great sense of humor because He is sending someone on a speaking tour who cannot speak.

It didn't happen like this automatically. I didn't always have this attitude. I could see my body deteriorate, and it was very difficult for me to accept—because I was such an active person.

Lucy: Charlie saw that he was putting our family through a physical and emotional strain, and for a while he thought it would be better if he died. But he always remembered what I said: "We would rather have him like this than not have him at all."

Charlie had gotten to the point where he weighed ninety-five pounds, and he probably would have died within a couple of days. At that point he realized he didn't have any more of his own strength left. That was when the Lord came into his life. From that time on, God started working in his life and helped him to realize that even though his body wasn't working, his mind was, and God could use him.

If Charlie Had One Wish...

———

BEING IMPRISONED IN A NONFUNCTIONAL BODY, UNABLE TO CARE FOR YOUR-SELF, IS UNIMAGINABLE TO MOST PEOPLE. YOU MIGHT THINK THAT IF WEDEMEYER WERE GRANTED ONE WISH, HE WOULD ASK TO BE CURED. NOT SO.

. . .

Charlie: Win the lottery! [*Lucy interrupts, "You can't say that!"*] I want to have a nine-course Chinese dinner! Seriously, I would hope and ask Him for more opportunities to share with people.

Healing me would be nice, but it wouldn't be my first priority. I have more of an impact on people the way I am, and I know God has a plan and purpose for me. I am more useful to God in my situation than if I were walking around.

Lucy: We feel we have been chosen—blessed—to undertake a journey, and we have a responsibility to share. It has opened our eyes to the hurt that is out there. We recently spoke at San Quentin [a high-security prison in California], and someone asked why we would speak there.

The reason was to share a message of hope and encouragement with all kinds of people. Often when people are confronted with a situation that seems insurmountable, they lose hope. They don't realize that hope—real hope—only comes through a personal relationship with Jesus Christ.

Charlie: Our philosophy is that when you come up against a brick wall, you must be determined to find a way around it, whether it is over it, under it, or through it. Often when people are confronted with difficult circumstances, they don't realize that it isn't so much the circumstance but how they react, how they respond, and their attitude.

Lucy: Charlie finally realized that he wasn't going to worry about what he didn't have and what he couldn't do, but make the best of what he did have and what he could do. People tell us there is nothing wrong with them, but they are not doing anything with their lives. Then they see this guy who can't walk, can't talk, can't breathe, can't eat, and he is traveling all over the country motivating and encouraging people.

Learning to Cope

ALS PATIENTS AND OTHER PEOPLE WITH SEVERE DISEASES ARE OFTEN IGNORED AND ABANDONED BY THEIR FRIENDS AND FAMILY. WEDEMEYER BELIEVES THAT THE PATIENT—NOT FRIENDS AND FAMILY—IS RESPONSIBLE FOR CHANGING THIS SITUATION.

. . .

Lucy: Once there was a young man whose family and friends wouldn't come to see him. Charlie told him, "You know what? Maybe things will go better if you change your attitude and change the atmosphere in your house. Don't dwell on what's happening. Be a part of life. No one wants to be a part of this negative, depressing situation."

Later this young man acquired a marvelous nurse who took him everywhere. One time they tried to go on a roller coaster! Charlie also explained—and this is something important for anyone who is facing either a terminal illness or a catastrophic situation—that a lot of times loved ones, friends, and family abandon you. It is not because they don't care—most just don't know how to cope.

They don't know how to talk to you. They don't know how to share. They don't know how to express their feelings. Charlie explained to him that was why the young man's dad didn't come to see him: he loved him so much he couldn't bear to see him in that situation.

If you are complaining and whining about things, you need to realize that it is a blessing that you weren't killed in a car crash or that you don't have cancer and have to go through radiation or chemotherapy. There are blessings in everything.

———

INTERVIEWING THE WEDEMEYERS WAS A LOT OF FUN. THE LAUGHTER STARTED DURING OUR FIRST TELEPHONE CONVERSATION WHEN LUCY TOLD ME, "CHARLIE HAS ALS, AND I HAVE ALZHEIMER'S, BUT BETWEEN THE TWO OF US, WE'RE FINE," AND I DIDN'T KNOW IF SHE WAS KIDDING.

• • •

Lucy: Humor is such a big part of coping. Once we were driving into San Francisco with our children to be interviewed on CNN. They gave us the questions they were going to ask, so I told the children we should go through them. One question was how they reacted when they were told their father had ALS. The two of them said, "What? You mean that's why he hasn't talked to us all these years!" We almost had to pull off the road, we were laughing so hard.

The biggest thing is to look for the humor in situations rather than focus on the negative, because you can get so bogged down in the tragedy of it all: having to have a nurse, having to be monitored, and having to have a machine. People say, "How awful. Poor thing. You have to be hooked to a machine." Charlie usually says, "Are you kidding? It breathes for me! I love it!" They don't think of those things. It's really a mind-set. Healthy people don't seem to have a lot of this kind of an attitude.

DURING THE FIRST YEARS OF HIS AFFLICTION, WEDEMEYER HAD A LOT OF PRIDE, SO HE REFUSED TO ACCEPT THE HELP OF PEOPLE OUTSIDE HIS FAMILY.

• • •

Lucy: Charlie is a perfectionist, so this has been very hard for him. It's difficult to let someone else comb your hair or shave your chin. The first years of dealing with ALS were horribly agonizing for Charlie. He would hold one hand with the other to try to comb his hair.

When the townspeople first approached Charlie to do a fundraiser to help when medical costs were starting to accumulate, Charlie's reaction was "No, thank you." Pride got in the way. Instead of focusing inward on your problem, you need to focus outward.

Often we have so much pride that we won't allow anyone to help, but it is only by allowing people to help that your frustrations will be eliminated. Charlie didn't want anyone to help, but it helps the person helping you, too.

We all have handicaps of one kind or another—some are just more visible. There are a million people who have situations much worse than ours. The Lord has blessed us compared to families coping with drug abuse, alcohol abuse, and maybe not physical problems, but emotional ones. So we go home and shout, "Thank you God!"

Anne McLaurin

. . .

FORMER DRUG ADDICT

$\mathcal{R}$ECOVERING FROM ADDICTION

• • •

Marijuana ... makes you sensitive.... Unfortunately marijuana makes you the kind of sensitive where you insist on everyone listening to the drum solo in Iron Butterfly's "In-a-Gadda-Da-Vida" fifty or sixty times.

P. J. O'ROURKE

Until eight years ago Anne McLaurin (age thirty-eight) was a drug addict. Her addiction started with smoking marijuana at the age of thirteen. By nineteen, she had progressed to speed, amphetamines, heroin, barbiturates, and LSD. To pay for her habit, McLaurin stole from her parents, sisters, and dealers.

McLaurin grew up as a child of alcoholic parents. At age twenty-three she married an American musician she met in Iran, and he turned out to be an abusive person with drug and alcohol problems. After about six years they were divorced. McLaurin was on her own with two kids and one more on the way.

In 1985 McLaurin finally kicked her drug habit, and she has spent the next eight years getting her life together. She has custody of her three children—and no mate. She's trying to make a living as a sewer-repair person, find good day-care, raise her kids, and—when all of this is done—fulfill her own needs, too. If you're in a self-destructive cycle, McLaurin's hindsights may help you.

McLaurin and I met at a Marie Callender's restaurant in Walnut Creek, California. I liked her right away because she told me that my hindsights about learning a foreign language and traveling more when I was in college amounted to yuppie fluff. Our conversation must have sounded strange, because after a while, our waitress stopped coming to the table.

Fixing the Right Problem

AS A TEENAGER, MCLAURIN DIDN'T KNOW HOW TO FIX HER PROBLEMS. DRUGS

WEREN'T A SOLUTION, BUT THEY WERE A WAY TO ESCAPE.

· · ·

I smoked a joint in the seventh or eighth grade, and it was the best thing that ever happened to me. I was very insecure, so I got this drug-induced fantasy world and fantasy person. When I was straight, I didn't like Anne that much.

I remember what I was like when I was seventeen: I was out there doing it [taking drugs]. Marijuana's very addictive. It's very difficult to stop smoking pot. It just progressed. Speed was my drug of choice. I really liked amphetamines. Then I liked barbiturates to come off of the amphetamines.

I stole, but I didn't burglarize. I would steal from my parents. I would steal from dealers when they left the room to get another stash. I would steal from my sisters. Honestly, I can't tell you I would change it [her past], because I did have some good times. Toward the end, though, my worst day straight and in recovery was better than my best day using.

Making Tough Choices

HAVING GONE THROUGH A STORMY MARRIAGE, McLAURIN HAS COME TO BELIEVE THAT IT IS BETTER TO BE ALONE THAN TO BE WITH PEOPLE WHO DRAG YOU DOWN.

· · ·

We were living in a nineteen-and-a-half-foot trailer, and I missed Anne—I missed me. I missed what I had. I have a lot of enthusiasm and a lot of initiative, and I was dying. It wasn't very long, it was probably six or seven years, the whole relationship.

It's easier to be lonely by yourself than it is to be lonely with someone. The loneliness you feel with someone when there's no communication—and the trouble and strife—is gut-wrenching. The kind of loneliness when you're *alone*, alone is much less painful.

I remember thinking it would be easier by myself. There was

alcoholism, and I was addicted to drugs, too. When you're living with someone that has a drug and alcohol dependency, and you also have one, you seem to set an example for each other to keep on doing what you're doing because you're both doing it, and nobody's sicker than anybody else.

There was some violence, and he wasn't home a lot. I remember I really tried toward the end of the marriage, when the kids started coming. When I left their dad in 1984, I was really angry because they were all babies—actually, I was pregnant with Dan. It took a few years to get over the anger at my life.

———

QUITTING DRUGS WAS MCLAURIN'S MOST DIFFICULT CHALLENGE. SHE COULD FACE UNCERTAINTY AND A SOBER EXISTENCE ONLY BECAUSE SHE WAS BOLSTERED BY THE HOPE THAT HER LIFE WOULD BE BETTER.

· · ·

We all come to a place where we get down on our knees and cry out to God. Yet I can't tell you how many times I would get down on my knees and cry out to God, and I would get right back off that floor and use the drugs that were sitting in front of me.

To stop using, you have to have hope. You're risking something that's familiar and secure even though it might be a real terrible, horrible existence. Stopping means you're going to give that up for something you can't see, you can't taste, and you can't feel. It's the unknown.

The most pain I went through was emotional. I would use drugs instead of having to deal with any kind of emotional pain. When I quit, I was bombarded with all these feelings that I couldn't make go away without drugs anymore.

———

BEING A SINGLE PARENT—MUCH LESS A SINGLE PARENT WITH A DRUG ADDIC-TION—IS HARD WORK, BUT MCLAURIN FOUND PEOPLE AND ORGANIZATIONS TO HELP.

· · ·

You have to do your homework; you have to pound the pavement. You've got to knock on doors. There are people out there to help you. That's all they are there for. They're loving, kind people from all walks of life.

The stress center told me about the crisis nursery. The crisis nursery told me about the food bank. The food bank told me about this other church where I could get some other food. Project Self-Sufficiency told me I could leave my kids at the YWCA. The YWCA told me about an early-childhood mental-health facility. They told me about this nontraditional employment program.

I went to a meeting, and I heard about the Employment and Economic Status of Women Commission. I sat in on one of their meetings, and I applied. So I get in there and then *boom*, things just happen. Never give up. Never give up. Never.

———

—

Challenging the System

. . .

Sarah Weddington

LAWYER AND PRO-CHOICE ACTIVIST

$\mathscr{S}$TANDING YOUR GROUND

. . .

If men could get pregnant, abortion would be a sacrament.

FLORYNCE R. KENNEDY

Most lawyers never argue a case before the U.S. Supreme Court. Then there's Sarah Weddington (age forty-eight). In 1971, only four years after she graduated from the University of Texas at Austin School of Law, she pleaded her first contested case before the Supreme Court. It was one of the most visible cases in the Court's history.

Weddington successfully defended Jane Roe's right to choose to have an abortion. She and her team won the case by a seven-to-two decision, and life has not been the same for her, or American women, since. In this landmark decision, the Court ruled that state laws prohibiting voluntary abortions in the first trimester were unconstitutional. The Court also severely limited states' rights to impede a woman's decision to abort in the second trimester, though it ruled that states could prohibit most kinds of abortions in the third trimester.

To many Americans, the right to an abortion is a matter of privacy and freedom of choice. To quote Justice Harry A. Blackmun's majority opinion, "The right of privacy...is broad enough to encompass a woman's decision whether or not to terminate a pregnancy." To many others, legalized abortion is government-approved murder. Weddington has been explaining and protecting this decision for twenty years. Whether you're pro-choice or pro-life, you'll see that this chapter is about devotion to a cause.

This interview took place the day before the twentieth anniversary of the *Roe* v. *Wade* decision, at the Hyatt Regency hotel near the San Francisco airport. Weddington was in San Francisco to make six speaking appearances in two days. Surrounded by businessmen in three-piece suits about to do battle in Silicon Valley, we discussed abortion and women's rights in the hotel lounge.

Getting an Abortion

ABORTION IS A PARTICULARLY PERSONAL ISSUE FOR WEDDINGTON BECAUSE WHEN SHE WAS A TWENTY-YEAR-OLD, THIRD-YEAR LAW SCHOOL STUDENT, SHE HAD ONE. AT THE TIME SHE GOT PREGNANT, SHE WAS DATING THE MAN SHE LATER MARRIED, AND SHE WAS SUPPORTING HERSELF BY WORKING SEVERAL JOBS. SHE KNEW THAT SHE WAS NOT PREPARED TO RAISE A CHILD, BUT ABORTIONS WERE ILLEGAL IN TEXAS UNLESS THE PREGNANCY THREATENED THE LIFE OF THE WOMAN. IN 1967 WEDDINGTON CROSSED THE BORDER TO HAVE AN ILLEGAL ABORTION IN MEXICO.

. . .

My experience had an impact in that it created a determination to do all I could to be sure that no woman had to go through being a fugitive from her own state; being a criminal; or having to go to a country where she had never been, where she didn't speak the language, didn't know who was going to be at the other end of the journey, or what was going to happen.

It also taught me the desperation that women feel and the lengths to which they will go if they think something is necessary for their own survival.

THE DAUGHTER OF A METHODIST MINISTER AND A CHRISTIAN IN HER OWN RIGHT, WEDDINGTON HAD TO COME TO GRIPS WITH BOTH HER RELIGIOUS BELIEFS AND HER PRO-CHOICE ORIENTATION.

. . .

I still feel comfortable with my decision—partially because I felt strongly about being able to finish school and help my future husband finish school after that. All those things would have been impossible if that hadn't been my decision. Also, I've learned that you make decisions the best way you can at the time, and you don't spend a lot of time regretting them. I made a decision, and I still think that, given all the information, it was the right one.

The reasons most people give me for being opposed to abortion are religious reasons. I respect their right to have them but not to try to force them on other people. Part of my faith is that we were created and given the right to make our own choices, and the issue is not what choice someone should make.

It's not: if you are religious, then you are opposed to abortion. There are many people who are very religious and who believe abortion should be an individual decision. The issue is who gets to make the choice: will it be you, the government, or a stranger? The government or a stranger making the decision is abhorrent to my understanding of human dignity and my understanding of the American legal system.

Winning *Roe* v. *Wade*

WEDDINGTON ATTRIBUTES HER SUPREME COURT VICTORY TO THE TEAM SHE WORKED WITH AND TO GOOD TIMING.

. . .

First, there was a combined effort by many very talented people. It is certainly true that no one person ever wins a case of this magnitude. One person argues it, but that person is the tip of an iceberg of others who have contributed to the effort.

Second, it was a time when the Supreme Court had not yet been stacked against us. Today, I don't think you could win the same decision, because Reagan and Bush have stacked the Court against it. So it was a time when the court was receptive.

Third, *Roe* v. *Wade* was presented to the Court at a time when women were just beginning to expand their options. Previously, if you became pregnant, you had to drop out of school. In many situations, you were forced to quit work, and you had no right to come back.

The essence of abortion and its effect on women's lives was so visible—even more so than today. It was a time when the court saw that the old ideas and old limitations that applied to women didn't have a legitimate basis.

———

In the aftermath of the *Roe* v. *Wade* decision, one of the complexities that has surfaced is Jane Roe's credibility.

. . .

At the time we were considering filing a lawsuit, we believed that it would be preferable to have a pregnant woman as the plaintiff. The courts traditionally do not take cases unless they are "genuine" cases or controversies.

Jane Roe was the first person we considered to be a plaintiff who was not early enough in her pregnancy to have an abortion. She had very little money. She had never finished the tenth grade. Her first child was taken away from her by her own mother on the basis that she was unfit to raise a child. She was a waitress and thought she was going to lose that job if anybody found out she was pregnant.

She was a woman the court would not have looked at and thought, This woman would make a wonderful mother; but instead, the court might well have understood why there are times in various people's lives when it is not right to have a child.

Even with Jane Roe as the main plaintiff, the case was fought on behalf of all women who were or who might become pregnant and wanted to have the option to have an abortion. The case, in terms of the brief, the oral argument, and the decision, talked far more about legal issues for women in general than it did for any one person. So the plaintiff was symbolic.

When Jane Roe first came to us, she asked if it would help if she'd been raped. It didn't because there was no exception under Texas law for rape. Abortion was lawful only to save the life of the woman. We asked if there was a police report or any witnesses, and she said no.

We didn't know what the truth was, and we sure didn't want to get into a trial situation where we were trying to prove she was raped. We certainly weren't trying to win a decision that said if you are raped, you may get an abortion. Also, we weren't going to say anything in court that we couldn't prove. There was never any mention in the case of how Jane Roe got pregnant.

Six months after the decision, Jane Roe did an interview with *Good Housekeeping*. When I read it, I was astonished because there were all these details about a rape. As the years went by, her story expanded. Then finally in 1989 Carl Rowan, the Washington columnist, interviewed her, and she admitted there was no rape. This had no impact on the case, but it's been a real P.R. problem.

If Men Could Get Pregnant...

I ASKED WEDDINGTON TO CONSIDER THE HYPOTHETICAL QUESTION, WHAT WOULD HAVE HAPPENED IN *ROE V. WADE* IF MEN COULD GET PREGNANT?

. . .

I think it would alter the discussion. Pregnancy makes women feel vulnerable—vulnerable to needing support and help, vulnerable to the effect that caring for a child will have on other opportunities and commitments, and vulnerable in the physical sense.

If men could really understand that—not just intellectually but emotionally—it would have an impact, because men are used to being in control of their lot. This is not to say we would not have discussion, because there are women who are very opposed to abortion; but given the number of men in power, it would alter it, and the legality of abortion would become far less of an issue.

For me, the decision is symbolic of the issue of who makes decisions and who is in charge. I say women ought to be. For the opposition, I think abortion is symbolic of every change that has happened in society in the last twenty-some-odd years that they don't like. It became tied to a whole range of other issues, but *abortion* is the code word.

There are a lot of women who have chosen the role of wife and mother. Some who chose it want everybody else to have a choice. Some want everybody to have to make the same choice.

There are those who, for their own sense of self-worth, need to feel superior to others. At one time in this country some people said, "I'm white, and you are black. Therefore, I am better than you are." That is unacceptable behavior now. Or some said, "I'm male, and you are female. Therefore, I am better than you are." This is also unacceptable now.

Now people say, "I am moral, and you are immoral. Therefore, I am better than you are." Pointing the finger at somebody else has almost become a way for some people to build their own self-esteem.

The Personal Costs of a Cause

ROE V. WADE HAS BEEN THE FOCAL POINT OF WEDDINGTON'S LIFE FOR THE PAST TWENTY YEARS.

. . .

Had I known the costs in advance, I still would have done it—but I would have thought about it a lot more. We started by just doing research—not realizing it would become a federal case. Certainly not the U.S. Supreme Court case—or that I would still be talking about it twenty years later.

Three years of my life were spent litigating the case. After that, I became president of the National Abortion Rights Action League. I have never stopped speaking on the issue. It's almost as if it controls much of my time. I would like to move on to other issues, but I cannot until I feel the decision is safe.

There have been times when I talked to various law firms about a job. They said they knew I was a really fine lawyer, but they wanted to know if I would do anything controversial — referring to the abortion issue. Of course I wasn't going to give up being involved even to be part of a law firm.

Another thing — it's not exactly a cost, but a consideration — is that all of us expect our lives to have a progression, that with early successes we build toward greater successes and later successes. I did *Roe* v. *Wade* in my twenties. I was in the White House as an assistant to President Carter in my thirties. Now, how do I top all of that in my forties?

I am not sure it is possible. Nothing I can do could have more impact on the lives of women, and nothing could be a more historic event than *Roe* v. *Wade*. So it feels unnatural, because I am never able to leave the issue to concentrate on other things, and because there is a very good chance that forty years from now, I'll still be best known as the lawyer who argued *Roe* v. *Wade*.

———

STILL, WEDDINGTON IS PROUD THAT SHE WILL BE KNOWN FOR HAVING AN IMPACT ON AN ISSUE OF VITAL IMPORTANCE.

. . .

Everybody would like to know they had an impact and they were part of something that was important. I do have that satisfaction. The other thing that keeps me going is that people come up to me and say with gratitude that the decision made a real difference in their lives. This kind of feedback reminds me of the importance of the issue and therefore keeps me going and working on it.

———

BECAUSE WEDDINGTON DEVOTED SO MUCH OF HER TIME AND ENERGY TO *ROE* V. *WADE* AND PRO-CHOICE ACTIVISM, HER MARRIAGE ENDED IN DIVORCE AND SHE NEVER HAD CHILDREN.

. . .

I'm sorry the marriage didn't last, but I don't blame my ex-husband. It was a time when it was very hard for a man to be eclipsed in the public view by his wife's successes. Now, especially when a marriage is established and is of fairly long duration, if the woman becomes more visible, a marriage can last, but it was particularly hard back then.

I have found so much pleasure and satisfaction in my work and my accomplishments, and I doubt that it would have been possible if I had children. I am so glad that all my cousins have children — that I can adore them. But I am just so happy now.

I ended up being fairly typical [divorced and no children], but I hope in a way younger women don't have to be. Something like 96 percent of men in top leadership positions are married, and 90 or 92 percent have children. Of women in those same positions, there are only slightly over 50 percent who are married and about 33 percent who have children.

This is partly indicative that twenty years ago we were fighting to get accepted into law school. We were fighting to get jobs. We were having to work so hard just to push the doors open that it did not leave the time and energy for the more personal aspects of life. What has changed in twenty years is that younger women are much more likely to assume that they are as able as men to be married, have children, and work outside the home.

There are times when I think it would be nice to get remarried. I regret that my marriage didn't last, but I was a divorce lawyer for years, and I've seen a lot of people get divorced who didn't have the pleasures of their work that I did. So I just don't spend time having regrets.

The Lessons of Social Activism

———

AS ONE OF THE MOST VISIBLE AND EFFECTIVE PRO-CHOICE ACTIVISTS IN THE WORLD, WEDDINGTON HAS LEARNED SEVERAL PRAGMATIC LESSONS ABOUT THE EFFORT TO EFFECT SOCIAL CHANGE.

. . .

First, life—and activism—are both processes. Every time you think you've won something, you had better remember that it is a process. The next day there is probably going to be some hedging or chipping or opposition. You are always going to have to be doing it. It never ends.

Second, everyone has different roles to play. A group that does things one way will criticize another that doesn't do it the same way. This is generally counterproductive. For example, I am much more comfortable working within the system, but there are other people who are much more comfortable working in a more public, rowdy way. All of us can make a valuable contribution.

Third, one person really can have an impact. It is incredible that the case I was part of as my first contested case went to the Supreme Court. I sometimes wonder whether I would take a case of similar magnitude today; at that point I was so young that I didn't know the chances were totally stacked against winning.

Fourth, people just out of law school—sometimes earlier—are able to contribute to the intense work it takes. When I was first out of law school, I might not have known where the courthouse was, but my focus had been the theory of law. Now I know where the courthouse is, but my knowledge of theory is not as fresh. In recent years I have had to deal with what the law *is*—not necessarily what it *should be*.

Right after school there is an enthusiasm, a passion, and an energy. You see things more simply; therefore, it is easier to be passionate. Sometimes the longer you are involved in something, the more complexity you see, and the harder it is to have that same single-minded determination that something is the right thing to do and you are going to do it.

Now I know the odds, and it would be much harder to have the same enthusiasm. Also, I was used to living as a student, and

I could afford to volunteer most of my time. Today that would be much harder because of mortgages and car payments and financial obligations.

Seizing Unexpected Opportunities

CURRENTLY, WEDDINGTON TEACHES AT THE UNIVERSITY OF TEXAS AT AUSTIN SCHOOL OF LAW. HER CAREER HAS FOLLOWED AN UNPLANNED AND UNPREDICTED PATH, SO SHE NOW COUNSELS STUDENTS TO PICK A GENERAL DIRECTION BUT TO REMAIN FLEXIBLE.

. . .

When I was in college, I was going to be a seventh- and eighth-grade English teacher. Then I tried making seventh-graders love *Beowulf* and decided to go to graduate school.

In law school if you had asked what I was going to do, I would have said, "I am going to practice law in some little Texas town." But I didn't get a job with a law firm, so I ended up doing *Roe* v. *Wade* and eventually was elected to the Texas state Legislature.

If you had asked me when I was a legislator what I was going to do, I would have said, "Stay here." Except somebody called from Washington, and I served in the White House. If you had asked me in 1980 what I was going to do next, I would have said, "Serve in some position with the second Carter administration." But we lost, so I got to start over.

If you had ever asked me what I was going to be doing in five years, never in my life would I have guessed the right answer. What I try to teach my students is to have an idea of where you are trying to go, and try to get there, but to think of it as a direction that offers the opportunity to course-correct.

Walter Stewart

. . .

SCIENTIST

$\mathscr{B}$LOWING THE WHISTLE

. . .

No good deed ever goes unpunished.

BROOKS THOMAS

Dr. Walter Stewart (age forty-eight) is a research scientist at the National Institutes of Health (NIH) in Bethesda, Maryland. He studies allegations of scientific fraud and mismanagement. In 1986 he and Dr. Ned Feder became embroiled in one of the most visible cases of scientific fraud in recent times— the David Baltimore case. It involved a research paper on transplanted genes by Dr. Thereza Imanishi-Kari, director of an MIT laboratory. The paper was co-authored by Dr. David Baltimore and four others, and it was published in the scientific journal *Cell*.

A researcher in Imanishi-Kari's lab, Margot O'Toole, could not replicate some of the data in the paper. Imanishi-Kari's notebook, in fact, contained reports of data that conflicted with data in the research paper. When O'Toole brought this to the attention of scientists in the lab, her charges were super-ficially examined by peer-review committees at MIT and Tufts University and dismissed. Stewart and Feder reopened the case when they heard about it. Though Imanishi-Kari was the only person accused of faking data, Baltimore led the efforts to end, and some say inhibit, the official investigation by the NIH—making it *his* case.

The case moved from the backwaters of the scientific community to front-page news because of Baltimore's prominence. He was co-winner of a Nobel Prize in 1975 with Howard Temin for research about how viruses can induce cancer. Eventually, because of Stewart and Feder's efforts, the House Oversight and Investigations Subcommittee of Congress held hearings to re-view the case. After five years of controversy, Baltimore requested a retraction of the paper, and Stewart, Feder, and O'Toole were vindicated. What happened to them illustrates how the system reacts when its sovereignty is challenged.

Stewart, Feder, and I met at a coffee shop in Bethesda, Maryland, a few miles from the NIH campus. Though both of them participated in the interview, Stewart did most of the talking. They are nerdy scientists more than rebels or troublemakers. They weren't seeking controversy as much as they were ignorant of how (and why) they should play the game.

The Cost of Whistle-Blowing

STEWART WAS TRAINED AS A RESEARCH SCIENTIST IN ORGANIC AND NERVE PHYS-IOLOGY. HE BECAME A SCIENTIFIC SLEUTH OUT OF CURIOSITY.

• • •

Eight years or so ago, Ned [Feder] and I got interested in the question of measuring how frequently scientific misconduct occurs. We had an idea for studying a sample of scientists. We did the study and eventually got it published, and life has never been quite the same since.

In this group of forty-seven scientists, we found that some two-thirds of the group had done at least one thing that appeared to be either careless or irresponsible during a three-year period. That is, in some way they flagrantly disregarded the standards of care that scientists are presumed to use in their work.

More disturbing, we also found that approximately one-third had done something that had the appearance of a lack of candor. To put it simply, they appeared to have lied in their work.

NATURE FINALLY PUBLISHED THE FINDINGS OF STEWART AND FEDER'S STUDY, AND SOON THEREAFTER STEWART LEARNED ABOUT THE COSTS OF WHISTLE-BLOWING.

• • •

It took three years to get the study into print. As a result of publishing it, we received over two hundred pages of letters threatening that we, our employers, and any journal that dared to publish it would be sued.

As we received on-the-job training, we came to realize that

people who report allegations of scientific misconduct are almost uniformly mistreated extraordinarily harshly by the system. They're subject to all forms of vilification and harassment. Professional destruction is usually the result of bringing the matter to anyone's attention.

It's like being a rape victim. They're told it's their fault. They caused the problem. I've seen reports, for example, blaming the whole thing on the whistle-blower, when there was clear, convincing evidence of misconduct on the part of the senior person.

The odds that whistle-blowers will get any degree at all of public vindication are almost zero. It is virtually impossible for a person even with certain, clear, and convincing evidence of scientific fraud to receive any public vindication and to do anything other than to end his career.

The Inevitable Presence of Dishonesty in Science

SCIENTIFIC MISCONDUCT, HOWEVER, IS NOT BLACK AND WHITE. EVEN STEWART ACKNOWLEDGES THIS. TO HIM, SOME DISHONESTY—OR EXAGGERATION—IS INEVITABLE.

. . .

Lying, cheating, and dishonesty in science, except insofar as it is inimical to good science, has never been a big problem. I would not challenge a scientist's ability to lie, cheat, or steal, so long as it doesn't get in the way of honest science.

Why? Because most science is, by definition and common experience, worthless. Science is a gamble and an adventure, and ultimately a dream that exists in the mind of a person. Very, very few of those dreams pan out to reality.

Many, many of the big leaps that make an extraordinary difference in the way science works exist just as dreams in the first instance—leaps like figuring out that you can grow monkey kidney cells to defeat polio, or perhaps what it will take to develop a cure for AIDS.

Nobody can sit down and say, "I can do this if I can assemble all of the resources." If you can do that, you're talking about engineering. That's an extraordinary, important part of our society, but that's the kind of thing that pharmaceutical companies do.

The small fraction of dreams that do work far and away pays for the huge fraction that don't. Society also benefits from sponsoring a search for truth. So all practicing scientists are committed to the idea that much science will by necessity be wasted.

What frightens me is that the dishonest, hypocritical, or trivial science and the various forces that corrupt science are hampering younger people's ability to do honest science. I've been told by hundreds of scientists that the Baltimore case had an extraordinarily chilling effect on young scientists who may wish to tell the truth about someone's misconduct or simply buck their bosses on a point of science where they think their bosses are wrong—not necessarily fraudulent.

Government Intervention in Science

———

DURING THE INVESTIGATION OF THE BALTIMORE CASE, THE OVERSIGHT AND INVESTIGATIONS SUBCOMMITTEE USED U.S. SECRET SERVICE FORENSIC EXPERTS TO DETERMINE WHEN LAB NOTES WERE CREATED, AND THE SCIENTIFIC COMMUNITY WAS ENRAGED.

. . .

Government intervention in science is a catastrophe for science. Science is and should be a self-regulating profession, and scientists should take a leading role in dealing with misconduct.

However, when a document's authenticity is questioned, the proper, appropriate, and correct scientific response is to settle the matter in as clear and unequivocal way as can be done. This involves forensic science. If you want to address a matter of forensic science, you go to the world's leading experts to get the most clear-cut answer.

The Secret Service has an international reputation for being state-of-the-art with respect to inks and the types of things that were involved in this case.

Also, when scientists fail to solve these problems themselves, they are in fact subject to the Constitution. The Congress that pays the money for this research can and should according to the Constitution hold those who spend it accountable for what goes on.

The outrage is not that the appropriate congressional committee had to deal with it and did deal with it. The outrage is that at no point in the process were scientists—either independently or with Tufts, MIT, or National Institutes of Health—willing to step in and take the sorts of steps that would have resolved this controversy on a factual basis.

Understanding the System

IN THE END, STEWART AND FEDER WERE VINDICATED AND THE PAPER WAS WITHDRAWN, BUT NOT BEFORE STEWART LEARNED ABOUT HOW THE SYSTEM WORKS.

. . .

What Baltimore did when he was informed by O'Toole that the paper lacked proper scientific support was not to simply pull out the evidence and examine it. At no point did he look at the evidence. He assumed from the beginning and carried consistently through to the end a hostile and menacing role toward those raising the problem.

In my view, there's no question that what he attempted over a period of years was to cover this problem up. Why? The conventional explanation is arrogance. I suppose his actions were arrogant, and so arrogance is an explanation, but were it not for a simply extraordinary set of confluence of circumstances, he would have gotten away with it.

To a certain extent, the explanation of arrogance avoids a much more unpleasant fact: arrogance is a property of a single person or a mistake in judgment. However, the system doesn't effectively discourage dishonesty. Indeed, it is extraordinary that Baltimore suffered any consequences at all. This is a much more disturbing explanation.

When I discussed the case with Baltimore, he told me a number of things that I dismissed as blustering. I've come to believe he is in fact an accurate and excellent student of what actually goes on. He said to me, "I've been told you're a reasonable person, but you're not behaving reasonably in this case." He said that if any of his colleagues had this information, they would simply have told him, "I'm sorry, I have something I should not have," and sent it back.

I found his description of how his colleagues would behave utterly ridiculous. He also threatened me and said he would have no choice but to humiliate me publicly. He said it was either his neck or mine. I was looking for a more scientific basis to solve the dispute; I didn't see why it had to involve either one of our necks.

His description of how his colleagues would behave was absolutely accurate. He did not achieve his enormous power and prestige in science through not understanding the situation or the way the scientific establishment works. Even after his colleagues found out that he had ignored critical things, almost without any exception they rallied around him.

I credit him in a completely straightforward way with understanding the system much more accurately, much more thoroughly, and much more objectively than I ever did. I came to realize he was right that the system works against the whistle-blower, but of course it doesn't mean the system can't be changed or things can't work unpredictably in one particular case.

Postscript

In April 1993, Stewart and Feder found themselves embroiled in another controversy when they used a computer program to examine a book for plagiarism. This led the National Institutes of Health to shut down their lab and assign both men to other jobs. An official explained the reason for this action by stating that Stewart and Feder had gone "beyond the mission" of the Institutes.

Stewart went on a thirty-three-day hunger strike to protest the Institute's actions. He ended this strike when his doctor advised him that he was risking a heart attack and when his goals unexpectedly received strong support from Capitol Hill. I talked to Stewart two days before he began the strike, and he mentioned that his wife told him that he could "stand to lose a few pounds anyway."

John Taylor Gatto

· · ·

GUERRILLA TEACHER

$\mathcal{L}$EARNING TO LEARN

. . .

A teacher like you cannot be found.
[Signed] Your student, Milagros

MILAGROS MALDONADO

John Taylor Gatto (age fifty-seven) was a copywriter for an advertising agency in New York City. After writing shaving-cream commercials and the like for three years, he could no longer see the significance of his work. He left the agency to become a substitute teacher for kindergarten through eighth-grade classes in Harlem. Soon thereafter, he met a third-grade student named Milagros Maldonado in a reading class for slow students. She was a good reader, but school authorities had labeled her "a bad reader with fantasies of being a good reader"—whatever that means.

Gatto bucked the system and arranged a special test for her. She passed it and was placed in the advanced reading class. Her thank-you note (above) hooked Gatto on teaching, and he stayed in the profession for twenty-nine years. He was employed at some of the toughest public schools in New York City. During his teaching career, Gatto won the New York City Teacher of the Year award three times and was named the New York State Teacher of the Year in 1991.

Gatto quit teaching in July 1991—while he was State Teacher of the Year—because the school superintendent dragged his feet on implementing Gatto's idea for an alternative school. Believing that the system was more interested in perpetuating itself than in educating its students, Gatto became an activist for better education. If you're thinking of changing a system—and even if you're not—you will probably find Gatto very inspirational.

I interviewed Gatto at the airport in Salt Lake City before he went to speak at a home-schooling conference. I met him at the gate along with people from the convention—twelve kids and three parents, to be exact. The kids had painted signs that said "Welcome to Salt Lake City," "Did you have a nice trip?"

and "Hello John Gatto." The scene looked more like grandchildren welcoming home their grandpa than students greeting a convention speaker at the airport. And Gatto, like a grandpa, collected all the signs to take home as souvenirs.

Challenging Accepted Beliefs

GATTO WASN'T ALWAYS THE RADICAL HE IS TODAY. WHEN HE BEGAN TEACHING IN THE EARLY SIXTIES, HE BELIEVED THAT STUDENTS VARY SIGNIFICANTLY IN LEARNING ABILITY AND THEREFORE SHOULD BE PLACED IN DIFFERENT CLASSES.

. . .

I believed that the Gaussian bell curve described human reality so well that people who fell two standard deviations away had to be morons or needed medical attention. But I kept seeing some kid produce a flash of brilliant insight which didn't fit with the numbers and pattern he was in. If that only happened once or twice, you would say, People are human; they mislabeled this kid. But it happened over and over again.

After I was teaching a couple of years, I went home and told my wife I was going to assume that the bell curve is nonsense, that people come equally equipped and that all the information I had to deliver was equally accessible to everyone. The results were so spectacular that I didn't want to believe them, because I had spent a lifetime believing in the bell curve, and I knew that rejecting it would get me in extremely hot water because our society is built around this idea.

I was teaching upper-middle-class students, and people told me this only worked because I was dealing with rich kids. So I transferred to a school with mentally disturbed kids. I worked there for five or six years and found that using the identical process—just saying "Educate yourself!"—worked. It's more complicated than this, but the bottom line is that teachers are much less important than they appear to be.

I couldn't teach there much longer because I was holding off administrators and politicians to run these experiments. I figured I would be able to do this with ghetto kids, who nobody gives a shit about—no matter what people say. So in 1987 I transferred to the school that produced seven of the nine rapists of the Central Park jogger. I had a 60 percent Harlem black class, and the other 40 percent was from Dominican Spanish Harlem plus a few Puerto Ricans.

Applying the same principles took a little bit longer but not much longer, and I got the same results. I had kids winning citywide essay contests who were on the record as not being able to read and write. Here are all these kids, and the bell curve is flattening in front of my eyes. It wasn't something that happened because I hoped it would happen. It happened because the core premises of teaching are wrong.

———

YOU WOULD THINK THAT THE EDUCATIONAL SYSTEM WOULD APPLAUD GATTO'S FINDINGS THAT STUDENTS ARE MORE CAPABLE THAN PREVIOUSLY BELIEVED AND WOULD EMBRACE HIS METHODS. NOT SO.

• • •

As the kids produced a record of success that was really unparalleled, rather than a stream of accolades descending on me in support, the exact reverse happened: I was ostracized, marginalized, and harassed. Strong attempts were made to drive me out of the teaching business.

Was it something personally directed against John Gatto? At first you wouldn't be human if you didn't think that it had to be personal. Gradually, I came to see that everywhere someone had set up a different code. The same thing happened to Jaime Escalante. Last year he was driven out of Garfield High. He didn't leave. [Escalante was a teacher in a ghetto area of Los Angeles whose students became outstanding calculus students. The movie *Stand and Deliver* is about him.]

Marva Collins, who taught Shakespeare and Plato to black eighth-graders in Chicago's inner city, was driven out of her public school. Her success doomed her because if one student breaks loose and floats to the top, that is a wonderful thing, and the dedication of

Marva Collins can be warmly rewarded. But what if a third of her class breaks loose? Suddenly everyone in the city is looking at all these sludge classes and asking if it is just barely possible that they aren't sludge classes.

No system can survive unless the myths of the system are honored and celebrated and worshipped.

False Standards

GATTO HAS COME TO UNDERSTAND THAT OUR EDUCATIONAL SYSTEM JUDGES CHILDREN TOO EARLY AND TOO OFTEN. THESE JUDGMENTS CREATE A FALSE SET OF STANDARDS AND CAN SERIOUSLY DAMAGE STUDENTS FOR THE REST OF THEIR LIVES. TO ILLUSTRATE HIS POINT, GATTO USES THE PROCESS OF LEARNING TO READ.

• • •

Reading is a process that is exceedingly easy to master—not just to learn, but to master. The only exception is if it is imposed at a certain age. The school system creates a set of winners who happen to be congruent with a certain level of reading at a certain age, and a whole lot of losers—some of them permanent losers and many of them different degrees of loser because the system has interfered with some psychic or sociological appointment they were keeping.

Kids automatically learn to read—I stress and underline *automatically*—between the ages of two and fourteen. People learn to read superbly well *if* the context around them seems to enjoy printed language. Nobody on earth can tell the difference between somebody who learned to read at two and somebody who learned at fourteen, by the time they are sixteen.

I've seen this confirmed so many times that I realized I was in the presence of one of the greatest scams in human history. I've seen two-, three-, four-, and five-year-old kids read so fluently and learn so easily, whatever social class they come from, that I am utterly convinced that it is exactly like walking: it is a physiological function.

As a theory this is intriguing, but actually seeing this over a period of years taught me that the system says, "I am sorry, but you are not keeping up with your first-grade classmates. We are going to put you in remediation for your own good." At six and at seven they say, "You are way behind even after remediation. We are going to put you in special education."

By that time, the kid has either developed a tremendously combative personality because the other kids are driving him in the corner, or he's turned into this jellyfish who thinks that he is not fit for human society. The structure and sequences of compulsory schooling mandate this disaster, not some personal failure of the kid.

The Guerrilla Curriculum

WHILE HE WAS INSIDE THE EDUCATIONAL SYSTEM, GATTO UTILIZED GUERRILLA TECHNIQUES TO PROMOTE THE EDUCATION OF HIS STUDENTS AND LEARNED BOTH THE PROS AND THE CONS OF TRYING TO CHANGE THE SYSTEM.

. . .

I spent my teaching career devising sabotage strategies—what I called the guerrilla curriculum—to underline the adversarial nature of good teaching inside the government compulsory school machine. It was not welcome. Good teachers and kids learning are not what schooling is about. Think of the word *school*, and you'll understand— fish swim in schools.

A great lesson I've learned—the bad lesson that all rebels learn— is that trying to change the system eats away at your life. You can't go home at five o'clock. The forces arrayed against you only have to work ten minutes each, and they've got you busy round the clock. By constantly intervening and throwing a monkey-wrench into the little experiments you're conducting, they can drive you to insanity, or they can destroy your family.

But let me tell you the good part now. If you deliberately set out to sabotage the system and you keep yourself flat against the wall, move fast, and don't give a profile that computers can home in on, then you can cause massive damage to a huge system. And this is one person doing it. If a handful of people are doing it, I think any system on earth could be brought to its knees—largely because the cohesion of the system doesn't exist. It's an illusion.

For five years I ran a guerrilla school program where I had every kid, rich and poor, smart and dippy, give 320 hours a year of hard community service. Dozens of those kids came back to me years later, grown up, and told me that one experience of helping someone else changed their lives, taught them to see in new ways, and to rethink goals and values.

My public speaking, like my teaching, is a test of what one nobody like myself can do without any resources. My answer is, An enormous amount! Not all the job, of course, but an enormous amount of it. It wouldn't take many of us to change the deal we give kids, and it is so much fun to work this way.

There are so many ways to teach kids right. There is no consensus about what is best—nor should there be. Artificial systems are the invention of a man or a group of social engineers—the best of them wildly deviate from human reality. The only way they can seem to work is by mutilating the people that are in them. Now mutilated creatures eventually—most of them, at least—learn to accept their mutilation and do the best with it.

———

AFTER TWENTY-NINE YEARS OF TEACHING, GATTO UNDERSTANDS WHAT IT TAKES FOR A TEACHER TO BE EFFECTIVE.

• • •

The government system won't let you be a teacher unless you expend an awful lot of effort conforming to it, but if you are going to stay in it—and be useful to kids—you've got to define yourself as a saboteur. You've got to see yourself as an independent agent, and since you can't remain employed as an independent agent, you're going to have to conceal that in some fashion. Then, when you see harm being done to children—by standardized tests, for example—you have to sabotage that process.

Don't ask me how that is done, but once someone begins to think like a saboteur, it is not hard to figure out. I will only say that when it's time to conduct standardized testing, all over the United States announcements are made by panicky assistant principals over loudspeakers that somebody has accidentally picked up Mrs. Jones's tests and could they please be returned at once. When that happened in my school, it wasn't an accident, and the tests weren't ever returned. There are dozens of creative and sophisticated ways to carry the idea of sabotage even further—beginning with teaching kids to critically analyze the process of schooling.

Teachers have to understand that they are independent and sovereign. If they don't, they are going to communicate some measure of damage to kids by not being real. If they are in the service of someone else's idea, they are not completely real. If they are true believers and absolutely sold on the existing system, then their teaching is close enough to an honest expression of themselves not to do much damage. But my experience with twenty-nine years in the business is that nobody thinks this thing works; thus, the cynicism of working for a paycheck, no matter how much damage the process inflicts, corrupts large portions of the teaching staff.

You have to free yourself of fear as a teacher or as a student. You do that by using your eyes and ears and a little research to figure out just how easy it is to make a living. It's fairly easy not only to make a living but to make a lot of money if that is your thing. Then you are freed from this constant threat that your future will collapse on you.

Once you have done that, you have to free yourself from defining yourself by other people's measures. You aren't really a "you" at all until you know yourself. You define yourself by testing yourself, falling on your face, getting up, and eventually a self-definition emerges that you can be comfortable with.

How to Encourage Learning

———

GATTO HAS TWO CHILDREN. THEY WENT THROUGH THE TRADITIONAL EDUCATION SYSTEM, THOUGH HE NOW BELIEVES THAT HE AND HIS WIFE SHOULD HAVE TAKEN A MORE ACTIVE ROLE IN THEIR EDUCATION AND PROTECTED THEM FROM GOVERNMENT SCHOOLING.

• • •

My son was a National Merit Scholar, and my daughter was a Presidential Scholar and National Merit finalist. Out of the millions of kids that compete for these awards every year, about 8,000 get them. I came to realize that being a National Merit scholar was a form of nonsense; and more than that, it was pernicious, poisonous nonsense. Both, my kids were taught to define themselves by other people's evaluations. Both had a real hard time digging out from under that garbage. That was my fault and responsibility, not theirs. I told you: I was slowly backed into seeing reality. I didn't want to believe it.

The right way for me would have been to gather ourselves together and for me to say, "This is the big world. We are all going to be learners in it. Because I am older, I'll protect you and put a shield around you. You test your hypotheses on me first. If I disagree with you, and you are absolutely certain you are right, then I'll protect you as you follow your own direction." That's what I should have done. Your family has to be the strongest idea in your kid's mind, and it can't be that unless it is the strongest idea in your own mind.

To encourage learning in a child, first you help him develop a self-identity. To do this, you have to encourage — not only allow — risk-taking from the get-go. I would say that nine months is probably not too early to start. That kid ought to be just bombarded with chances to take risks. He wants to crawl around, and he's going to fall off the step into your living room? You can calculate that this is not going to kill him or break his little head, and then let him do that.

When it seems like a kid is playing or goofing around, the kid's figuring out who he is and how he thinks. Once you've got a self-identity in place, and that can probably happen clearly by the time you are two, you've solved half of the problem. Sixty percent of the kids I encounter didn't have that, and they are going to flounder for the rest of their lives. I'm not sure whether it is possible to ever be completely confident in your identity if you aren't allowed to fashion it early.

Second, by the time you are three, if you don't have a clear sexual identity—if you don't know the roles assigned to your gender and you don't like your gender—then you've got trouble for the rest of your life. You may very well have a success in the world's eye—a lot of money in your bankbook and six kids—but you've got a lot of trouble.

Third is a belief in risk-taking. This means you feel that the world is such a safe place that any risk you take is OK because nothing much bad can happen to you. You've got to know where the limits of trust are, and nobody can tell that to you. You've got to find that by getting slapped down. It's a misconception to think you are doing somebody a favor by sparing them that.

So those three things: a self-identity, a sexual identity—if that bothers people, give them my phone number—and a belief in risk-taking. After that it is hard work. The harder the work you can lay on a kid, intellectual and physical, the more complicated his brain will grow.

I'm teaching grown-ups what I learned teaching kids so that someday we won't need compulsory schooling at all—as we didn't for the first 250 years of American history. And by the way, my daughter will be teaching my granddaughter at home, so the National Merit folks will have to look elsewhere for future victims.

———

Dave Foreman

• • •

ECO-WARRIOR

$\mathcal{S}$AVING THE EARTH

. . .

We abuse land because we regard it as a commodity belonging to us. When we see land as a community to which we belong, we may begin to use it with love and respect.

ALDO LEOPOLD

Dave Foreman (age forty-six) is an eco-warrior. He is waging a war against land development and industries that destroy the ecosystem. In 1980, frustrated by the growing bureaucracy of existing conservation groups, Foreman co-founded Earth First!, a radical environmental-action group. Believing that traditional methods of reform were insufficient, Earth First! advocated and practiced eco-terrorism—the use of sabotage to thwart logging and land development.

Foreman believes in deep ecology, the concept that the Earth is one big system with interdependent and equally important species of flora and fauna. In Foreman's opinion, it is more important to save the planet than any single species—including humans. Foreman has dedicated his life to changing the way people think about the environment. His interview is about working within the system, working outside the system, and eventually realizing that one must do both to succeed.

I met Foreman in Tucson, Arizona. He was late for our interview because he was stuck in traffic while driving back from a white-water rafting trip. I expected a rabid terrorist of a person—a veritable Green Rambo. Instead, I met a sunburned, middle-aged nature lover in an Aloha shirt who, with his round face and twinkling eyes, would make a terrific Santa.

Maintaining Your Ideals

———

BEFORE HE STARTED EARTH FIRST!, FOREMAN WORKED FOR THE WILDERNESS SOCIETY FOR EIGHT YEARS. HIS EXPERIENCE YIELDS A VALUABLE LESSON ABOUT HOW ORGANIZATIONS CAN CHANGE.

. . .

The conservation groups back in the seventies were different than they are today. The big, mainstream groups like the Wilderness Society still had connections to the past. For example, Bob Marshall's [the founder] two brothers were still on the Wilderness Society Council even though Bob had died in 1939. Bob was my hero, so when I met these two guys it was like touching John Muir.

There was that wonderful camaraderie of conservation. The people working for conservation groups in those days were grass-roots conservationists who had come up through the ranks. Ernie Dickerman, one of the lobbyists at the society, was a Great Smoky Mountains hiker who had been an original member of the Wilderness Society in 1935. It was also a wonderful bunch of folks to work with. It really was a family.

Things happened in the seventies on several levels. One, we had just been through most of the Carter administration. Unlike the Clinton administration, the folks that Carter appointed to office said, "We are conservationists too." "Leave it to us." "Don't worry about us." "Don't lobby us." "We'll take care of it."

We thought we could take it easy on the Carter administration because they would do a good job for us, and quite frankly, we got the shaft. The Forest Service's second Roadless Area Review and Evaluation (RARE II) occurred during the Carter administration, and we played the game. We were very moderate. We actually sold out, and we still wound up losing.

The other thing that happened was that conservation groups were changing very radically. Professional fund-raisers were becoming the tail that wagged the dog, and groups were getting hooked like junkies on a direct-mail treadmill. A new person was hired as executive director of the Wilderness Society who was very business-oriented, but he did not appreciate what the Wilderness Society was.

There are problems when professional staff people in D.C. are setting policy instead of the conservationists back in the field. There are problems when you spend a huge amount of your budget every year on direct mail—Greenpeace is sending out 40 million pieces of direct mail a year.

You can't compromise on your principles. You can certainly make deals and compromise in specific instances, but you don't sell out your principles. Also, organizational structure determines a great deal of philosophy. Certain organizational structures make it very hard to be visionary, idealistic, and to maintain an *esprit de corps*.

While you need efficiency, competence, responsibility, and people where the buck stops—in an organization that is working for something idealistic—the organization is not the bottom line. The Sierra Club should be more sierra than club. The Wilderness Society should be more wilderness than society.

Pushing the Edge

———

FOREMAN SAW THE NEED FOR A MORE VISIBLE AND MORE CONTROVERSIAL FORM OF ENVIRONMENTALISM. HE LEFT THE WILDERNESS SOCIETY TO FILL THAT NEED.

• • •

I guess what I've always done as a conservationist is look for the empty niche, for what needs to happen and what nobody else is doing. It seemed to me that the environmental conservation movement needed a big boost, that issues needed to be dramatized, and that the envelope needed to be pushed.

Earth First! did that. A perfect example is the ancient-forest issue in the Pacific Northwest. When Earth First! was started, there was no ancient-forest issue. In 1980, Howie Wolke [a co-founder of Earth First!] and I were the first people to call for a stop of all logging of old-growth forests in the national forest. Nobody had ever thought of that before. Conservation groups had shied away from some of those issues.

———

. . .

It's one way for the people without power to thwart things. The very word *sabotage* goes back to the French word for wooden shoe — *sabot* — because wooden shoes were thrown into the gears of machinery.

When *The Monkey Wrench Gang* [by Edward Abbey] was published in 1975, it was sort of group therapy for a lot of folks in the movement who were frustrated. It was a good release. It was vicarious. By 1980 it had attained mythic stature, so while we weren't out front advocating monkey-wrenching when we started, it was part of the mythos.

The Boston Tea Party is a perfect example of monkey-wrenching, but like so many other things, it's a real chancy tactic. It is one that a person has to think very carefully about and be very rigorous about.

Another negative aspect is that it tends to attract kooks. Earth First! became the "in" radical group of the eighties, so people became attracted to it who didn't understand the history of Earth First! and the frustration that led to it. They were just angry people, or they wanted to be where the action was.

———

. . .

In a way, the arrest is a great compliment. It says as much as anything that what we had done during the 1980s was effective. There are very, very few things I would do differently. You've got to remember that when we started Earth First!, we didn't expect it to last that long.

The groups of John Muir, Aldo Leopold, and Bob Marshall were being transformed into something else, and there was a feeling that we had been compromising too much and making so many deals that we were forgetting our vision.

Earth First! was a tool to do a specific job: to try to get the conservation movement back on track, to get conservationists back to their roots, to keep us from compromising too much, to get away from organizational maintenance, and to talk about biological diversity. Earth First! succeeded beyond my wildest dreams.

The Power of Diversity

AS FOREMAN GAINED INTERNATIONAL EXPOSURE AS AN ECO-WARRIOR, HE FRE-
QUENTLY CRITICIZED EXISTING CONSERVATION GROUPS SUCH AS THE SIERRA CLUB—
PERHAPS TOO HARSHLY.

. . .

Throughout the whole time of Earth First!, I was a member of the Nature Conservancy and the Sierra Club. I was critical of them because there are problems when you pay people $200,000 a year in a volunteer group. There are problems when you hire political operatives instead of conservationists to be lobbyists.

Public-interest groups should not be immune from public scrutiny and criticism. That is how we get better. That is how we improve ourselves. The mistakes I made were that some people took my criticism too personally. My criticisms were probably a little harsh and flippant—those types of things I would change.

FOREMAN'S OPINION OF OTHER GROUPS IS LESS DOGMATIC AND MORE BROAD-
MINDED THAN HIS REPUTATION. HE BELIEVES DIVERSITY STRENGTHENS THE ENVIRON-
MENTAL MOVEMENT.

. . .

One of the things that is so wrong with advocacy and activism in our country is that most people feel that they have to argue for their way and that there is one way to do things. I don't believe that.

There are 10,000 different ways and styles and tactics and approaches to protect the biological diversity of Earth, and we have to use them all. What is beautiful about the conservation movement—the many groups involved and the volunteers involved—is that you get that diversity.

You get people working their own way with their own strengths—working on the issue that they really believe in. That gives the movement a great deal of strength.

The Value of Human Life

———

EARTH FIRST! GOT ITS NAME FROM THE BELIEF THAT THE EARTH SHOULD COME FIRST—EVEN BEFORE HUMAN LIFE. FOREMAN EXPLAINS WHAT HE SEES AS THE RELATIONSHIP BETWEEN HUMANS AND THE EARTH.

• • •

Humans are part of the Earth. We cannot live without Earth. Earth can certainly go on without us. As James Lovelock says, We were arrogant to think that human beings will ever destroy life on Earth, but Earth may very well rid itself of humans.

We have to recognize that life has been on Earth for nearly four billion years. Human beings have been here for a little over 100,000 years. Civilization has been here for 10,000 years. Industrialism has been here for 200 years.

Let's try to put things into a little bit of perspective. Human beings aren't going to be around forever. We are not the end point of creation or evolution. We aren't something separate from and superior to the rest of life. We are another species, and unless we develop some wisdom, we aren't going to be here much longer.

———

BUT WHAT WOULD FOREMAN DO IF CUTTING DOWN YEW TREES COULD SAVE HIS MOTHER'S LIFE?

• • •

I think it is a lot more complicated than that. If you cut down all the yew trees right now, how much Taxol could be produced from them to save how many people? Then what do you do for everybody else who is going to get cancer? And most people are getting cancer now because of industrial pollution.

We seem to have this terror of death in modern American society or modern civilization that says you have to do anything to prevent death—even cause a person to suffer horribly. I remember ten years ago when my mother was in critical care in the hospital with emphysema and had a respirator and everything else. She pulled the respirator out. She asked me to do it because she didn't want to live that way. I didn't do it, but she did it. I really respect her for that. She made a value-based choice.

Certainly human life is valuable, but we are all going to live a certain number of years. None of us is going to live forever, and what kind of legacy do we leave? The quality of life is more important than the quantity. Do we leave the world a better or a worse place because of our life? Those are more important questions.

———

—

Changing the World

. . .

Anita Roddick

• • •

ENTREPRENEUR

COMBINING PRINCIPLES AND PROFITS

. . .

A visitor arrived inquiring about Zen. Master Nan-in (1868–1912) silently poured him a cup of tea and continued pouring until the cup overflowed. "Why do you continue to pour after the cup is full?" asked the visitor. "To show you," replied Nan-in, "that you are like this cup: so full of preconceptions that nothing can go in. I can't tell you about Zen until you have emptied your cup."

ZEN TO GO BY JON WINOKUR

Anita Roddick (age fifty-one) is the founder, evangelist, and soul of The Body Shop. To say that the company embodies her aspirations and concerns is an understatement—she *is* The Body Shop. The Body Shop, for those of you who haven't slathered banana conditioner on your hair, is a skin-care, hair-care, and accessories retailer that started in the United Kingdom in 1976. Today, there are over 900 Body Shop outlets around the world.

The mission of The Body Shop is to combine profits with principles. Profits are easy to understand. Roddick's principles include refusing to sell products tested on animals, buying goods from underdeveloped parts of the world, and training Body Shop employees to be effective salespeople and responsible citizens of the world. Roddick's story is about a corporate executive combining social responsibility with entrepreneurship.

Our interview took place in Roddick's hotel suite in Morristown, New Jersey. Roddick, who resides in her native England, was in the United States for a meeting of The Body Shop's American franchisees. I expected her to be taller than the petite five-feet-two-inches she is because I'd seen her in pictures standing a head taller than male Kayapo and Yanomami Indians. Her hair, however, was no surprise. It was every bit as wild and curly as befits this uninhibited woman who challenged the status quo of business.

"Bloody Survival"

IN 1976, RODDICK WAS FORCED TO SUPPORT HERSELF AND HER CHILDREN WHEN HER HUSBAND DECIDED TO FULFILL HIS DREAM OF RIDING A HORSE FROM BUENOS AIRES TO NEW YORK CITY.

. . .

When Gordon wanted to go off for two years to ride his damn horse, I was left with the kids, and I had two options. One was I find a job, but I was not employable because I was a teacher who was fairly radical.

Forget entrepreneurial dreaming. For me, it was if I didn't make the money, the kids wouldn't be fed, and there is not much more to the need to survive than that. The hindsight there is bloody survival.

Also, I wanted to be in control of my own life and put my stamp—my thumbprint—on something. Being a teacher, I could see the playground I could have. And constantly, constantly—this is a prerequisite in my life—I have to learn.

This is such a thirst because I have such a fear of dying. My entire life is run by that fear. Even sleep to me is like a sliver of death. I'm a good Catholic girl brought up to believe that I deserve nothing. I've lived my life, honest to God, like I not only don't deserve to have it, but petrified at the thought of how finite it is.

RODDICK BUILT A BUSINESS THAT PRODUCES ABOUT $300 MILLION IN SALES PER YEAR—A LEVEL OF SUCCESS THAT IS FAR BEYOND HER EARLY EXPECTATIONS. HER APPROACH TO BUSINESS WAS NOVEL FROM THE START.

. . .

We didn't know how to run a business in a traditional way— that a business's purpose was to earn a profit. If we had known that, we probably would have screwed up everything because we would have been confined by the language of business—that everything had to have a quantitative measurement to it.

We ran a business which was an extension of our playground or of our living room—an extension of the things we cared about. We didn't even know what marketing was. We didn't know what a profit-and-loss sheet was.

We just wanted to not stop what we were doing in our home, in the streets, and in the causes we were espousing twenty-five years ago. We couldn't understand why it could not continue in the workplace.

Why The Body Shop Succeeded

IN SPITE OF HER UNCONVENTIONAL METHODS OF DOING BUSINESS, RODDICK ATTRIBUTES THE SUCCESS OF THE BODY SHOP TO TRADITIONAL CONCEPTS LIKE GOOD PRODUCTS AND HONEST MARKETING.

. . .

The products are good. We could not have succeeded with a bad product. We didn't have an advertising budget for that. We didn't know how to seduce a customer with some complex images.

There was a close understanding of women because there was me organizing and getting the products made. Over the course of the past seventeen years, the decision makers in terms of the products, manufacturing, development, and even language were all women, and that puts a different wash to things that are said.

If you take a look at the language of The Body Shop, it is one step away from puritanical. There are no claims. Instead, it's this is in it, this is why it's in it, and this is what it does—the story of the product. This is almost a clarion call in an age where sellers work overtime to seduce buyers.

That is number one. Two and three, we had a good smell. Nobody thought of using smell to capture the senses in terms of the total senses. From the very first day when nobody would come in the shop, I dripped the perfume down the road. They were all early-memory smells like fruits and flowers—they weren't very sophisticated combinations or formulations.

The other thing was that my shop was totally nonintimidating. Remember, this was 1976, and the entire cosmetics industry was run by Max Factor and Revlon. It was the time when everything had to have a scientific edge to it—the magic X ingredient. We didn't know anything about that, so we just told the stories about the natural ingredients.

TO GIVE THE BODY SHOP GREATER VISIBILITY, RODDICK FORMED PARTNERSHIPS WITH VARIOUS ORGANIZATIONS INCLUDING ENVIRONMENTAL GROUPS. THE BODY SHOP SPONSORED GREENPEACE POSTERS, FOR EXAMPLE, AND THE SAVE THE WHALES CAMPAIGN. THESE ALLIANCES DIDN'T WORK, BUT RODDICK LEARNED A VALUABLE LESSON ABOUT DEPENDING ON OTHERS.

. . .

Do projects yourself. Don't go in with anybody else. We learned that early, and we don't associate with any large corporation or environmental group. They are too pedantic and too conservative, so now we use them as resources.

I love Greenpeace in one sense because they understand they had to be confrontationists—which they did well—to get profile. But working with Greenpeace was difficult. When you come in with real enthusiasm for a cause, and then suddenly this group says they won't run this campaign in Germany because it came out of England—that's a pain in the neck.

Greenpeace was fine, but it took them years to make a decision. Everything fell to the lowest common denominator. Everything had to be decided so democratically. You can't run a business or an idea democratically. You have to have somebody there who has got the vision and the speed and the passion that people should follow.

I've never seen a more territorial, conservative, back-smacking, backbiting group than I have in nongovernmental organizations, and especially environmental groups. There is just no love of the shared interest or the notion we are playing out the biggest suspense story ever told: we are going to die as a species if we don't get our act together. The sense of territory and sense of nonsupport is mind-boggling.

The Downside of Going Public

IN APRIL 1984, THE BODY SHOP WENT PUBLIC. THIS MEANS THAT ANYONE CAN BUY SHARES OF THE BODY SHOP STOCK, AND EMPLOYEES CAN REAP FINANCIAL REWARDS BY SELLING THEIR STOCK, BUT IT ALSO MEANS—TO RODDICK'S CHAGRIN—THAT THE PRESS AND FINANCIAL ANALYSTS CONSTANTLY REVIEW THE COMPANY'S PERFORMANCE.

. . .

When things are OK you don't worry about it, but when the shit hits the fan.... Would we go public again? Absolutely. Why? Because we needed to raise our profile. Why? Because retailing was run by the property owners. We had to get a high profile to fight the property owners.

The offering worked, and the timing was brilliant. It had nothing to do with us. It was the timing: it was the eighties, we were sexy, we were young and eloquent. I certainly wouldn't have gotten the high profile if I'd had acne and been a bald-headed man, and I am very aware of that.

Is it working for us now? Absolutely not. I think the City [the U.K. equivalent of Wall Street] has the least business responsibility. They have no real interests in your profit. The fact that we make £21 million of profit [approximately $30 million] without firing anyone in this recession is of no value to them. What is of value is the difference between your last interim report and the next one.

The best thing for our company is to ignore the City's needs and just keep running the company in the way it should be run. I hope we do that. Sometimes when we flounder I think, Christ, what is going to happen? Then Gordon and I get together and say, What the hell! The purpose of this company is to keep it alive. We can't be at the mercy of these speculators.

I would love for us to be able to debate the notion of growth. When is enough enough? When are we valuable in terms of the human spirit or qualitative measurements and not just quantitative measurements? How is that value going to be eroded the bigger we get? I want to be able to say to Gordon, "No new shops this year—let's play with the customers and the staff." But that can't be done because we sold out on the economics of more.

I don't regret going public. I'll tell you why—I think it is a female philosophical thing: I am the sum total of what I've done. It just would have been easier not to have taken this route—we wouldn't have such intrusion into our lives by the press.

Sharing Your Vision

———

RODDICK HAS EXPANDED THE BODY SHOP FROM ONE STORE IN BRIGHTON, ENGLAND, TO OVER 900 STORES EMPLOYING THOUSANDS OF PEOPLE AROUND THE WORLD. SHE HAD TO LEARN TO SHARE HER VISION OF THE COMPANY AS IT GOT LARGER.

• • •

In my thirties, I feathered my nest and looked after the kids. In my forties, I only wanted to be surrounded by people I loved. In my fifties, now I think, What have I left behind and what have I done? Being brave in areas where no one else has gone sets us apart from the cosmetics industry and from any retailer—indeed, many businesses.

What we have is an absolute sense of passion. Where the passion comes is not the product. It comes with the principles, the idea of being brave, and the idea of bringing in things where the human spirit comes to play.

When the efforts of our main shop in London released five Moroccan prisoners of conscience, the employees were on a high for months—more so than selling $20 million worth of moisture cream. That is number one: giving employees a sense of empowerment.

In terms of education and information, we are interesting and entertaining. We have our own video and film production company. We produce videos once a week for every shop. They are not just what you do to put this product on the shelf. We bring in human rights and my travels around the world.

Another thing is I spend six months of the year traveling to my shops. I am not sitting around in some office. I also bring employees over to England, so there is a real sense of connectedness.

We also celebrate our people an enormous amount. The biggest celebration is being able to go on a volunteer program where you take three weeks' paid sabbatical and work in Rumania, Russia, Mexico, Guatemala.... You end up becoming an active citizen, and your values change when your experiences change. Why the hell would they ever want to work for another company?

We also have an absolute anal fixation on aesthetics. There is a carnival spirit in our offices. In our warehouse there are huge bananas floating around the ceiling. It's very theatrical and full of visual surprises, inspirational quotes, and scenes out of a famous French Impressionist's paintings.

We pay people well, and they are shareholders. We have a lot of economic experiments. For example, in England, we allocated twenty shops to our staff. After five years, they own them—they pay them off with their profits, not by going to a bank to raise the money. They would never get the money from a bank, because they are all under thirty and female.

———

BECAUSE OF ITS IDENTIFICATION WITH SOCIAL ACTIVISM, THE BODY SHOP ATTRACTS EMPLOYEES WHO WANT TO IMPROVE THE WORLD—NOT JUST SELL HAIR-CARE

AND SKIN-CARE PRODUCTS. THIS REQUIRES RODDICK TO REITERATE THAT THE BODY SHOP IS A BUSINESS.

. . .

I am a trader. I am not a government organization. I am just a trader. I just choose to put my profits into social causes, not self-aggrandizement. That is my choice.

Many people want to work for The Body Shop because they want to work on community projects or environmental issues. They are wonderful, but I am paying their wages. The products are being sold to pay their wages. This little girl said we can't relate to our causes at Christmastime because we have to sell. Sell more, I say! Then we can do more for the causes.

Family Issues

WHEN RODDICK STARTED THE BODY SHOP, SHE COULD NOT SPEND MUCH TIME WITH HER DAUGHTERS BECAUSE THE BUSINESS WAS GROWING RAPIDLY AND HER HUSBAND WAS AWAY. OUT OF NECESSITY, HER MOTHER TOOK CARE OF HER DAUGHTERS.

. . .

I come from an Italian working-class family. It was an extended family. The rich have a nanny, and the poor have their mums or their grandmothers. I don't regret that. They don't regret that—I hope I am speaking for them!

There was no option. You didn't work, you didn't eat. The girls understood the work. They came to love it. They had extraordinary people around them at an early age. They were party to conversations of such futurist thinking. So what they lost in terms of my time...I think they would be bored with me anyway.

I brought up my kids with a work ethic. The day the shop opened, they breathed it, lived it, and they know better than anybody the values and the ideas and the real dreams of this company. They were spoiled completely for any other job [*laughs*], and I am glad

I encouraged them to go out and get a job—just to see what it is like—because this is a remarkable company.

———

THE BODY SHOP HAS TRULY BECOME A FAMILY BUSINESS. WHEN RODDICK'S HUSBAND RETURNED FROM HIS ADVENTURE, THE TWO OF THEM RAN THE BODY SHOP TOGETHER—AND LOVED IT.

. . .

I don't see how anybody can *not* do it. He is not an easy person, but my God, when the chips are down and you feel so low that you say, "Oh, I've screwed up this one really badly," there is always this wonderful viewpoint that says, "It's not that bad. Look at it this way. Look at it the other way."

I couldn't imagine him being in another job where I have to go home and relate the day's events. But you've got to separate physically where you work. If you have finite areas of interests, there has to be a formal, well-mannered way of inviting people into each other's space.

The enjoyment of getting his viewpoint in my areas of design, graphics, education, and product development is fantastic. It doesn't mean I always embrace it, but it is fantastic. He always drags me to talk to the City folks to be the eccentric viewpoint of the company—which I play very well—just to frighten the backsides off these buggers. I say, "Why don't we not open up another shop for two years and just play?" It gets their little white necks going even whiter.

Being True to Yourself

———

WHEN THE BODY SHOP OPENED ITS FIRST STORE IN THE UNITED STATES IN THE SUMMER OF 1988, RODDICK DIDN'T PUBLICIZE HER "AGAINST ANIMAL TESTING" PHILOSOPHY. SHE ALSO DIDN'T SELL REFILLS. RODDICK CHANGED HER PRINCIPLES TO ENTER A NEW A MARKET.

. . .

Before we opened The Body Shop in the U.S., the lawyers advised us so much that we began to feel like we would have to modify the way we did business. We didn't want to end up playing the lawsuit game, so we accepted our lawyers' advice.

A statement like "Against Animal Testing" had always worked for us before, but now it was presented to us as a red flag that would unnecessarily outrage the bull. How we were seduced into dropping that statement, I'll never fully understand, because it was a huge moral mistake. Now we're trying to redress that error by running huge campaigns against animal testing.

We were also warned to drop the refill policy. Refilling had always been a core value, and to abandon such a fundamental point of policy in the biggest consumer market in the world was a terrible betrayal of our ideals, but we'd been told insurance costs would be insuperable. Our insurers were cool to the whole thing, but after a lengthy delay, the U.S. shops got their refill bars.

I think we were too careful in the beginning. After a year of that, we woke up to the fact that we should stick to our guns. What did it teach me? Fight harder. Even though I ran the company — or was supposed to — I had to fight these demons because they carried more weight than simple reason. The lesson is that whatever happens, the last things to be tampered with — indeed, never to be touched — are the essential values on which a company was founded.

———

Myrtle Faye Rumph

. . .

COMMUNITY ACTIVIST

CHANGING THE 'HOOD

. . .

What happens to a dream deferred?
Does it dry up
Like a raisin in the sun?...
Or does it explode?

LANGSTON HUGHES

Myrtle Faye Rumph (age sixty-one) received her fifteen minutes of fame when *The Wall Street Journal* and *People* published stories about her in 1992. These publications didn't write about Rumph because of her wealth, status, or notoriety. They did it because she started the Al Wooten Jr. Heritage Center in south-central Los Angeles.

She started the center after her thirty-five-year-old son, Al Wooten, Jr., was killed in a random drive-by shooting in 1989. Some of her family members wanted to take the law into their own hands, but Rumph stopped them and vowed to make things better in her south-central Los Angeles community. With little fanfare or government support, Rumph has built an oasis in the middle of a dangerous ghetto.

Inside the center's 2,000-square-foot building, Rumph and her volunteers are making a difference in the lives of neighborhood kids. Kids come to the center after school and on weekends to participate in educational and cultural programs. It is one of the few places they can feel safe and even have fun. Rumph's story is about healing pain by helping other people.

The center is located in the area where rioting erupted after the Rodney King trial. Rumph and I talked at her facility in a dusty storage room containing old, donated computers. It was the only room where my tape recorder could pick up Rumph's soft voice over the din of kids playing.

The Wrong Place at the Wrong Time

———

Rumph's son, Al Wooten, Jr., was walking with two friends on a street near his house when he was killed in a drive-by shooting.

• • •

The police thought maybe it was a gang initiation 'cause sometimes they require you to kill a person to get into the gang. When he was killed, the police didn't call me; they just took him to the hospital.

He lived through the night and died the next morning. Seven-thirty in the morning, flat on my back in my bed, something hit me, and I jumped straight up in my bed and started screaming. I didn't know what it was. It felt like something was going out of me.

My husband was in the other part of the house, and he came in the back bedroom to see what the problem was. I said, "I don't know what happened. It's like I was having a bad nightmare." Later I found out that my son died at the same time...so very weird.

Healing Through Helping

———

Al Jr.'s killer was never found, but Rumph turned her anger and despair into something positive and healing.

• • •

I started the center because my son was murdered while walking the street. I don't want to see murderers being raised. It was very disturbing to me that it was not safe to walk the streets and that society had created people that could kill strangers. I started this organization to fight whatever took him away from here.

Gang members shouldn't think about the person they've killed, because that person is at peace. They should think about the people left behind. When my son was killed, it was devastating for my family. Everybody was upset, and they were ready to find the person and kill him. When you shoot someone, they are gone, but we suffered and are still suffering because of our loss. My husband and I had a moving company at the time of my son's death, and I ran the office. I could no longer function in the office. When I went to work, I would be sitting at my desk crying. I couldn't answer the phone.

———

IT'S BEEN YEARS SINCE RUMPH'S SON WAS KILLED, AND SHE IS STILL RECOVERING. THE CENTER IS THERAPEUTIC FOR RUMPH, TEACHING HER THAT HELPING OTHERS IS A WAY TO HELP YOURSELF.

• • •

I'm still not over it. It's been over three years, and I still have bad times. Sometimes just driving along, if I think about him, it's devastating. But it don't last.

When it first happened, I felt like I was not going to recover and it was the end of the world—so much pain. You just feel like you're over-whelmed and you're not going to make it. But day by day you go on, and after about a year you start feeling a little better. It just takes a long time.

When I worked at the center, I felt the pressures leave. So I got more and more involved in it, and the more I got involved in the center, the better I felt. After about a year of working at the center, I found it was the only place I was happy.

My family probably thought, It'll die down—she's just grieving, and she's trying to hang on to her son. But I knew that wasn't it. It was something deep inside of me that I had to do—a driving force of some kind. I just had to do it no matter what. The more involved I got, the better I felt.

An Outpouring of Care

———

RUMPH'S PHONE STARTED RINGING THE DAY *THE WALL STREET JOURNAL* ARTICLE BROKE. SHE DISCOVERED THAT MANY PEOPLE CARED AND WANTED TO HELP—PEOPLE SHE DIDN'T EVEN KNOW.

I started getting calls early on the morning of the eighteenth [May 1992]. The first call I received was from Tennessee, and the lady says, "I read the article, and I would like to send you some money to help." And she did.

The phone rang like that all day from different people. One lady called me and said she was from a foundation: "I'm reading your article for the second time, and I'm crying." I said, "I haven't even seen it yet." So she says she'll send me a copy and some money. She sent $500 and two copies of *The Wall Street Journal*. Things like that. We received phone calls all the way from Cuba.

I think a lot of people read about what we were doing here, and they were just so overwhelmed that out of all of this chaos, this riot, all this stuff here, somebody out here was already trying to make a difference.

A lot of people have volunteered their time. We had a gentleman in San Luis Obispo who called me and said he would love to bring about twenty-five of our kids from L.A. over there to show them a different world. He took five weeks off of his job, and he raised over $4,000 to sponsor this trip. They went up there on the Amtrak and stayed for a week.

A lot of people don't know how, but they would love to help. People all over America really care, and if they could find a way to help the situation, they would.

Taking Control

RUMPH'S CENTER IS A SANCTUARY IN THE MIDDLE OF POVERTY, DANGER, AND DESPAIR. SHE DIDN'T WAIT FOR SOMEONE ELSE TO DO SOMETHING. SHE TOOK CONTROL.

. . .

It's up to us as a people—black people—to change our own destiny. One way to accomplish this is sticking together, and another way is doing things for ourselves. Have your own business if it's possible, and open them in your own communities.

It might take a lot of years, but it can happen. I started this center, and now we are putting a market up front to just help service the community and the kids. They will have a place to shop without spending a lot of money, because we keep our prices low for the community.

We have to help ourselves instead of waiting for the government to help us or give us a job. Get out and make your own job. My father worked for himself, and he taught us kids to take care of ourselves. It stuck with me. If you think about the negative, you will become negative. No matter what situation I find myself in, I always try to focus on the positive.

I've taught my children that nobody is going to help them — they've got to do it for themselves. If you want to get somewhere in life, it's up to you. Despite the prejudice and nit-picking, you can still do it if you really want to.

———

PART OF TAKING CONTROL OF A BAD SITUATION IS BEING RESPONSIBLE FOR YOUR CHILDREN AND BEING AN ACTIVE PARTICIPANT IN THEIR LIVES.

• • •

Kids come to the center, and their parents don't know where they are. They're here all day, and yet we never receive a call. Parents should show their children that they care. Keep letting them know that you really care and that you want to know where they are.

I married real young, and I got a divorce and had three kids for nine years by myself. I didn't have a lot of money, but I took my kids to places that didn't cost money. If you want to be with your children, you can.

When they get older, they'll say, "I know she cared because she tried to keep up with me." Take them on a picnic. Take them to the beach — whatever you can do to be with that child. They will feel like you put them first. Just being with a parent means a lot.

The Role of Education

WHEN RUMPH LOOKS BACK OVER HER LIFE, HER BIGGEST REGRET IS NOT GETTING A TEACHING DEGREE, SO NOW SHE WORKS TO ENSURE THAT THE KIDS AT HER CENTER DON'T MISS OUT ON AN EDUCATION.

. . .

The schools were segregated in east Dallas, where we lived, so I only went to school up through the ninth grade. Eventually we moved to west Dallas, but the all-black high school was in east Dallas. It cost money to go every day, and my father had nine kids. There was no money for bus fare.

I don't know what I could have done, but I just wish there had been a way. Now everybody who wants an education can get it—no matter how old you are, you can still get it, like I did later. I had three kids, but I went back to school through mail, and I also attended some classes at night.

People don't think it's important, but it is. I made sure my kids had every opportunity to go to school—college if they wanted to. Kids here at the center, hopefully I'll be able to influence them. That's the main subject around here: Get your education.

Judith Heumann
. . .
CRUSADER

$\mathscr{F}$IGHTING PREJUDICE

. . .

Action is the antidote to despair.

JOAN BAEZ

Judith Heumann (age forty-five) contracted polio at the age of one and a half, and she has been a quadriplegic ever since. This means that she has only limited use of her four limbs. She requires the help of attendants to put her to bed each night and to get ready for work each morning, but during the day she is self-sufficient for most activities.

Don't feel sorry for her, though. She is assistant secretary for special education and rehabilitative services in the Department of Education in the Clinton administration. She is a champion for the rights of disabled people. Her story is about the fight to change society's perception of a minority group.

Prior to joining the Clinton administration, Heumann was an executive at the World Institute on Disability, a public policy, research, and training organization. She played a crucial role in lobbying for the passage of Section 504 of the Rehabilitation Act and for the Americans with Disabilities Act. In 1990 she won the first Henry B. Betts Award for her activism on behalf of people with disabilities.

I met Heumann at the World Institute on Disability in downtown Oakland, California. The office was buzzing as people—with and without disabilities—worked side by side. Some of them blew into tubes to move about and run office equipment. They may have been *disabled,* but they sure didn't look *handicapped.*

Fire Hazard Turned Crusader

FORTY YEARS AGO, THERE WERE FEW LAWS TO ENSURE THE RIGHTS OF DISABLED PEOPLE. BACK THEN, HEUMANN WAS ONCE LABELED A FIRE HAZARD AND DENIED SCHOOLING.

· · ·

I was in and out of the hospital from when I was eighteen months and had polio until I was about three years old. My first recollections of disability are from when I was about four, when I was in a place called the Institute for Rehabilitative Medicine in New York City.

I was there for three months for rehab. I went on Monday mornings and came home on Friday nights. I didn't like being separated from my family. Once I fell out of my wheelchair because they didn't put a seat belt on me, so there aren't a lot of fond memories about it.

My family was not into sending me out for surgery or to different rehab centers. They felt they had a responsibility to be involved, so they had a therapist come in, and my father used to do exercises with me. I was always very grateful for staying more in the house than being sent away.

When I was five, my mother took me to the local public school, and the principal said I couldn't go to school there because I was a fire hazard. The average parent doesn't know anything about legislation or litigation, so my mother took me home.

If something like this happened today, it would be against the law. Using the Constitution, there may have been something my parents could have done, but I couldn't expect my parents to have a clue about it, because they were immigrants.

———

THE DISCRIMINATION HEUMANN FACED IN THIS SCHOOL WAS NOT AN ISOLATED INCIDENT.

· · ·

I would only remember a little if another school had accepted me the next day, but what disabled people experience isn't a one-time situation. You are discriminated against over and over.

Eventually I realized that it was also happening to my friends, so we began to work on trying to make the problem go away. Then one day I woke up, and I realized I was spending an awful lot of my time in this area. I didn't plan to be a civil rights leader.

For me, the need to help create a movement, and to allow disabled people to be a part of that movement, is very important because my life wouldn't be what it is today if I didn't have the support and friendship of other disabled people.

Breaking Barriers

AS ONE OF AMERICA'S MOST VISIBLE DISABLED-RIGHTS ACTIVISTS, HEUMANN LEARNED HOW TO FIGHT PREJUDICE. IN RETROSPECT, SHE SAYS THE FIRST STEP IS FOR PEOPLE TO GET TO KNOW EACH OTHER.

. . .

When I was a teenager, I recognized that nondisabled people were not going to make the changes, because they didn't think I represented enough people. Changes didn't come about easily for any minority group. Women fought for their rights. Racial minorities fought for their rights. Older people fought for their rights.

Disabled people are fighting for their rights because we've recognized that the majority—whoever that is—hasn't taken the responsibility and initiative to make changes. It's our responsibility. It's a necessity if for no other reason than to allow my own life to be a better life.

How do you get non-Japanese people to not discriminate against Japanese people? By being in contact with Japanese people and learning that they are not any different. Maybe you're a good person or maybe you're not a good person, but it has nothing to do with whether you are Japanese or disabled.

As communities become more accessible, nondisabled people are slowly beginning to become less afraid of us. I underscore *slowly*. When a movie theater wasn't accessible, nobody in wheelchairs ever showed up, so people thought people in wheelchairs didn't want to go to a movie theater. Now, as places become accessible, you see lots of disabled people in the community.

———

THROUGH THE ADVANCES THAT HEUMANN AND OTHER DISABLED-RIGHTS ACTI-VISTS HAVE MADE, SHE'S LEARNED ABOUT THE PACE OF CHANGE AND EFFECTIVE COALITION-BUILDING.

. . .

I've begun to realize that change takes a lot longer than I would like it to take, and there is so much that needs to be changed that it's not all going to happen in my lifetime. What we haven't done effectively enough is work in conjunction with other minority groups and women.

Part of the problem is that a lot of racial minority groups don't want to work with their own disabled people because the stigma against disabled people is so significant. You can't go to African-American, Japanese, Chinese, or Jewish disabled people and find that they feel accepted by their own community.

You can't just say that since you are a minority, it means you understand the kinds of discrimination other people have faced. When black people weren't allowed to sit in the front of the bus, they could still get on the bus. Ultimately, they were able to sit anyplace they wanted. However, if the bus doesn't have a lift or a floor which is low, telling me that you're not going to deny my right to get on the bus doesn't change anything.

The Real Handicap

———

DO YOU KNOW THE DIFFERENCE BETWEEN BEING DISABLED AND BEING HAND-ICAPPED? BEING DISABLED MEANS HAVING A PHYSICAL OR MENTAL CONDITION SUCH AS QUADRIPLEGIA. BEING HANDICAPPED, BY CONTRAST, IS A CONDITION THAT IS THE RESULT OF THE WAY PEOPLE VIEW YOU BECAUSE OF YOUR AFFLICTION.

. . .

I don't feel a disability is anything negative. It's been the discriminatory attitudes and practices that have been put before me and against me that have resulted in my life being difficult. I don't fantasize about being a nondisabled person. I have no interest in doing away with disability.

I have a great life. I travel all over the world. I meet people all the time. My disability allows me to try to be an agent of change. I wouldn't have this opportunity if I was just a Jewish girl from New York. I've met people with disabilities who are great friends of mine that I wouldn't have met otherwise. I've met people who have an inner strength that other people haven't necessarily gotten in touch with.

If someone said you could be white, would you want to be white? No, right? Because it's who you are. That's what we are saying—it's who we are. The answer isn't to make everybody a white, Protestant, nondisabled, hearing, seeing person in order to be able to fit into society. The answer is to look at the kinds of prejudice that face us and remove it so that one doesn't have to feel that in order to be accepted, one has to change who one is.

When people grow up nondisabled, they look at people who have disabilities and think they don't want to be that person. At best, maybe they feel charitable and give some money, but being me is something people don't aspire to. People don't aspire to be somebody in a wheelchair. Or blind. Or deaf.

Nondisabled people see disabled people as vulnerable. I am not saying nondisabled people hate disabled people, but we represent vulnerability, and people are afraid of being vulnerable. People don't like to have to ask other people for help. Maybe it's acceptable for older people to be given assistance by their family, but people like their youth.

Disabled people present a different type of a challenge for them. I can have very strong adverse feelings about you, but I am not worried about waking up like you [Japanese] tomorrow. You are not going to wake up being a woman, and you are not going to wake up being black, but you may very well wake up one day being disabled.

Maybe hate isn't what you would feel, but maybe you don't want to be around us so much because we make you uncomfortable. You may be thinking, Maybe it will happen to me tomorrow and maybe it won't happen to me, but I'll deal with it if and when it happens.

Adjusting to a Disability

ALTHOUGH HEUMANN HAS BEEN DISABLED ALMOST ALL HER LIFE, SHE HAS EXTENSIVE EXPERIENCE WITH PEOPLE WHO ARE DISABLED AS A RESULT OF AN ACCIDENT OR A DISEASE.

. . .

When nondisabled people become disabled, they have to deal with their own prejudice against their new selves. Even when they accept themselves for who they are, in many cases they are isolated from other disabled individuals. People who have just become disabled should, as quickly as possible, meet others who have accepted themselves as good people with their disabilities.

A disabled person can ask me questions about how to adjust. What are the problems? What do I do when I feel sad? What do I do when I feel angry? What do I do when my husband wants to leave me or when my kids don't accept me or my mother won't let me do things? I can help you feel more self-assured about the new you. A nondisabled person can't do that. They don't have the same experience.

Newly disabled people also need to get help for their families and friends to begin the process that will allow them to accept the disability, too. It is very common to hear newly disabled people talk about how they lost friends and how people stopped treating them the same way as they did before.

Finally, they need to learn about the laws and do everything they can to maintain the life they had before. They are still the same people. A lot of things have changed, but the thing is to try to keep a positive perspective on who they are even though their life is changing. The most important thing is to move into the new situation and do everything they can to accept who they are.

Using the Bathroom

IN ADDITION TO HELPING NEWLY DISABLED PEOPLE ADJUST TO THEIR NEW LIVES, HEUMANN TEACHES PEOPLE TO UNDERSTAND HOW A DISABLED PERSON LIVES.

• • •

People have asked me all kinds of questions about sex and other things which they wouldn't ask other people. I've always answered those questions because I felt I was putting myself in a situation where I was saying I would answer their questions. If you allow people to ask questions, you understand the depth of what people don't understand and how they don't think we are like them.

I used to teach a class of seven-year-olds, and once I was reading them a story. A little boy raised his hand and asked, "How do you go to the bathroom?" I could have said that this wasn't the time to answer it, but I chose to try to explain as much as I could so the kid could see it was OK to ask the question.

Not all disabled people like questions being asked of them about their disability, so they might basically say, "Get lost, I don't want to answer that question." That doesn't mean you shouldn't ask another disabled person a question, and maybe you should consider how many times people tell you to get lost, because maybe you are asking the wrong question.

SINCE HEUMANN BROUGHT IT UP AND I DIDN'T KNOW THE ANSWER, I ASKED

. . .

Do you see the hand control on my chair here? I push it back, and then I put this leg over here and open my foot pedals. Then I put my wheelchair up against the toilet, and I turn around. I don't sit on the toilet. I need somebody to help me get my pants down. I kind of hang over the toilet if it is too low. If the toilet is the right height, I can just slip over onto the toilet and go to the bathroom just like you.

———

—AND JUST LIKE YOU.

Del Martin and Phyllis Lyon

...

LESBIAN ACTIVISTS

To know oneself, one should assert oneself.

ALBERT CAMUS

In their minds, Del Martin (age seventy-two) and Phyllis Lyon (age sixty-eight) are married. The legal system, however, considers the San Francisco couple strangers, even though they have lived together for forty years. Martin and Lyon's story is about what it was like to be a lesbian in the fifties and how they worked to reduce oppression, build a community, and sustain an organization.

Martin and Lyon are social activists. Among their causes are the rights of gays, lesbians, and other victims of discrimination and violence. Their work started in 1955, when they helped form the Daughters of Bilitis, the first lesbian organization in the United States. In 1964 they co-founded the Council on Religion and the Homosexual. In 1972 they were among the co-founders of the Alice B. Toklas Memorial Democratic Club, and they wrote a landmark book called *Lesbian/Woman*, which was one of the first books about lesbians that reached the general public.

In 1976 Martin published *Battered Wives*, a book that became a catalyst for the mobilization of the battered women's shelter movement. In 1990 the ACLU of Northern California honored both Lyon and Martin with its highest award, the Earl Warren Civil Liberties Award, for their decades of service and inspiration to the community.

Martin invited me to the home she and Lyon share in San Francisco. It is a simple house on a hill above Castro Street, an area with a large, active gay and lesbian community. It's appropriate that their house overlooks Castro Street, because Martin and Lyon are, in a sense, the caretakers of the people who live there. Their story is about making a place for yourself when you don't seem to fit in.

On Being a Lesbian in the Fifties

MARTIN AND LYON BECAME AWARE OF THEIR SEXUAL ORIENTATION AT A TIME WHEN BEING LESBIAN OR GAY WAS EITHER UNHEARD OF OR FORBIDDEN.

. . .

Martin: Like most lesbians in our age bracket, I thought I was the only one who was different. In those days, nobody talked about sexuality, and certainly not homosexuality. Most of us knew we had feelings for other women, but we didn't have any words for it, and we didn't have any knowledge about it. I thought, I am the only one, and I'll just keep quiet about it.

I certainly had crushes on women in my teen years. When I got married, I didn't have a crush on a woman at that point. I thought I was in love with my husband. Later, I fell in love with the woman next door. It was a case of unrequited love, but it did force me to question my sexual orientation.

Now people ask, "Couldn't you go to the library?" We didn't have a word to look up! Then, when we finally did learn the terms *homosexual* and *lesbian*, all we found was very negative material describing people we could not identify with.

Forming the Daughters of Bilitis

BACK IN THE FIFTIES, LESBIANS IN SAN FRANCISCO HID "UNDERGROUND." THE ONLY PLACE FOR THEM TO MEET WERE GAY BARS, UNTIL MARTIN, LYON, AND SIX OTHER WOMEN FORMED THE DAUGHTERS OF BILITIS. (*BILITIS* COMES FROM "SONGS OF BILITIS," A POEM BY PIERRE LOUIS, WHO JOKINGLY TOLD PEOPLE THAT HE FOUND THE POEM IN A CAVE ON THE ISLAND OF LESBOS AND THAT BILITIS WAS A CONTEMPORARY OF SAPPHO.)

. . .

Lyon: When Del and I got together in 1953 in a little apartment on Castro Street, we didn't know any other lesbians and felt very isolated. We went to the lesbian bars, where it seemed everybody knew each other. We didn't know any of them, so we sat in the corner and wished we could get to know them. But we were too shy to do anything about it.

We finally met a couple of gay men who lived around the corner from us, and eventually they introduced us to a lesbian friend. We finally knew one other lesbian in the city! Not long after that, she called us and asked us—this was in September of 1955—if we would like to be involved in starting a social club for lesbians. We said, "Oh yes!" immediately, because it meant that we were expanding our circle of friends.

Daughters of Bilitis was the idea of a working-class Filipina woman who wanted a place where lesbians could go and dance and be safe—dancing was not allowed in lesbian bars, and they were subject to raids by the police. We spent about a month, the eight of us, talking about how the club was going to function and what we were going to do.

In the process we gave it a name, the Daughters of Bilitis. The woman who suggested it said we could say it was a poetry club or a women's lodge and that lesbians would know what it meant, but nobody else would. Del and I had never heard of Bilitis. I don't think that any of the others in the group had heard of it except for her. We didn't know that we would be explaining the origin of the name for the next thirty years.

Fighting Back

————

THE DAUGHTERS OF BILITIS, LIKE OTHER GAY AND LESBIAN ORGANIZATIONS, WAS HARASSED BY LAW-ENFORCEMENT AGENCIES. MARTIN AND LYON LEARNED TO FIGHT BACK, AND THEY LEARNED THAT PEOPLE CAN'T BE ACTIVISTS UNTIL THEY'VE DEVELOPED SELF-ESTEEM.

. . .

Martin: At the beginning, it was very scary because of gay-bar raids. The police would tell your employer. They would list people in the newspaper. If you were a child, your parents could send you to a shrink or have you institutionalized. People could lose their jobs if they were found out.

Lyon: Lose your children—your life could be ruined.

Martin: There were a lot of suicides in those days.

Lyon: The tenor of the times was that many homosexuals, if arrested in a gay-bar raid, pleaded guilty because they thought they were guilty simply for being homosexual—although this was never against the law. We were labeled illegal, immoral, and sick, and our work as individuals and organizations focused on these three political issues.

We decided there were other things besides being a social club that we might want to do. We saw the need for education about our rights and the need to help lesbians feel better about themselves through peer counseling and group discussion. We also saw the need for law reform and for participation in research projects to help educate the public as to who lesbians really are.

Martin: The whole thing is to fight back. As Tish Sommers [founder of the Older Women's League] once said, "Don't agonize—organize." The best way to get over our fears was to increase our numbers, our knowledge of the law and our rights, and what to do in case of arrest. We knew we had to educate our own. In the early days, we spent a lot of time peer counseling—trying to get people to accept themselves.

Historians think we were just acquiescing to what was going on—which is a lot of baloney. First, you had to help people build some self-esteem and some self-confidence so they could cope in the world. You can't have a movement until you have some self-esteem.

Power Struggle

———

THE DAUGHTERS OF BILITIS DISSOLVED IN 1970 BECAUSE OF AN INTERNAL POWER STRUGGLE. ITS DEMISE YIELDS VALUABLE LESSONS ABOUT KEEPING AN ORGANIZATION GOING.

. . .

Martin: What led to the demise of DOB was that in 1970 the national president and the editor of *The Ladder* [a publication that started as the Daughters of Bilitis's newsletter] conspired to take the magazine away from the organization and took the mailing list into Nevada—which made any attempt to deal with it a federal case. We had seen similar situations arise in other organizations and knew it would take years and years in the courts to resolve ownership of the magazine.

As a result, at the national convention in New York in 1970, we decided to dissolve the national organization because putting out the magazine had been its main focus. That left the chapters free to function on their own. Two years later, the magazine folded because it didn't have the backing of the national organization.

Lyon: It seems weird, but we could never quite understand people who were really fighting to become the national president. Being president meant you did a hell of a lot of work, but no one even dreamed of getting paid for doing stuff like this in those days. I guess there is just something about positions and titles—power corrupts, and absolute power corrupts absolutely.

The lesson is that members need to be aware of what is going on in their organization and beware of leaders who begin to assume ownership. Splits or disagreements need to be dealt with before they become major conflicts.

———

THE RADICALESBIANS, A GROUP OF LESBIAN ACTIVISTS WHO BELIEVED WOMEN

WERE OWED REPARATION BECAUSE OF YEARS OF OPPRESSION, TOOK OVER THE NEW YORK CHAPTER OF THE DAUGHTERS OF BILITIS. BECAUSE THEY DIDN'T CHARGE FOR MEMBERSHIP, THEY COULD NOT AFFORD TO MAINTAIN THEIR FACILITY AND EVENTUALLY CLOSED DOWN.

. . .

Lyon: The closure is sad because Daughters of Bilitis was a coming-out place. Other groups had different ideas and ways of doing things, but why destroy an organization that really had a function in the community?

There were more and more ideas about how to go about getting what we all wanted: acceptance and equal rights. Some felt that the best way to gain media attention was to be obstreperous: to break up meetings and to demonstrate. Others chose to work quietly within established institutions, forming a caucus, and when large enough, introduce, debate, and sometimes successfully change policy.

We need to use every imaginable avenue toward trying to get what we want. Nobody knows which one will succeed. There is no one way to effect social change.

Catalyzing Social Change

MARTIN AND LYON HELPED FOUND THE DAUGHTERS OF BILITIS BECAUSE NO OTHER ORGANIZATION FOR THE LESBIAN COMMUNITY EXISTED. SINCE THE DAUGHTERS OF BILITIS CLOSED, MARTIN AND LYON HAVE BEEN WORKING WITHIN EXISTING INSTITUTIONS TO CATALYZE SOCIAL CHANGE.

. . .

Lyon: The lesbian and gay movement is like the church. Some people stay in their denominations to fight from inside. Others have gone outside to find other churches or to build new congregations that are more positive. I think you need to do both.

Martin: I think it would be great to have new institutions, but how do you get there? I don't see how we can achieve rapid change, so we've been trying to bring about changes within the system.

We have the Democratic Party and the Republican Party, but there have been lots of tries at other parties without much success. We joined the Peace and Freedom Party at one point but decided that sitting around coming to consensus was never going to get us very far.

We have seen a lot of changes in the Democratic Party since the early sixties, when Assemblymen Phil Burton and John O'Connell told us that they couldn't do anything without being accused of being for sin and being thrown out of office. They said we needed to get the church behind us if we wanted to make changes in the law.

––––––

ANOTHER LESSON MARTIN AND LYON HAD TO LEARN IN ORDER TO BECOME EFFECTIVE ACTIVISTS WAS TO PROMOTE THEIR CAUSE WITHOUT ANTAGONIZING PEOPLE.

• • •

Lyon: One time we had the opportunity to speak with a group of young seminarians from Fresno. They were at least open-minded enough to visit us. A gay man started out with a tirade against the church. I agreed with what he said, but when he finished, I realized he had lost the audience.

When the seminarians got down to the lobby of the building, I talked to them a little bit and tried to explain why he was so angry. That was a lesson learned: you can be very strong about what you say, but you are not going to win friends and influence people if you are trashing their innermost ideals.

––––––

MARTIN AND LYON ALSO LEARNED THAT ACTIVISTS MUST CONSTANTLY EDUCATE PEOPLE ABOUT THEIR CAUSE.

• • •

Lyon: We have learned one other thing that for sure needs to go on forever, and that is education. In the seventies, the movement concentrated on political organizing and making change through litigation and legislation. For the most part, it left out the educational component, but there will always be people who don't know very much about lesbians and gays.

Martin: We still need people out in high schools and colleges and churches and all over the place, explaining who we are and what we are all about.

———

RECENTLY, IT HAS BECOME AN ACCEPTED PRACTICE TO REVEAL A NOTABLE PERSON'S GAY OR LESBIAN LIFE-STYLE—TO "OUT" THEM—IN ORDER TO INCREASE PUBLIC AWARENESS OF THE NUMBERS OF GAYS AND LESBIANS IN ALL SECTORS OF THE POPULATION.

• • •

Martin: Back when we came out, everything was so secret, so everyone was using pseudonyms. If you were walking down the street and saw a lesbian you knew who was with somebody else, you didn't speak unless she spoke to you.

We've always encouraged people to come out, because it makes a difference, and we always believed that people had to come out in their own time and their own way. As far as outing is concerned, I am still opposed to it.

Lyon: I don't believe in outing either, except that I think if I knew somebody who was gay and who was being terribly detrimental to the gay and lesbian cause, I would be for outing that person. But not just because he or she is famous.

Well-known people are coming out and talking about their sexuality now more than ever, and as more people see that they aren't being shot or they are not losing their livelihood, more and more people will come out.

Martin: During the Briggs Initiative [aimed at outlawing lesbians and gays and their supporters from the school system], we learned the main reason it's important to come out. The people who knew some of us personally were on our side, and the people who thought they had never met one of us were adamantly opposed.

More people seeing us as human beings instead of mythical monsters made a lot of difference.

Are Lesbians Born or Made?

————

ONE ISSUE THAT HAS BEEN DEBATED FOR DECADES IS WHETHER LESBIANS ARE BORN OR MADE. MARTIN AND LYON HAVE THEIR OWN THEORY, BUT THEY DON'T REALLY CARE WHY THEY ARE LESBIANS. LIKE MANY INTERVIEWEES, THEY RETURNED THE DISCUSSION TO THE IMPORTANCE OF BEING TRUE TO ONESELF.

. . .

Martin: We agree with the Kinsey people: that circumstances in your life probably determine the direction your sexuality will take. In other words, we all have the capacity to respond to either sex. This was evident when some women in the feminist movement, frustrated by the treatment and attitudes of the men in their lives, turned to women.

Lyon: So it is nature/nurture—a little of this and a little of that. Nobody really knows. There is a division within the gay movement as to whether it is biological. Some people believe that they were born gay. If it is biological, then it means it is natural, and therefore we should not be discriminated against.

Martin: In the beginning, all the research was about gay men. Nobody really cared too much about lesbians. After all, they were just women. But for a man to act like a woman, to give up his male privileges, was unthinkable to the researchers, who were mostly male.

Lyon: The great concern about what causes homosexuality is so it can be cured. I am not particularly interested in that. We are happy the way we are!

————

—

Doing Your Own Thing

. . .

Herbie Hancock

· · ·

MUSICIAN

$\mathscr{S}$HARING WITH OTHERS

. . .

Where there is music there can be no evil.

CERVANTES

It is an understatement to say that Herbie Hancock (age fifty-three) is a talented musician. He plays the acoustic and electric keyboard and writes music. His albums have won three Grammies: two for best rhythm and blues performance and one for best instrumental performance. His sound track for *'Round Midnight* earned an Oscar in 1987 for best original score.

If there's a single word to describe Hancock, it's *versatile.* He is one of the leading jazz pianists in the world, but he's equally accomplished at playing pop as well as rhythm and blues. In addition to *'Round Midnight,* Hancock composed soundtracks for *Blowup, Death Wish, A Soldier's Story,* and other films. He produced Wynton Marsalis's first album, and he hosted Showtime's series of cable television specials called *Coast to Coast.*

Hancock's story is about crafting a career out of doing something you love. In his case, the something is music, and the love started at the age of seven. When he was eleven years old, Hancock played the first movement of Mozart's Concerto in D Minor with the Chicago Symphony. Donald Byrd, the great trumpeter, made Hancock a part of his band when Hancock was twenty.

I interviewed Hancock while driving him from the Oakland airport to his hotel in San Francisco. That Hancock would fly into the Oakland airport instead of the San Francisco airport to save $200 is an indication of what an unpretentious, down-to-earth person he is.

Turning to Music

HANCOCK, A MASTER MUSICIAN, STARTED PLAYING THE PIANO WHEN HE WAS VERY YOUNG BECAUSE OF HIS OLDER BROTHER.

. . .

I'll give you the real deal from the real beginning. I have an older brother. He is three years older than me. When he could shoot marbles, I could only mess up the game. When he could first throw a football, my hand couldn't get around it. I wound up being the mascot of the team, so sports was kind of a nightmare for me. [*Laughs*.] Being a mascot for a team, you feel like a pet [*laughs*] — like some subhuman dog or something. To this day, I have no real interest in sports.

When I was seven and my brother was ten, we all started taking piano lessons. For the first time, I was on an even keel with my brother. We started taking lessons, and he wasn't better than me — I wasn't better than him, either. I would practice and play the piano all the time, and he would divide his time between practicing and playing sports or playing with the guys and stuff like that.

————

AT THE BEGINNING OF HIS TRAINING, HANCOCK LEARNED TO PLAY CLASSICAL MUSIC. HE BELIEVES THAT HIS BACKGROUND IN CLASSICAL MUSIC GAVE HIM A SOLID FOUNDATION FOR HIS FORAYS INTO JAZZ, RHYTHM AND BLUES, AND POP.

. . .

A lot of people think, "I don't want to be bored. I just want to do my thing," but the standards that were part of the European culture — Bach, Beethoven, and Mozart — still prevail as a foundation for any music that comes out of America. Classical music started so long ago that there are certain standards that we Westerners are accustomed to.

I would encourage someone to study classical music, because I did it and it worked. That doesn't mean that is the only way to do it. It may be possible to become a professional and qualified musician without having to go through classical music, but from my experience, it was classical music that helped me to play jazz. I think there is a strong relationship between jazz and classical music.

There is a big influence from French Impressionistic music that is inherent in modern jazz. Even the founders of modern jazz —

Charlie Parker and Dizzy Gillespie and Bud Powell and those guys from the early and mid-forties, and Miles Davis—listened a lot to French Impressionistic music. They also listened to contemporary classical music. They listened to people like Stravinsky and Bartok. And Ravel, Debussy, and people like that.

———

LATER, JAZZ PROVIDED YET ANOTHER LAYER OF PREPARATION FOR HANCOCK'S EXPLORATION OF OTHER STYLES OF MUSIC.

. . .

One of the things I decided when I was a young musician in my twenties was that I wanted to be the most versatile musician in New York. I got to the point where I was doing a lot of studio work, so I would be called to play all kinds of music. I have been on records of Connie Francis doing country music and Eydie Gorme.

There are a lot of different kinds of music I've gotten into, and what I've found is that a foundation in jazz has made this possible for me. The foundation in classical led to my foundation in jazz. Classical music is the glue, but the bricks and the mortar are jazz. That has made it possible to go into those different areas: rhythm and blues, dance music, pop, country, and blues.

Learning from Others

———

HANCOCK'S TURNING POINT AS A PROFESSIONAL MUSICIAN OCCURRED IN 1960, WHEN DONALD BYRD INVITED HIM TO BE THE PIANIST FOR HIS BAND. THREE YEARS LATER, HANCOCK JOINED THE QUINTET OF ANOTHER JAZZ LEGEND, MILES DAVIS. THROUGH HIS RELATIONSHIPS WITH BYRD, DAVIS, AND OTHER MUSICIANS, HANCOCK LEARNED ABOUT PEOPLE INSPIRING EACH OTHER.

. . .

One day the phone rang, and it was Miles. He asked me if I was working with anybody, and I told him no, although I had been working with Donald Byrd at the time. Donald had already heard through the grapevine that Miles was going to call me, so he told me that if Miles called, to tell him I was not working with anybody else.

I have to give credit to Miles for not only being a direct influence on me through his music and his playing, but also the fact that he had the vision to recognize young talent, nurture that talent, and give that talent a platform to develop itself and go on to become an influence in another area of music.

There couldn't have been a finer band that I could have been with. All the guys in the band were a major influence on me. What I learned is that since we all live in some kind of society, what we develop as our own comes as a result of borrowing from the rest of our environment, including the influences of people—whether it is our parents or friends or relatives—or our religions.

Our own personality is there waiting to be developed. It takes those influences to prod, nurture, or feed the development of our own personalities. In other words, we are not alone. We borrow from each other and give to each other constantly. Everybody is really important, because one word said to one person could change that person's life in a way that you may not be aware of, and that person may not be aware of it either.

Versatility Over Synergy

MANY MUSICIANS FORM A GROUP AND PLAY TOGETHER FOR YEARS. THE ADVANTAGE OF THIS METHOD IS THAT THE GROUP DEVELOPS A HEIGHTENED SENSE OF SYNERGY. BY CONTRAST, HANCOCK HASN'T HAD A GROUP SINCE 1973.

. . .

I had the choice of doing what was the standard approach of forming a band and developing that band by changing the personnel little by little throughout the years. I started off doing that when I first left Miles back in 1968, and that happened all the way through 1973.

Then I did an album called *Headhunters* in 1973 because I wanted to explore another avenue of my interest—rhythm and blues—which was also part of my heritage. What I chose to do was not have a permanent band, because I wanted to do so many different kinds of music. I really didn't think I could find a single group of musicians that could do all of those areas to my satisfaction, and I've never regretted that.

The downside to what I did is that it becomes extremely difficult, if not impossible, to develop the kind of synergy that comes as a result of musicians having worked together for years and years and years, like the Modern Jazz Quartet or Weather Report. I made that choice because I felt that this versatility was much more important to me, and the reaching out and the pioneering kind of attitude was much more important to me than the development of that synergy.

Prima Donnas

HANCOCK'S REPUTATION AS A PERSON IS THAT HE'S A COOL GUY WHO DOESN'T TAKE HIMSELF TOO SERIOUSLY OR CONSIDER HIMSELF TO BE ABOVE HIS FANS.

. . .

I've always hated the fact that there are prima donnas in the entertainment business. It is something I never respected and never thought was necessary. In a lot of cases, entertainers who exhibit those kinds of characteristics do so because of a real lack of confidence in themselves.

They have been given so many accolades and been patted on the back and so revered by an adoring public that there is an imbalance between how they view themselves and how the public views them. This puts them in a very weird space.

It helps when you have to pay some dues to achieve certain things. When there are some struggles and some challenges in your life, it really helps you to see a value in and a dependence on other people, and the value and the reality of the interdependence of people.

That audience out there that buys my records pays my rent and pays for my family's rent and food. Those people have their jobs. They are taking their hard-earned money to buy my records. For me to just ignore them or act like I am better than them makes no sense at all.

On Being Black

———

HANCOCK GREW UP IN AN ALL-BLACK NEIGHBORHOOD IN CHICAGO, WHERE HE LEARNED ABOUT BEING BLACK AND TAKING RESPONSIBILITY FOR HIS LIFE.

. . .

As a matter of fact, the only white people we knew were people collecting money: the insurance man and bill collectors [*laughs*]. I didn't know any white kids. I just knew the people that came to take money from my family.

I went to a mixed high school, but most of the kids were white. I think something like 20 percent of the kids were black. I remember the first day I went to high school, which was the first time I really met white kids, running home and saying, "Mom, they are just like me. They are just like we are."

I had heard these stories from my folks about when they were kids in Georgia. My father was born in 1910. My mother was born in 1916. So of course they told me all the sensational stories like the signs that said Colored, and my mother going into a drugstore to get a Coca-Cola and the guy behind the counter saying, "Little girl, I will sell you the Coke, but you can't drink it inside."

My mother took the glass and threw it and broke the mirror that was behind the counter, turned her back, walked out of the place, and never turned back. I mean they could have killed her. Nobody did anything. They probably couldn't believe the balls that this little girl had.

I think that there is a tendency for white people to think that it's unfortunate to be born black. It's not! I am very proud to be a black American. I feel that being black gives me certain advantages. Pity? I don't want pity. I don't think black people want pity. I don't think that black people want excuses for their destiny, but circumstances have made it easy to grab for that.

I can't feel like a strong person unless I take responsibility for my life. I don't want to have any excuses like blaming the white man for this or that situation or things that happened to me. I have to take responsibility for my own life and learn from the adversities of life.

Frankly, there haven't been a whole lot of adversities for me as a black man in America. Maybe because I am an artist. Maybe because I was born in Chicago and have lived in big cities all my life. Maybe because I developed a certain kind of confidence from having traveled around the world and being around a lot of different kinds of people.

It's unfortunate to be born and not grab the fruit off the vine yourself and shape your own destiny and utilize the challenges in life, whatever they are, to move yourself forward. It's not always easy, but I'm tired of black people making excuses.

I am sick of that. I really don't want to hear that anymore. I realize that everybody's life is different, and that my life may have been a lot easier than others, but I wasn't born with a silver spoon in my mouth. I was born in a poor family, but I had the good fortune of having a mother who gave my brother, my sister, and me hope from the very beginning.

Keeping an Open Mind

———

HANCOCK FIRST USED AN ELECTRIC PIANO BECAUSE MILES DAVIS TOLD HIM TO. THIS IS HOW HANCOCK LEARNED TO KEEP AN OPEN MIND AND INVESTIGATE THINGS FOR HIMSELF.

. . .

     I started off on acoustic piano. That was a period of time when I was a jazz snob. I didn't want to hear rock and roll or rhythm and blues. Jazz was the music, and it was the hot stuff. It was the music with real meaning, and everything else — electric instruments and all that — was below it.

     I remember walking to the recording studio for one of Miles's recordings, and I looked around for the acoustic piano and didn't see it, so I said, "Miles! What do you want me to play?" He said, "Play that over there." It was an electric piano. I thought to myself: That toy? I am going to play that toy? I mean, OK, Miles is the master. I'll play it.

     So I turned it on, and it had a volume control. It was a Fender Rhodes electric piano. I played a chord on it, and it sounded so mellow and so pretty. I could turn it up and play loud. For the first time I could play as loud as the drums. So I said, "Fantastic!"

     I learned a lesson from that. I had never played an electric piano before. I didn't have any personal experience. I took what someone else told me and accepted it as the truth without checking it out myself. If I hadn't respected Miles so much, I would have lost out, because later on I used that instrument to make some of the best records I ever made.

———

Ruth Graham

. . .

DAUGHTER, WIFE, MOTHER,

GRANDMOTHER, AND GREAT-GRANDMOTHER

$\mathscr{F}$INDING A PERSONAL MINISTRY

. . .

Where there is no wife, there is no home.

YUGOSLAVIAN PROVERB

According to *Webster's New World Dictionary, grace* is defined as "beauty or charm of form, composition, movement, or expression." Ruth Graham (age seventy-three) is the embodiment of grace. She has nothing to prove, no one to compete with, and she's wholly at peace with herself.

Ruth Graham measures her life by the Bible's standards and values—not other people's. She is the daughter of Presbyterian medical missionaries, the wife of the Christian evangelist Billy Graham, the mother of five children, and the author of several books. She grew up in Tsingkiang, Jiangsu, China, where her father ran a hospital. She went to boarding school in Korea when she was thirteen. This chapter is about devotion to God and family.

Ruth Graham and I talked in her husband's study in the offices of the Billy Graham Ministry in Montreat, North Carolina. It is a simply decorated, wood-paneled office with a fireplace. One of the most interesting mementos is a stack of Bibles that look as old as sin. In the middle of the interview, Billy called from their house (about a half-mile away) to ask her why he smelled burnt toast. She told him she had already checked, and things were OK. When she hung up, she explained to me that their house is made of logs, so the smell of anything burning is a serious concern.

Being Married to Billy Graham

IN 1935, WHEN GRAHAM WAS SIXTEEN YEARS OLD, HER FAMILY SPENT A FUR-LOUGH YEAR IN MONTREAT, NORTH CAROLINA. A YEAR LATER SHE FINISHED HIGH SCHOOL IN MONTREAT, AND IN 1937 SHE ENTERED WHEATON COLLEGE IN ILLINOIS. AT THE TIME, SHE INTENDED TO GO ON A MISSION TO TIBET AFTER GRADUATION.

. . .

I had already been there [Wheaton] for three years, and Billy was a transfer student from Florida Bible College. I was going up the steps of Blanchard Hall one day, and he was coming down two at a time. I just thought to myself, There is a young man in a hurry.

I taught Sunday school at Moosehart and Rural Bible Crusade. Before going, we would meet in the lobby of Williston Hall, which is one of the dormitories. I heard this man praying, and I thought, There is a man who knows to whom he is speaking, and thought nothing more of it.

One day—it must have been some weeks later—he came over in the library and asked me if I would go to the *Messiah* with him. I said I would. He picked me up at my dorm, and we walked the six blocks to the campus.

It's strange, but when I prayed that night, I just said to the Lord, "If you would let me spend the rest of my life with that man, I would consider it the greatest privilege imaginable."

I didn't know what I was asking for. Looking back, if I had known what was coming, I might not have had the nerve. [*Laughs*.] But that was it. I never said any more. It sort of took off from there— sort of slowly.

————

FOR THEIR ENTIRE FIFTY YEARS OF MARRIAGE, GRAHAM HAS SHARED HER HUS- BAND WITH THOUSANDS OF CHRISTIANS AROUND THE WORLD. HER EXPLANATION TO THOSE WHO ASKED HOW SHE COPED WITH THIS WAS, "I'D RATHER HAVE BILL PART-TIME THAN ANYBODY ELSE FULL-TIME."

• • •

Looking back, being married to anybody but Bill might be boring. There were times when I envied—not really *envied*, because I think that is the wrong word—wives who have their husbands at home more, and a more normal, more usual sort of life.

I just thank God for the privilege that He has allowed me to be married to the man that I think is the finest man I know. So it has been a privilege to share him with the rest of the world. It's not always easy, but He never promised it to us easy.

———

BILLY GRAHAM'S LONGTIME RIGHT-HAND MAN, T. W. WILSON, DESCRIBES RUTH'S INFLUENCE ON BILLY IN THIS WAY: "THERE WOULD HAVE BEEN NO BILLY GRAHAM AS WE KNOW HIM TODAY HAD IT NOT BEEN FOR RUTH."

. . .

I would not recommend any other young person try to do what Bill did. When Bill started, there weren't other young preachers in the country. I can think of one or two other evangelists—a lot of wonderful preachers, but I am thinking of evangelists who are on the road preaching. Today there's not the same need.

For a young man to go into this type of work with his eyes open…it can be very attractive, in a sense, if you stay in hotels and if you have room service. You are more or less free. You don't have to come home to a tired wife and scrappy kids and try to help them through supper and have a good time and tuck them in bed.

You are saved a lot of hassle, and yet the hassle is a part of the ministry. People talk about the Lord's work, and you think of going out and preaching or working as a missionary. The Lord's work is also the home and the family. So today I would urge young men to make mighty sure that God is calling them to this.

Before we were married, Bill was pastor of a little church in Wheaton, and they gave us a shower before we were married. The shower consisted of little sayings on pieces of paper. The best one, the one I've never forgotten, is that if two people agree on everything, one of them is unnecessary.

The important thing is to know when to disagree. You never disagree when tired or preoccupied or sleepy. That doesn't leave us much time…. [*Laughs.*] Never disagree with your hair up in rollers. Try to look as nice as you can. Tone of voice is very important. Rules of courtesy are very important.

See, I come from a long line of strong-minded, hardheaded individuals. Some people are much more flexible, milder, I would say, so there were times...but we celebrate our fiftieth this August.

Raising Children

BECAUSE BILLY WAS AT HOME "PART-TIME," GRAHAM RAISED HER CHILDREN WITH THE HELP OF GOD, HER PARENTS, AND THE LOCAL COMMUNITY.

. . .

There have been times when I wished we could have him [Billy Graham] at home more. Especially, this has been hard on the children, and it has been hard on him, although I don't think he realizes how much he missed seeing them as they were growing up.

I remember Anne, when she was little, sitting out in the yard, and a plane went overhead. I saw her look up and wave her little hands and say, "Bye, Daddy! Bye, Daddy!" I guess she just associated planes with her daddy.

I don't think the children remember the absences as much as they remember the times when he was home, and each one has happy memories of their father. He is a very caring person, and I think when they were little they thought that everybody's father traveled.

I tell you, if I didn't have God and know He was there with me, I couldn't have managed. And also, our wonderful friends. We live in a unique community. It used to be mainly for retired ministers and retired missionaries. We had the kindest neighbors.

The important thing, if a man feels like God has called him on the road, is to settle his wife where she would be the happiest. She — not he — may have to choose. In some places I don't think I could have made it, but at the time Mother and Daddy lived right across the road here, and we lived right next door.

THE GRAHAM'S FIVE CHILDREN FACED GREAT PRESSURE TO EITHER CONFORM TO

. . .

We never put pressure on them. They were just not aware that their father was.... He was special to them, but they didn't realize that he was well-known. Courtesy takes care of a lot of things. Courtesy for strangers, courtesy for one's superiors, courtesy for everybody — and a desire to help. Because their father was special doesn't mean that they are. They have to earn the right to be respected.

The tourists were pretty bad at first. If they drove past, we knew they were Episcopalians. If they stopped and looked down, we thought they were Presbyterians. If they stopped and came down to the road, we knew they were Baptists. [*Laughs*.]

For all the handicaps they got from being a child of Billy Graham, there have also been certain privileges: trips that they have been able to make, a global point of view that they've caught from their father, and friends from all over the world. There are many pluses along with the minuses.

———

Gentleman's Quarterly and other magazines have written about the Graham children. One son in particular, Franklin, has drawn media attention because of his interest in motorcycles, guns, and fast cars.

. . .

My father loves motorcycles. My father had a Harley-Davidson in China. He got it because it was the only thing you could get through those narrow Chinese streets back in the old days, but he had fun on it too. I remember a lot of the missionaries had Harley-Davidsons. He had a sidecar at the time; mother and we kids could ride in the sidecar.

I remember one time...our city straddled the Grand Canal, and eighty miles north of us lived the Currys. Uncle Ed—everyone was uncle and aunt to the missionary children — Uncle Ed Curry and Daddy got out on the canal with the motorcycle—it was frozen over.

One got on the motorcycle, and one got on ice skates. The one on the motorcycle would aim for every object in the canal—the Chinese children threw rocks and sticks into the canal. The one behind would have to quick-jump to keep from hitting the same thing.

I cannot see anything wrong with enjoying something like a motorcycle. If it were immoral or illegal, no. His love for guns goes way back to childhood, and as long as Franklin doesn't misuse it, I see no harm in it.

The Success of the Billy Graham Ministry

THE BILLY GRAHAM MINISTRY HAS BEEN IMMENSELY SUCCESSFUL IN BRINGING PEOPLE TO CHRISTIANITY. RUTH GRAHAM ATTRIBUTES ITS SUCCESS TO THREE FACTORS.

. . .

One, I attribute our success to the sovereignty of God; two, to the cooperation of the local churches; and three, to prayer. People have really upheld him in prayer, which has kept him going. I don't know why God chose him, but I do know that he couldn't have gotten along without the prayer of the local churches.

It's a good thing, because when he leaves a town, the baby Christians are left to be nurtured by those local churches. It makes a tremendous difference if they have that support and guidance and backup of the local churches and the local Christians.

I cannot overstate the power of prayer. When I get upset about something, our son Ned is fond of saying, "Mother, God is not a *little bit* sovereign." We know we live in the devil's world, but God is still omnipotent. He is sovereign.

THE BILLY GRAHAM MINISTRY PROVIDES A SHARP CONTRAST TO THE SCANDALS SURROUNDING JIM AND TAMMY BAKKER AND JIMMY SWAGGART. GRAHAM BELIEVES THESE SCANDALS ILLUSTRATE THE CORRUPTING POWER OF MONEY AS WELL AS THE FORGIVENESS OF GOD.

. . .

My hindsight about those is really grief and pity. When my husband was in Rochester, Minnesota, the last time to go to the Mayo Clinic, the doctor who was in charge took him over to see Jim Bakker [at the Federal Medical Center in Rochester, Minnesota]. Bakker had no idea who was coming.

He just came into the room, and his job was to clean something like forty toilets a day. He had on these dirty whites and tennis shoes. He had lost a lot of weight, and he was so humble.

I am convinced he is a true man of God; he just got misled. He came from a very poor family. Both he and his wife did. So often when you come from a very, very poor family — I mean really just an outhouse and no indoor plumbing — and suddenly run into all that kind of money and fame, you may not know how to handle it. It's kind of intoxicating.

I never met Jimmy Swaggart. I know he is an enormously talented person. I used to watch him occasionally just for entertainment value — which is not the reason for watching — but he could sing, he could play. He is just a gifted person.

What happened I don't know, but someone said — and I think this makes sense — "It's the airplane that crashes that makes the news." There are thousands of preachers out there preaching their hearts out. True to the Lord. True to the Gospel. No one ever hears of them. But they faithfully go on year after year. They are good men. Godly men.

God Works in Strange Ways

WHILE GRAHAM WAS IN SCHOOL IN KOREA, SHE HATED BEING AWAY FROM HER FAMILY AND MISSED HER HOME, BUT THROUGH THIS EXPERIENCE SHE HAS COME TO BELIEVE THAT GOD HAS GOOD REASONS TO *NOT* ANSWER PEOPLE'S PRAYERS.

• • •

When I first went to North Korea, I was one little homesick girl. I was thirteen, and it must have been 1,400 miles from home.

I was so homesick I cried myself to sleep night after night after night, until they were having prayer meetings for me in the school.

We used to get stationery from Japan rolled like scrolls and decorated with cherry blossoms, and I wrote what must have been a twelve- or fifteen-foot letter home, begging to come home. I was convinced that if I would go home to learn from mother how to keep house and learn all the things that she could teach me, I would be much better prepared for life than if I went through high school.

They just made me stay on. I am so glad. Looking back, I am so grateful for those three years that I spent in Pyongyang. God has not always answered prayer the way I've asked, but in the long run I am glad He didn't. What He did instead was so much better.

There are things today that I am still concerned and praying about that haven't reached a final solution, but I know because in the past He has never failed, that He is not going to start failing now. My prayer is that I won't fail him.

———

Langston Earley

. . .

AIDS PATIENT

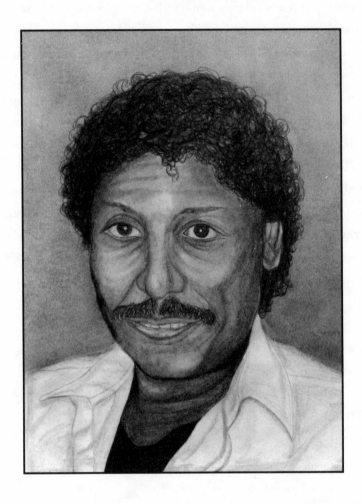

$\mathscr{B}$EING TRUE TO YOURSELF

. . .

One time I got a letter from a woman complaining about some people who had just moved in next door. There was a guy with long hair and a couple of women with short hair. It was clear from her letter that these were gay people, and she wasn't happy about having them move into her nice neighborhood. She said, "We're disgusted with these types. What can we do to improve the neighborhood?" My answer was "You could move."

ABIGAIL VAN BUREN

During our interview, an alarm attached to Langston Earley's (age thirty-nine) pillbox went off. The pillbox is a gift from Earley's lover, John. He uses it to hold the dozen or so pills he must take every day to combat AIDS. Among the medications he takes are AZT (to slow the progress of AIDS), Bactrim (to prevent pneumonia), Fluconazole (to control yeast infection), Tagamet (to increase T cells), and Naltrexone (also to increase T cells—it's mixed with Robitussin cough syrup to dilute the dosage enough to reduce side effects).

Earley is black—and gay—and he has AIDS. Other than that, he is like most people trying to make a living and maintain a relationship. This interview isn't about a man with AIDS who regrets that his sexual promiscuity led to a life-threatening disease. It's not about the positive effects that contracting AIDS has had on his life. This interview is about being true to yourself—sexually, professionally, and racially.

I interviewed Earley in the piano bar of the Boston Harbor Hotel. Earley brought John to the interview for support, although he hardly spoke until the interview was over. There we sat: one black-American gay man with AIDS, one white-American gay lover, and one straight Japanese-American writer. The odd squad.

Setting Up Boundaries

THE EFFECT OF AIDS ON EARLEY'S LIFE DOMINATED OUR INTERVIEW. LOOKING BACK ON HIS LIFE, HE WISHES HE HAD BEEN TRUER TO HIMSELF—A HINDSIGHT PERTINENT TO MOST PEOPLE, BUT PARTICULARLY APPLICABLE TO SOMEONE WHO CONTRACTED AIDS THROUGH SEXUAL CONTACT.

. . .

I know I got AIDS sexually, because I have never done any intravenous drugs or had a blood transfusion or any of those other methods. I can't imagine any other way that I would have been infected.

One of the things I thought about is the whole issue of sexual experimentation, monogamy, and having more than one sexual partner. What would I feel if I could go back and have fewer sexual partners? I would probably be less sexually adventurous and that sort of thing. But the more I thought about it, the more I began to think that all those experiences are a part of what made me who I am today.

There is a lot I like about who I am today, and I don't know if I would want to give that up. What I finally did realize is that if I could change anything about my sexual history, it would be that I would have been truer to myself at certain times.

When asked to do something that I didn't necessarily want to do, I would say "Not now" instead of saying yes to please the other person. I am not talking about anything that caused me pain or that I didn't perhaps enjoy doing at other times.

But the funny thing is that a lot of the things that are recommended in terms of safe sex—for instance, concentrating more on touching and affection as opposed to "sex equals penetration"—is what I like anyway and what I would ask for most of the time.

A lot of times I did things to accommodate the other person because I wanted to make them happy. Maybe if I had trusted my instincts more or set up firmer boundaries about what was OK with me and what was not, I might have reduced the opportunities for infection.

———

DESPITE THE FACT THAT HIS LIFE-STYLE HAS LED TO AIDS AND SEVERE PAIN, EARLEY IS GLAD AND PROUD TO BE GAY.

. . .

Kawasaki: Do you wish you were straight?

Earley: No.

Kawasaki: Not at all?

Earley: No.

Kawasaki: Despite the disenfranchisement of gays and all this stuff that goes on?

Earley: That would be like asking, "Do I wish I were white?" Even if we were at whatever place we come from before we hit Earth and they said, "You can be a member of a minority group where people give you a lot of shit all the time and you have to fight for everything and you'll have to be twice as good to get half as far as anybody else. Or, you can have a whole lot of advantages."

Learning from Illness

———

WHEN EARLEY BEGAN TO SUFFER FROM AIDS, HE LEARNED ABOUT THE NATURE OF PAIN.

. . .

After going through a lot of pain and distress, I realized that once the crisis was over, I quickly began to forget what the pain felt like. I'd always been afraid that I wouldn't be able to handle the pain. When I talked to other patients, I'd often think, God, I couldn't handle that—how did they make it?

What I've found is that the brain seems to have a remarkable ability to mask the memory of pain and allow you to get on with your life. I don't know how much this ability can deal with without overloading, but it's pretty neat to know it's there!

WHEN HE STARTED GOING TO A SUPPORT GROUP, EARLEY HEARD PEOPLE SAY THAT THINGS WERE GOOD. SOME EVEN SAID THAT AIDS IMPROVED THEIR LIVES. AT FIRST HE THOUGHT THEY WERE NAIVE OR STUPID.

. . .

One of the reasons why I contacted you was because I was going through a period during which I was a little surprised that my answer to the question, If you could go back and not be infected, what would you do? wasn't what I thought it would be anymore.

When I first got diagnosed and started going to a support group, guys talked about how positive their lives were and how, in some ways, they didn't mind having AIDS. I thought that was very Pollyannaish and kind of crazy, but now that it has been almost two years, I can see that there have been a lot of positive changes in my life that probably wouldn't have happened if I hadn't gotten infected with this disease.

For example, I don't deal with things that aren't good for me anymore. I express my anger more easily—at this point it's hard for me to justify sitting on my feelings. I don't have time to take care of other people's reactions.

Before, the idea of starting a business was the kind of thing I wished I could do, but it always felt like something other people do. Since being diagnosed, I've done some occasional consulting to supplement my disability benefits. If a cure was found tomorrow and I was off disability, I would be working to build this into a full-time business. I don't think I'd have had the nerve to attempt it before I got sick.

If I could have experienced these changes without AIDS, that's what I would choose to do, but I don't know if the average person is able to work though some of these issues without a catalyst like this. People I've spoken to with other chronic or fatal diseases have gone though the same thing.

Magic Johnson

———

MAGIC JOHNSON'S DISCLOSURE OF HIS HIV-POSITIVE STATUS HAS DRAWN CONSIDERABLE ATTENTION TO AIDS AND BROADENED PUBLIC AWARENESS OF THE DISEASE.

. . .

My first reaction was I was sorry for him just like I'm sorry for anybody who gets it, but I'm really glad it happened, because a lot of people feel like they know him on some level. Now they know someone with AIDS, and now they are thinking about it differently.

Until a large number not only of straight people, but famous, well-loved, or whatever-you-want-to-call-it straight people and children start dying, then not much is going to happen in terms of defeating the disease.

If 25,000 children died tomorrow, they'd do something, but right now the average person still defines AIDS as being something that affects disposable communities: gay and minority. It's also very easy to say it's their own fault for being drug users or whatever.

It's very important that people know they know gay people. It's getting very important that people realize that they know someone with AIDS. At that point energy will really get devoted to finding a cure.

A lot of times I've met people who were pretty homophobic until they realized their brother, sister, mom, or dad is gay, and all of a sudden the issue of gay rights became something different to them.

Coming Out

———

IN 1970, AT THE AGE OF SEVENTEEN, EARLEY LOST HIS VIRGINITY IN A TWO-DAY PERIOD WHEN HE SLEPT WITH A MAN AND THEN A WOMAN. AFTER SEVERAL YEARS,

HE BECAME EXCLUSIVELY HOMOSEXUAL—IN EFFECT, COMING OUT TO HIMSELF—THOUGH HE HID HIS GAY ORIENTATION FROM MOST OF HIS ACQUAINTANCES. LATER, IN 1975, HE DROPPED PRETENSES ALTOGETHER.

. . .

There's three stages to coming out. There is coming out to yourself—which some poor devils never accomplish. There's coming out to the people close to you, and then there's coming out to the rest of the world.

When I came out, my initial reaction was to have this life in the evenings but to go to work every day and have another life. Then I found myself thinking, Why am I doing this? This doesn't make any sense. It's not consistent with the way I want to live my life, and it takes a lot of energy.

Gay people should come out whenever they can and however they can. I don't think that you can confront discrimination if you're invisible. For most of my adult life—or most of my life since I've become aware that I'm gay—I've been out in pretty much every area of my life.

Some people can't handle coming out. I have a theory that in some ways minority men have an easier time with coming out. The reason is they've already adjusted to the idea of being a member of an oppressed group.

When I came out, I had to adjust to a lot of the cultural stuff I was raised with, but in many ways my reaction was, This is just one more minority to add to the list. I've seen white gay men have real difficulty because for the first time in their life they realized that someone might try to harm them, hold them back, or even think they deserve to die simply because of who they are.

Going Back

WHEN EARLEY TOOK A JOB IN 1987, HE WENT BACK INTO THE CLOSET. HE

. . .

It was one of the stupidest things I ever did. We oppress ourselves even more than other people oppress us. I didn't lie and say that I was straight. I just didn't talk about it.

Toward the end, I began doing things like showing up at company functions with John, and they knew he was the man I'd been living with for a few years. Part of my reason for doing it wasn't just for me to be comfortable or to be proud. There was a certain passive-aggressive element to it; I knew it shook them up.

It would have been better for all of us if I'd been more up-front, because it's not about who I am sleeping with. It's about who I love. If I was given an award at work, and I was supposed to receive the award at a banquet, everyone else getting an award would want their wife or husband to be there and share their moment of pride.

How could I go and leave him behind because I don't want them to know about me? That completely robs me of my joy. It takes away from him, and to some degree it's insulting to him.

Earley's Lover

———

AS I MENTIONED BEFORE, JOHN, EARLEY'S LOVER, SAT WITH US DURING THE INTERVIEW. THIS IS HOW EARLEY DESCRIBES THEIR FIRST MEETING.

. . .

It's a cheap, tawdry story. I got home one night, and I was totally hysterical. I was ready to shoot everyone I worked with, and I decided I had to go out. I didn't care if I didn't see anyone I knew or if I didn't talk to anyone, but I had to be in a room full of queens.

We met at the bar — a bar I told all my clients that they'd never meet anyone in and form a real relationship. [Earley was once a social-services counselor.] In a disco. I met my lover in a disco. It's so humiliating. [*Laughs*.]

I ASKED JOHN ABOUT FALLING IN LOVE WITH A MAN WITH AIDS.

· · ·

John: It sucks. It really stinks because your first instinct is to go away.

Kawasaki: Why didn't you?

John: Because I love him.

Steve Wozniak

• • •

HACKER AND HUMANITARIAN

ESIGNING A LIFE

. . .

Man is still the most extraordinary computer of all.

JOHN F. KENNEDY

You know you've arrived when you can go by a single name like Madonna or Cher. Among early personal-computer owners, Steve Wozniak (age forty-two) is simply known as Woz. His name is associated with the magic and romance of the Apple I and Apple II because he and Steve Jobs are the legendary "two guys in a garage" who started Apple Computer.

Three people were responsible for Apple's early success: Steve Jobs, Mike Markkula, and Woz. Jobs was the charismatic leader who came up with the idea of selling preassembled, ready-to-use computers. Mike Markkula, a rich and semiretired investor who made his millions at Intel, never worked for Apple but provided capital, credibility, and industry know-how. Woz was the engineer. He liked to build cool computers to impress the members of the Homebrew Computer Club, an eclectic group of renegades interested in microprocessors and computers.

This chapter is about the early days of Apple and choosing your life's work. Woz and I met for this interview in his offices in Los Gatos, California. *Lab* would be a better way to describe this facility, because it is jammed with Macintosh computers and printers as well as audio and video equipment. Almost anyone's mom would faint at the disarray here, and just about anyone's dad would faint at the cost of the equipment lying around.

The Start of Apple Computer

WHEN WOZ WAS DESIGNING THE APPLE I, HE NEVER THOUGHT THAT THE PROD-UCT WOULD LAUNCH A MULTIBILLION-DOLLAR COMPANY. HE WAS JUST HAVING FUN—APPLYING HIS ENGINEERING SKILLS TO BUILD GADGETS FOR HIMSELF AND HIS FRIENDS.

. . .

Apple was a total accident of history. I was building projects like terminals for Hewlett-Packard and heard about a club starting up. I designed the Apple I in a closed room in my lab at Hewlett-Packard and in my apartment in Cupertino. I just built it for myself and started showing it off at the Club [the Homebrew Computer Club] by passing out schematics. It was like a science project I was showing off to friends. It wasn't done to be a product to be sold.

Steve Jobs came to one of the club meetings, and he saw that people were interested in my schematics. He came up with an idea— he had worked in surplus-electronics stores—Why don't we make a PC board for $20 and sell it for $40? I didn't know if we would make our money back, but I finally went along with his idea. When you are young, it is a neat, thrilling idea that you could have a company. It didn't have to be for money.

We never knew exactly what the next step was. What was right in front of you was obvious, but you could never look three, four, or seven steps ahead. We thought we were going to sell PC boards for $40, and maybe we'd make $1,000 back. We wound up getting orders for $500 computers right away, but it was a total surprise.

All the designs and all the software for the Apple I were my ideas. The electronic features—how many chips did what and right down to how many slots—were all my choices. What the computer looked like, how it would be sold, and how it would be presented to people were Steve's. Working with Mike Markkula, he came up with ideas to make the Apple II a salable device.

———

WHY DID WOZ AND JOBS CAUSE THE BIRTH OF THE MOST IMPORTANT INDUSTRY SINCE AUTOMOBILES, WHILE OTHER COMPANIES MISSED IT? MAYBE IT'S BECAUSE WOZ AND JOBS WERE BEATNIKS AND HIPPIES—TRYING TO START A REVOLUTION, NOT BUILD AN INDUSTRY.

· · ·

Apple came about from a couple of kids with an idea of building a little cheap product, trying to hawk it, finding sales, and stepping into magic. I came from a group that was what you might call beatniks or hippies — a lot of technicians who talked radical about a revolution in information and how we were going to totally change the world and put computers in homes.

If people who were smart in business had looked at us in the category of small computers and thought Apple was going to become a huge company, they would have started something inside their companies. Mike Markkula told us a company like Apple — a brand-new, little company that is just starting up — can get in and hold on to a certain amount of the market and grow with the market. He turned out to be right, but at first I thought he was just making up the hugest number possible.

———

Woz and Jobs were not completely alone in their dream of creating a computer revolution. Two companies, Imsai and Altair, created computers at about the same time as Apple.

. . .

Altair and Imsai approached the world as if there were a lot of technical people that would buy kits of parts because they know how to solder them together. It was so easy for Altair and Imsai to put a bunch of chips in a bag and not have to learn how to manufacture a computer.

Stores wanted a product that they could sell a lot of. A lot of people — even technicians — would walk in the door and want to buy a completely built Altair, so the store would buy an Altair kit, build it in the back room, and sell it at an already built price. We paid a local company $13 per computer to solder all the parts for us. Why should we give a kit to a customer who is going to make mistakes and force him to spend twenty hours soldering everything together when we can do it for $13?

With the Apple II, we went a step further and told people they didn't even have to plug in transformers or keyboards or monitors. It came as one complete box, and the only problem was hooking it up to a TV set. There was a second company that had a product to do that.

That was when the terminology started going toward *personal* computer. *Personal* meant one computer for one person, but there was also a difference between hobby computer and personal computer: a hobby computer was a kit, and you had to be a technician. It had a bunch of weird binary lights on it. A personal computer had a keyboard that you could type on, and the output went to your TV set.

Building the First One for Himself

WOZ DESIGNED THE APPLE II TO BE A COMPUTER THAT HE WOULD LIKE TO OWN AND COULD AFFORD TO BUY. EXPERIENCE HAS TAUGHT HIM THAT THIS IS ONE OF THE BEST WAYS TO DESIGN ANY PRODUCT.

• • •

There was no market research — nobody asking how many characters you should have on the screen or if you should have this mode of color. My approach was to look at the chips that were available and gut-feel the set of features and the compromises as I went along.

Cost was a real issue because I was building the first one for myself, and I had to be able to afford it, so it had to be low-cost. I like things with very few chips because I consider that good design. It came out much tighter than if I had been given a set of specs, because then I would have just designed by brute force by adding on circuitry.

SHORTLY AFTER APPLE WAS FOUNDED, COMMODORE AND RADIO SHACK INTRODUCED READY-TO-USE PERSONAL COMPUTERS. BUT THEY, TOO, SOON FAILED. (DON'T WORRY ABOUT THE JARGON WOZ USES IN THIS SECTION—THE MESSAGE IS TO BUILD FLEXIBILITY AND LONGEVITY INTO PRODUCTS.)

• • •

What I really compare our computer to is two other computers that came out after ours, intended to be prebuilt, ready-to-run computers. They were the Commodore Pet and the Radio Shack TRS 80. Why did we win out over them? The Pet and the TRS 80 were not expandable, and you could not plug cards in them. We were expandable to 48 kilobytes of RAM [random-access memory]. Once you got to a spreadsheet program, it needed more than 8K of RAM, so it couldn't run on the Commodore Pet or the TRS 80, but it could run on the Apple II.

The reason why Apple was a big winner dates back to an earlier story—the IBM 360 computer. It's been called the most successful computer of all time. It had an architecture so that as the machines expanded, every program ever written would always run. You shouldn't tie yourself into a limit on memory that is shorter than what you could maybe see a couple decades ahead. An engineer should think, I don't want my machine to become obsolete. You got to feel like you are the owner, and this is your machine.

Changing of the Guard

IN 1983, STEVE JOBS RECRUITED JOHN SCULLEY FROM PEPSICO TO BE PRESIDENT AND CHIEF EXECUTIVE OFFICER OF APPLE WHILE JOBS RETAINED THE TITLE OF CHAIRMAN. THIS WAS SUPPOSED TO BE APPLE'S TEAM FOR THE FUTURE: THE BRILLIANT, YOUNG TECHNOLOGIST AND THE SEASONED, PROFESSIONAL MANAGER. IN 1985, SCULLEY OUSTED JOBS.

• • •

Steve was a great visionary, but a lot of the things that happened to us at Apple were accidents and luck, and not because we could think things out properly. The world was going to get into small computers, and we had some of the right products at the right time. I think Steve felt that a lot of his thinking had caused the world to get into computers in the year when microprocessors were going to cost $5 and RAMs were going to cost $5.

Steve's idea of running the company was to build the best technology, but the market will sometimes choose a worse technology at a higher price for reasons such as familiarity, knowing other people that are getting into it, the way the marketing is done, and sales agreements. He had his purist's ideas. Maybe he was trying to build a machine for himself at a time when we had to build a machine for customers.

Steve was very, very bright—he might have been the brightest person at Apple, but he didn't handle people well. He left bad sentiments all over the company. I think a lot of managers were upset over Steve wanting to direct what they were doing, being very rude, and talking to people in a way that didn't make them feel like they were smart and respected—like they didn't know what they were doing unless they did it his way.

All this came up to John, and I think he started having to take actions to save the company. I am sure he would have left Steve a lot of freedom to create great, great things—to do the kind of work he wanted to do—but John had to save the company and get some things done. I think Steve felt that he couldn't do the great things for the world at Apple and that he'd have to go outside of Apple.

Making It

WHEN APPLE MADE ITS PUBLIC STOCK OFFERING, WOZ MADE SEVERAL HUNDRED MILLION DOLLARS. AFTER REFLECTING UPON THIS, HOWEVER, HE REALIZED THAT HE HAD "MADE IT" LONG BEFORE APPLE WENT PUBLIC.

• • •

Making it financially is making it. People might say they are successful if they achieve something they really wanted to achieve, but if you were successful at achieving what you wanted to achieve and didn't have the financial success, I don't know if you could say you made it.

Maybe [*changing his mind*] either fame or fortune is making it. You could, in other words, be an educator and get very famous for what you are doing. You could call this making it, because wherever you go, people would say, "I heard your speech," "I heard your seminar," "I really agree with your points," and "I think you've done a great thing with this project." Maybe you didn't make money, but you could still say you made it.

I had my happiness before I had money. I had a whole big internal religion—no church or anything—but a whole line of thoughts and philosophies of how to live life and how to be happy forever. I had that down. I was a real healthy, pure person. I never used any drugs or smoked marijuana or anything like that. I never even drank wine until I was thirty.

———

SINCE HIS RETIREMENT FROM APPLE, WOZ HAS STARTED SEVERAL COMPANIES, BUT MOSTLY HE'S BEEN DOING PHILANTHROPIC THINGS LIKE TEACHING FIFTH-GRADERS HOW TO USE COMPUTERS, DONATING COMPUTER LABS TO SCHOOLS, AND PROVIDING FUNDS FOR NONPROFIT ORGANIZATIONS.

• • •

I am doing what I grew up being taught was right. I read books to my young children, and in all the books there are good people who are doing things for others—Goofy wins a big race over Big Bad Pete, and he gives the money he won to build a baseball diamond for the orphans. If you are lucky enough to be successful, then try to do something to help your community.

Life After Apple

———

MANY ENTREPRENEURS HAVE DIFFICULTY GIVING UP CONTROL OF THE COMPANIES THEY CREATED—PARTLY BECAUSE THEIR COMPANY BECOMES THEIR *LIFE* AND PARTLY BECAUSE THEY THINK NO ONE CAN DO THE JOB AS WELL AS THEY CAN. NOT WOZ.

• • •

It got to the point where there were enough engineers, so I was just another engineer, and I wasn't really critical. I would talk to the press more than anything, so I went to my boss one day and had him lower my salary below the engineers who were doing the real work.

Also, I had my children and a family. I've got six kids now. They are my first priority in life. There is no way in the world I could be an engineer and take all this time away from my family. Children mean a lot to me because of things I was taught as a child—about how great we were—and the good memories of what fun it was to play and be a kid.

In the sixth grade, I decided I was going to be an engineer, and then I was going to be an elementary school teacher. That's what I've done. I could have had a lot of fun in Apple and been involved in some great things going on in the world, but I really feel better about what I am doing.

———

It seems that Woz has life all figured out: design a product you love, make a lot of money, retire young, and do something for people.

• • •

Find something you are good at, work on it, and eventually you can succeed and make your life. Don't just slack off and think you will just go through life doing a job. You should try to do incredible things—put a lot of hours into making a lot of things very, very good.

When you are young, skip a bunch of parties and just stay up late at night working on programs and technology. If you are starting out in a company, spend the extra hours. Talk to people and get that report just right. You have a lot of free time when you are young, so put it into what you are good at before you wind up with a life with many commitments, meetings, bills, and mortgages. Spend time when you are young, and that will give you a lot more freedom when you are older.

I want to be remembered as a good computer designer who

designed things with very few parts and wrote code that was very amazing and tricky and ingenious. I want to be remembered as a good father who cared about children. Every step of my life has been incredible. I have a lot of freedom. I get to do a lot of traveling and see a lot of things. I've got wonderful children. Nobody could have a life better than mine.

———

—

Contemplating History

. . .

Hans Bethe

· · ·

THEORETICAL PHYSICIST

$\mathcal{U}$NDERSTANDING NUCLEAR WEAPONS

. . .

In the course of time, the present conflict between Communism and Democracy, between East and West, is likely to pass just as the religious wars of the 16th and 17th century have passed. We can only hope that it will pass without an H-bomb war. But whichever way it goes, the H-bomb will remain with us and remain a perpetual danger to mankind.

DR. HANS BETHE

Although he is a Nobel Prize winner, Dr. Hans Bethe (age eighty-six) may be best remembered for his role as director of theoretical physics for the Manhattan Project, the frantic effort started by the United States Army in 1942 to create an atomic bomb. He and other nuclear physicists were recruited by Robert Oppenheimer to work on this project at the Los Alamos National Laboratory in Los Alamos, New Mexico.

The group was successful, and on August 6, 1945, the United States dropped an atomic bomb on Hiroshima, Japan. It destroyed about four square miles of the city and killed 71,000 people. On August 9, 1945, the United States dropped a second atomic bomb on Japan, this time on Nagasaki, and killed 40,000 people. On August 14, 1945, the Japanese surrendered.

Bethe was born in Strasbourg (at the time in Germany, now in France) and taught in Germany until 1933, when he moved to England and shortly thereafter to the United States. From 1933 to 1975, Bethe held a chair in physics at Cornell University. He was awarded the Nobel Prize for physics in 1967. In this chapter, Bethe reflects on America's creation of nuclear weapons.

My interview with Bethe took place in an office in the library at the Los Alamos National Laboratory. Los Alamos is built on the Pajarito Plateau, a beautiful place that rises out of the desert floor. Juniper and piñon trees grow along the way up, and there are ponderosa, fir, spruce, oak, and aspen trees at higher levels. I couldn't help but wonder how such destructive weapons could have been built there.

The Manhattan Project

ALTHOUGH MOST ACCOUNTS OF THE MANHATTAN PROJECT DEPICT THE CREATION OF THE ATOMIC BOMB AS A HERCULEAN TASK WITH A SHORT DEADLINE, BETHE SAYS IT WAS EASY.

. . .

It was obvious it would succeed. There was nuclear fission [first achieved by Enrico Fermi in December 1942] releasing tremendous energy — making possible a chain reaction. This made it obvious that you could make nuclear weapons.

You have to have very good people with great enthusiasm and a feasible project. We spent some time thinking of possible obstacles and finding out that everything was all right. Once we had the material, it was obvious that the bomb would be built.

ONE OF THE CRUCIAL STEPS OF THE PROJECT WAS GARNERING THE SUPPORT OF THE U.S. GOVERNMENT. MOST ACCOUNTS SAY THAT THE CRITICAL EVENT WAS ALBERT EINSTEIN SENDING A LETTER IN SUPPORT OF THE PROJECT TO PRESIDENT ROOSEVELT. BETHE DISAGREES.

. . .

I suspect the first important person this [Otto Hahn's discovery of nuclear fission] persuaded was Vannevar Bush [a prominent physicist and advisor to the U.S. government]; then Bush and others got Roosevelt interested in it. Roosevelt had received the famous letter by Einstein, which had no real effect, but he remembered it. It was not Einstein who set it going.

Bombing Hiroshima and Nagasaki

THE BOMBING OF HIROSHIMA AND NAGASAKI KILLED TENS OF THOUSANDS OF PEOPLE. SOME HISTORIANS BELIEVE THAT DROPPING THESE BOMBS WAS UNNECESSARY

AND THAT THE UNITED STATES SHOULD HAVE SIMPLY EXPLODED A BOMB IN AN UNIN-
HABITED AREA TO DEMONSTRATE THAT IT HAD NUCLEAR-WEAPON CAPABILITIES.

. . .

In hindsight, I think the correct action was taken. This meant the end of the war, and I don't think the end of the war would have come that soon otherwise. Emperor Hirohito himself intervened and said, "We must stop."

The emperor would never have been taken to a place where he could see a demonstration. I think the emperor was impressed by the suffering at Hiroshima—that suffering was terrible, and I'm terribly sorry about that, but I believe it was that suffering which induced the emperor to give in.

I don't believe that Japan would have done this without bombing Hiroshima. Nagasaki? That's a different matter. I think the second bomb was not necessary and should not have been dropped.

AFTER WORLD WAR II ENDED, A CONTROVERSY AROSE OVER WHETHER OR NOT THE UNITED STATES SHOULD BUILD A HYDROGEN BOMB. THE DECISION TO PROCEED WAS MADE LARGELY BECAUSE OF COLD WAR FEARS THAT THE SOVIET UNION WAS DEVELOPING A SIMILAR WEAPON.

. . .

Building a hydrogen bomb was the wrong thing from the beginning. There was no need to further increase the power of the bomb. The atom bomb was quite enough. We have been lucky that no nuclear weapon has been used since Nagasaki. No hydrogen bomb was ever used, but that's luck.

I think, even before the test of the hydrogen bomb, the statesmen had become aware of their responsibility. Now it is true that maybe the hydrogen bomb emphasized it still more. There was a proposal by Fermi and Rabi [Isidor Rabi, professor of physics at Columbia University] in 1949 to approach the Soviets to propose that we both refrain from developing the hydrogen bomb.

I thought that was a good idea. I am somewhat uncertain that it would have worked, though, because I have read part of Sakharov's memoirs, which said it wouldn't have done any good to have approached the Soviet government. [Andrei Sakharov is the Soviet physicist who was responsible for the development of the Soviet hydrogen bomb. He won the Nobel Peace Prize in 1975 for his work supporting the nuclear-test-ban treaty, international peace, and improved civil rights.]

He said the Soviet Union was clearly set on the path to the hydrogen bomb—that if we had approached them, they would have reacted by saying one of two things: a sign of weakness by the U.S.; or else it is deception—they say it so that we don't develop it, and in the meantime they will do so.

That's Sakharov's opinion, but Sakharov was not in the government. I believe that Stalin indeed would have rejected it. But Malenkov [Georgi Malenkov, the Soviet Communist Party leader who took over following Stalin's death] and then Khrushchev, that was a different matter.

The way we should have acted was proposed by Vannevar Bush. He was the wartime boss of all scientific research during the war. In 1952, he headed a committee set up by the State Department to discuss what one could do toward reducing the warlike attitude of both sides—that is, partial disarmament.

He proposed, "Let us develop the hydrogen bomb"—which by that time, summer of 1952, had gone a long way—"but let us not test it. Let us declare: we have fully developed the hydrogen bomb. We don't want anybody to have it. We will not test it. But if any other country tests it, we are ready to do so." I think that was a much better approach than the Fermi/Rabi approach.

The Role of Scientists

WHEN IT COMES TO AN INVENTION LIKE A HYDROGEN BOMB, MANY SCIENTISTS BELIEVE THAT IF IT CAN BE BUILT, IT SHOULD BE BUILT, AND THEN IT SHOULD BE LEFT UP TO POLITICIANS TO DECIDE WHAT TO DO WITH THE TECHNOLOGY. OTHERS, LIKE BETHE, THINK THAT THE GOVERNMENT SHOULD DECIDE IN ADVANCE WHICH WEAPONS SHOULD BE DEVELOPED.

• • •

Let's go back to 1951. A very likely, very promising way of making a hydrogen bomb had been invented by Edward Teller [a Hungarian-born nuclear physicist who was one of the primary forces in the development of nuclear weapons in America] and Stanislaw Ulam [a Polish mathematician from the University of Wisconsin who worked for Teller at Los Alamos]. What should have happened is that we should have gone to the government—in fact, we did, in the form of the Atomic Energy Commission—and said, "We do not think that it is a good idea to develop it, but you decide whether we should."

When the hydrogen bomb became feasible in the spring of 1951, there was a meeting in Princeton, New Jersey, which involved the Atomic Energy Commission and its General Advisory Committee. By that time, I'm sorry to say, I as well as other scientists were convinced that we should do it. I did not have the wisdom of Vannevar Bush. At the meeting in Princeton, we decided to go full speed ahead. And we did. In a year and a half—even a little less—it was all ready for test, and it was tested. I don't believe we could have prevented the development at that time.

BETHE HAS COME TO BELIEVE THAT DECISIONS OF THIS KIND SHOULD BE MADE IN THE BEST INTEREST OF THE WORLD AS A WHOLE—NOT JUST A SINGLE COUNTRY.

• • •

Scientists should go to the government and say, "This is what I believe I can do. Do you want me to do that?" Then the secretary of energy would go to his scientific advisory committee and see whether the idea is scientifically reasonable.

Nine out of ten will not be, and that would end it. On the tenth, I would then bring together a committee of wise men who have in mind not just the strength of the U.S. but the welfare of the whole world. Let that committee—which might easily involve some British, French, Japanese, and Germans—listen and decide if this is an advantage for the welfare of the world or not.

If they decide it is undesirable and that it is bad for the peace of the world, then I would not try to get any support for it.

Forgiveness

———

BETHE'S DAUGHTER IS MARRIED TO A JAPANESE NATIONAL WHO LIVES IN JAPAN. OUR CONVERSATION ABOUT THIS TOPIC IS AN ILLUSTRATION OF FORGIVENESS.

• • •

Kawasaki: Isn't it ironic that your daughter is in Japan, studying Japanese art, married to a Japanese man, and you helped create the atomic bomb?

Bethe: No.

Kawasaki: No?

Bethe: When the war was over, it was over, and as you probably know, the United States has been very generous to both Japan and Germany. Many people have made the joke: "Let's make war on America!" [*Laughs.*]

———

Chuck Colson

· · ·

PRESIDENTIAL AIDE

$\mathcal{D}$ISCOVERING TRUTH AND MORALITY

. . .

You shall have joy, or you shall have power, said God; you shall not have both.

RALPH WALDO EMERSON

Chuck Colson (age sixty-one) used to be a plumber—not the kind that fixes pipes, but the kind that fixes leaks for the government. In Colson's case, the particular part of the government he worked for was President Richard Nixon and his senior executives, and the particular leak was the *Pentagon Papers.*

The *Pentagon Papers* was a study of America's involvement in Vietnam called *The History of the U.S. Decision-Making Process in Vietnam.* It was leaked to *The New York Times* by Daniel Ellsberg, a former Rand Corporation analyst who helped compile it. President Nixon was incensed that such a highly confidential document was leaked, and he ordered that the leaks be plugged and Ellsberg be investigated.

At first Colson and other senior members of Nixon's staff recruited E. Howard Hunt and G. Gordon Liddy for legitimate tasks at the White House. Later, however, these two men were directed to engineer a break-in at Daniel Ellsberg's psychiatrist's office to find material to discredit Ellsberg. Colson and his fellow plumbers later used burglars to break in to the Democratic National Committee headquarters at the Watergate office building to steal vital information about Democratic campaign plans and activities.

The plan went awry when the burglars were caught by the police, and the Watergate scandal began to surface. As part of the prosecution process, Colson pled guilty to smearing Ellsberg, and he served seven months in federal prisons at Fort Holabird in Maryland and Maxwell Air Force Base in Alabama. A short time before his trial, Colson became a Christian, and after his release he founded Prison Fellowship, a Christian outreach service for prisoners and ex-prisoners. Colson's is a cautionary tale that is applicable when the ends seem to justify the means.

This interview was conducted on June 17, 1992, twenty years to the day after the break-in at the Democratic National Committee headquarters. We met in Colson's office at Prison Fellowship in Reston, Virginia. A sign on his desk says "Faithfulness not Success"—a reminder of where he's been and where he's going.

Prison Fellowship Ministries

COLSON HAS BEEN A SPECIAL COUNSEL TO THE PRESIDENT OF THE UNITED STATES, A CONVICTED FELON, AND A CHRISTIAN LEADER. IN THIS JOURNEY HE LEARNED ABOUT THE TRUE NATURE OF HUMANKIND.

. . .

I'd studied political philosophy in college and was a student of Locke and Burke and the Enlightenment thinkers. I really believed in the social contract theory. I believed in the capacity of man to form a just social order.

In that respect, I suppose I was a Rationalist in the Enlightenment mold. A political idealist. I had a lot of deep conservative political convictions, and I believed in what Kant called the categorical imperative—the idea that you could, on your own, with your own wisdom, develop a rational, moral code and live by it. And that it would be the best for everyone if everybody did that.

For me Watergate was a shattering realization that all of this is untrue, because while you can arrive at the right conclusions rationally, you don't have the will to carry them out. And you have the infinite capacity to delude yourself and rationalize.

Watergate was a profound turning point not only in the sense of turning my life over to Christ, but in realizing the sinfulness of man and our infinite capacity for deluding ourselves. Tolstoy put it right in *War and Peace* when the central character said, "Why do I know what is right and do what is wrong?"

The Danger of Pragmatism

ACCORDING TO COLSON, THE WATERGATE DEFENDANTS THOUGHT THEY WERE WORKING WITHIN THE BOUNDARIES OF THE SYSTEM TO ACHIEVE WHAT THEY BELIEVED TO BE A MORAL GOAL: THE RE-ELECTION OF A PRESIDENT.

• • •

We were pragmatists—supreme pragmatists. I don't think anybody ever sat around and said, "Let's figure out how we're going to break this law and get away with it."

That was never the idea. The idea was, Let's stretch it to the limit. Let's do what was done before by the Democrats, only do it better. They bugged us in the 1968 campaign—we'll bug them in the 1972 campaign.

It was a dog-eat-dog mentality. It was the ends justify the means, but it was not a deliberate, conscious breaking of the law. I went to Bob Haldeman [another top-level Nixon aide] and told him this is dangerous and that we could be getting into a criminal situation here. He said, "We've just got a public-relations problem."

The Prison Experience

COLSON SERVED SEVEN MONTHS IN FEDERAL PENITENTIARIES. HE CAME TO VIEW HIS PRISON SENTENCE AS AN EXPERIENCE THAT LED HIM TO HIS LIFE'S WORK.

• • •

It was a shock to be in prison the first day. Everything you brought with you was taken away; you were stripped naked and stood in a bare-walled receiving room and thrown a dirty pair of underwear.

But by that time, I had been a Christian for over a year—long enough to begin to understand what my faith was really about. I was able to say to myself, "Obviously, I'm here for a purpose. I'm going to make the best of it. I want more than anything else to be a witness for Christ inside this prison."

. . .

I have dealt with people in the Christian community with less scruples and integrity than many of the people I knew in prison. Solzhenitsyn was absolutely right: he said the line between good and evil passes not between principalities and powers but through the human heart.

Sometimes people make wrong moral choices with very serious consequences and end up in prison. Sometimes people make wrong moral choices and get away with murder. Anybody who looks at the people in prison and says that's where we have all the bad guys had better go look in a mirror in a hurry.

One of the great myths of Christianity is that once a person is converted, they never sin again. We're fighting a constant battle. We're like running up a hill that's well-greased, because you make a couple of steps forward and then you slide back.

This is especially true for a Christian who does not recognize the constant temptations that he is subjected to daily, who doesn't have a good accountability system, who doesn't have people who will tell him the truth, and who isn't willing to submit to other people.

He becomes even more dangerous than the pagan, because the Christian believes he is now sanctified: He who believes that he is now without sin is farther away from the kingdom of God than anybody else. A Christian who thinks, "Now I'm a Christian; I'm converted, so I can't do any wrong"—that's the guy you really want to be careful with.

Redefining the Good Life

. . .

The good life before my conversion was wealth, power, money, influence, limousines, people saluting, and being invited to the best parties, which I used to turn down because it was fun to be able to say that the British ambassador invited me to dinner and I turned him down.

You lose a lot when you are so caught up in what the world thinks is important and powerful. You lose what is much more important and much more fundamental, and that's your own family. I shortchanged my kids and family. I've been trying to make up for it since, but you never really make up for it.

Most people spend most of their lives on a treadmill going nowhere. They keep thinking they'll find the good life with one more step up. Get me that sports car. Get me that second house at the lake. Get me that promotion. Get me that corner office that looks out on 17th and Pennsylvania. I discovered all of those things were empty and meaningless. The good life is the fulfilled life, and a person can only be fulfilled when they've made peace with God.

You start out in college extremely idealistic. Then you get into your thirties, and you realize that you're struggling enough just controlling your own family and environment. You're less concerned with changing the world than you are with changing your own immediate circumstances and environment.

By the time you get into your late fifties and sixties, you begin to realize that your biggest job is just keeping yourself straight and changing yourself. You look back at how naively idealistic it was to think you were going to change the world. Anybody who can get through life keeping their own priorities straight has done a pretty good job.

———

Condoleezza Rice

. . .

PRESIDENTIAL AIDE AND EDUCATOR

$\mathcal{U}$NDERSTANDING THE FALL OF COMMUNISM

. . .

My fellow Americans, I'm pleased to tell you today that I've signed legislation that will outlaw Russia forever. We begin bombing in five minutes.

RONALD REAGAN (JOKING WHILE TESTING A MICROPHONE, AUGUST 1984)

You might think that in order to become a top government official and a professor, a person must attend expensive prep schools and prestigious universities. Not so. Professor Condoleezza Rice (age thirty-eight) is a black woman who spent her childhood in Birmingham, Alabama, where she attended segregated schools. She grew up to become one of President George Bush's top advisors for Soviet affairs (from 1988 to 1991) and a top-rated professor at Stanford University. She is currently the provost of Stanford University—its second-highest administrative position.

As special assistant to the president for national-security affairs and senior director for Soviet affairs for the National Security Council, Rice hob-nobbed with Mikhail Gorbachev, Boris Yeltsin, and George Bush when the Berlin Wall came down and the Soviet Union fell apart. How did this black woman from Alabama who wanted to be a concert pianist rise to such a lofty position? And what is her interpretation of the fall of communism? In this chapter, Rice provides a unique perspective on both personal and political history.

Rice and I met in her office in a simple, one-story building on the Stanford campus. I thought she'd be in a modern, high-security area, but any student could—and they frequently do—walk right into her office.

There Are No Victims

———

RICE MADE HER WAY TO THE SIDE OF THE PRESIDENT OF THE UNITED STATES AND NEAR THE TOP OF STANFORD UNIVERSITY THROUGH HER ABILITY, HARD WORK, AND THE HELP OF HER FAMILY AND COMMUNITY.

. . .

I was born in Birmingham, Alabama, and moved to Colorado when I was about thirteen. Birmingham was doing just about everything it could to make sure black children did not succeed—like spending less money on black schools or taking new equipment from black schools and giving it to white schools.

It was that nefarious, but we had extremely dedicated teachers who were determined that these actions weren't going to work. We had a community, including my father's church, where there was tutoring every evening, as well as ballet lessons, choirs, and social clubs. The community made up for the lack of an education infrastructure in the city.

My community was saying: Life may be tough, and there may be a lot of racism out there, but you have no excuse. I don't want to hear that they did it to you because you were black...just keep pushing ahead.

There are no victims in this society. There are trials and tribulations and difficulties that stem from race and gender and whatever, but I believe you must take responsibility for yourself. You have to believe that you can take charge of your life.

———

PERHAPS RICE'S BELIEF IN PERSONAL RESPONSIBILITY AND RESOURCEFULNESS IS A FAMILY TRADITION.

. . .

When you perceive yourself as a victim, you are powerless. When my granddad was about twenty or twenty-one, he decided he needed to get book-learning. He was growing up in Ewtah, Alabama, on a farm raising cotton. He asked what was the closest college that would take a colored boy, and people told him Stillman College in Tuscaloosa.

He went there and told them he was going to pay for college with cotton. They said he couldn't pay with cotton, so he asked how the other boys were going to school, and they told him they had scholarships and that if he wanted to be a Presbyterian minister, he could have a scholarship, too.

He replied, "Oh, didn't I tell you? I want to be a Presbyterian minister," and we've been Presbyterian ever since. What would possess a man in Ewtah, Alabama, circa 1919, to figure out a way to get book-learning? My grandfather had a reason to have a gripe. He had a reason to feel like a victim. He was free—sort of—but he was in the deepest of Jim Crow Alabama.

My other grandfather worked three jobs to buy property so that they could have a place to live and educate all five of his children. These are people who took charge of their lives. I can't believe that life is more complicated today than it was for them.

Assuming People Are Good

———

WHEN RICE STARTED STUDYING FOR HER MASTER'S DEGREE, SHE LEARNED A VALUABLE LESSON ABOUT JUMPING TO CONCLUSIONS.

• • •

When I was in graduate school, I had an incident that taught me to be a little more careful about jumping to conclusions. I went to Notre Dame as a master's student. All I knew about Indiana was that it was the home of the Ku Klux Klan. It was my first time away from home, and I was all revved up to protect myself and be careful.

The first day I was in South Bend, I went driving to pick up some things for my room. I had a brand-new car, and it overheated. I pulled to the side of the road, and I walked back to a service station. The guy said, "You'll have to pull it over here."

I immediately flashed on it. I thought, You racist so-and-so! I said, "Why do I have to pull it over here?" and he said, "Well, I thought if you pulled it over here in the shade, it might cool off faster."

———

YEARS LATER, A SECRET SERVICE AGENT JUMPED TO THE CONCLUSION THAT RICE

. . .

My first reaction was not that I thought he was racist. He was nasty, but I wouldn't call it abusive. Frankly, I was pretty mad and nasty to him, too. When he wasn't looking, I pushed past him and went out onto the tarmac. Then he came over to me and said, "You are not supposed to be out here." And I said, "What is your name?" He said, "I don't have to tell you my name. Who are you?" I said, "I am the president's special assistant for Soviet affairs. Who are you?" He gave me his name, I reported him, and I figured that was the end of it.

I can feel racism at a thousand paces — I grew up in Bull Connor's Birmingham. [Eugene "Bull" Connor was the commissioner of public safety of Birmingham. He refused to protect the Birmingham Freedom Riders and instructed the police force to use fire hoses and dogs on black demonstrators.] Because I am black and female, there was an immediate assumption that everything was racial. The guy was an overzealous field agent. I challenged his authority, and he didn't like it. Do I think that somewhere subliminally for him, I didn't look like the president's special assistant for Soviet affairs? There are not that many black, female Soviet specialists, so maybe it was a genuine mistake. I didn't take it as a personal insult.

By the time it got into the press, it was a huge incident. By the time it got into some of the black press, it was as if I had been knocked down. I had people calling from all over the country. Even my father called. The president asked Brent Scrowcroft about it. I was mortified.

The biggest lesson is that things aren't what they seem — especially when the press gets hold of them. Being black, it's easy to come to a conclusion about any slight. I have learned that until further evidence, I'll assume innocence. There is enough racism around that you don't have to go looking for it.

The Fall of Communism

RICE WAS A FIRST-HAND WITNESS TO THE FALL OF COMMUNISM. ULTIMATELY, SHE ATTRIBUTES THE ASTOUNDING COLLAPSE OF THE SOVIET POLITICAL SYSTEM TO THE DENIAL OF INDIVIDUAL RIGHTS.

. . .

The Soviets didn't trust individuals and believed that the state or some set of bureaucrats or ideologies was better at organizing human beings than they were at organizing themselves.

There are two ways to think about human history. One is that states and organizations find the truth, get everybody to fit into a blueprint, and end up in nirvana. The other is that individuals come up against something they consider an assault on their rights and batter it until it comes down.

Ultimately, human history progresses that way. The Soviet Union was a society that tried to program symphonies — Shostakovich [Dmitri Shostakovich, a Soviet composer] was told that one of his symphonies wasn't socialist enough. How can you tell if a symphony is socialist? In that kind of society individuals don't blossom. They have no reason to take responsibility for themselves or anybody else, and they just shrivel up. Incentives and initiative, and all of the things that make human beings what they are, disappear.

The thing that boggles my mind is that communism succeeded as long as it did. I was not one of the people who said it was going to crash in 1989 — or 1992 — but even at the time, and certainly in retrospect, it was a crazy way to organize human beings: trying to make everybody basically the same except a very small layer of people who got richer while everybody else got poorer.

I believe that Jimmy Carter never understood what he was dealing with. In some ways Reagan understood *too* well. He scared the living daylights out of most of us who had studied the Soviet

Union when he started down the road of a very aggressive, high-risk, nonaccommodationist policy.

Those people had nuclear weapons, right? Calling them an evil empire and saying that they were going to end up on the ash heap of history seemed to me slightly dangerous and none too diplomatic. I can remember reading that speech and thinking, Oh my God!

Reagan was determined that he would build up America's military forces and challenge the Soviets everywhere on the globe, whether it was supporting the Contras in Nicaragua or the Afghan rebels in Afghanistan.

I don't think Reagan caused the fall of communism. It was a fundamentally weak system from the inside out, but his policies were the final nail. All of a sudden the communists were treated as a fundamentally weak society that we thought we could defeat—not accommodate, defeat.

I thought it was risky at the time, but it turned out to be the right way to go about it. Had he come ten years earlier, I think they might have just pulled themselves up by their bootstraps and taken on the challenge. But ten years later, they were—thank God—too weak to do so. Timing is everything, and the timing was right.

Nuclear War

IN ADDITION TO HER EXPERIENCE WITH SOVIET AFFAIRS, RICE IS AN EXPERT ON NUCLEAR ARMS. SHE BELIEVES THAT THE POTENCY OF NUCLEAR WEAPONS HAS MADE THEM, IRONICALLY, IMPOSSIBLE TO USE.

. . .

The history of warfare is using technology to kill. So going from the crossbow to the rifle to the tank to the airplane has been a steady progression of getting better weapons. Then you have the ultimate weapon, and the paradox was that it was unusable, so you were forced to go back and develop better relations with adversaries.

There is no way to prove this, but I believe that nuclear weapons were so terrible that nobody could use them, and that is why we did not have a war during the Cold War. At least in Europe and probably in parts of Asia, nuclear weapons prevented human beings from giving way to their worst instincts.

It didn't matter that you had Joseph Stalin, who was paranoid, or Nikita Khrushchev, who I think in some ways was more of a risktaker than Stalin. It didn't matter that there were two hostile ideologies in the United States and the Soviet Union. We continued to have wars, and we continued to perfect better ways of warfare. But the big wars, the wars to reshape the international system—like the war of 1914 or 1941—are no longer possible.

Paradoxes

RICE SEEMS TO BE A PARADOX: SHE IS BLACK, FEMALE, PRO-CHOICE, AND REPUBLICAN. SHE IS LIVING PROOF THAT THINGS ARE NEVER AS SIMPLE AS THEY SEEM.

• • •

President Bush is a man to whom I would trust my life. I had the strongest sense of his absolute confidence in me. He was completely able to put aside the fact that I was black and female and deal with me as his principal aide on Soviet policy. Individual relationships are transcendent: you establish a level of trust and confidence in a person, and other factors are nonissues.

Bush's inner circle was male—Scowcroft, Baker, Cheney, Powell, Brady, and Sununu—but I think this is partly generational, and within ten years that will not be an issue. You will see women who have grown up together and been around their male counterparts.

If one of the people I worked with in the administration became president or secretary of state, I'd be a part of that inner circle. Baker and Bush have known each other for thirty years. You don't replace that kind of intimate knowledge of somebody just for the sake of gender or race.

One reason I am a Republican is that I would rather be ignored than patronized. Though the Republican Party has not done a good job of explaining, reaching out, or demonstrating that it can be a home for black Americans who hold certain principles, it comes down to how you feel about the role of government and how you feel about individualism.

There is a policy history with the Democratic Party that appeals to blacks, but the Republican Party should appeal because of its emphasis on the individual and on its belief in the stagnating role of the government.

Pushing Your Luck

––––

I POSED MY FINAL QUESTION: "WHAT IF CLINTON CALLS YOU UP AND ASKS YOU TO CONTINUE?" AND RICE GAVE ME HER INSIGHTS ON WHEN TO QUIT.

• • •

I had the best possible set of circumstances: I worked for a president I admired and for a boss that I adored [Scrowcroft], with whom I had a wonderful relationship and terrific access. I am still very close to most of the staff people I worked with in the State Department and National Security Council. It was the best possible time: the end of the Cold War. We saw Eastern Europe liberated; we helped unite Germany. We did great things.

I am not going to try that again! To go back so soon and have to deal with events that are far less dramatic would be anticlimactic. Maybe ten or fifteen years from now, it would be fun to do it again under different circumstances. The lesson is: Don't push your luck.

––––

Harold Gordon

. . .

HOLOCAUST SURVIVOR

$\mathcal{P}$UTTING PAIN ASIDE

. . .

A Jew survived the gas chambers, having lost every one of his relatives. The resettlement officer asked him where he would like to go. "Australia," he replied. "But that's so far," said the officer. "From where?" asked the Jew.

RABBI JOSEPH TELUSHKIN

B2209 is the prisoner number tattooed on the inside of Harold Gordon's (age sixty-two) left forearm. He is a Holocaust survivor whose only crime was being a Jew when the Nazis were trying to conquer the world. In 1993, shortly after retiring from running a service station for forty years, Gordon self-published a book about his Holocaust experience called *The Last Sunrise.*

Gordon grew up in Grodno, Poland, a city of 60,000 people, of whom about one-third were Jews. His father was a barber; his mother, a homemaker. He had a brother who was eighteen months younger. In September 1939, when Gordon was eight years old, the Nazis attacked Grodno. Soon afterward, the Russians made a nonaggression pact with Germany to partition Poland, and Russia received the part of Poland that contained Grodno. Here the Gordons thought they would be safe from the Nazis. However, in June 1941, the Nazis took over Grodno. One of the Nazis' first acts after conquering the territory was to round up Grodno's 20,000 Jews and to imprison them in a Jewish ghetto completely surrounded by a brick wall.

One night the entire Gordon family and about 3,000 other Jews were marched out of the ghetto to a detention camp called Kelbasin. Gordon and his father were able to escape from this camp, but they were separated from his mother and brother. Gordon never saw his mother or brother again. After their escape, Gordon and his father had nowhere to go except back to the ghetto in Grodno. They hid in the ghetto until the Nazis had removed all 20,000 Jews, and then, for lack of a better plan, they walked seventy miles to Bialystok, another Jewish ghetto.

In 1942 the Nazis transported Gordon and his father from Bialystok to

Buchenwald, one of the infamous death camps, where they worked as camp barbers, shaving the heads of fellow prisoners to reduce problems with lice. Nine months later, they were transported to another death camp—Auschwitz—to be executed. Gordon and his father were in line to be gassed when they were pulled out by a Nazi officer to work in the crematorium as laborers. One of their tasks was to retrieve the clothes of fellow prisoners who had been ordered to strip and step into the gas chamber. They lived in Auschwitz for one year.

In 1943, when Gordon was thirteen, he and his father were transported from Auschwitz to Oraninburg, a detention camp near a Nazi airplane factory. After Allied planes destroyed the factory, Gordon and his father were taken to Sachsenhausen, where they stayed until the spring of 1944, when they were transported to Dachau, another death camp. By the spring of 1945, the war was going poorly for the Nazis, so Dachau was deactivated. To dispose of the remaining prisoners, the Nazis started them on a sixty-mile death march to Tyrol.

On the third day of the march, two American planes attacked the Nazi guards overseeing the prisoners, and Gordon and his father escaped in the confusion. Early in the morning of May 5, 1945, they were rescued by a column of American tanks as they hid in the forest from the Nazis. At that point they were badly malnourished and near starvation. For two months, they lived in a "Displaced Persons'" camp. Eventually, Gordon found a job working for a battalion of American soldiers as a kitchen helper. After a year, Gordon and his father accumulated $1,200 and were able to buy boat passage to the United States. Gordon was fifteen years old when he arrived in America.

I first met Gordon when my wife and I were vacationing in Monterey, California—after I thought I had finished interviewing people for this book. He was standing in a bookstore hawking his book. Since my wife and I have a soft spot for authors, he reeled us in for two copies. Since I know a good story when I see one, I reeled him in for an interview. His story is about one man's efforts to understand and then move beyond a personal atrocity.

Where Was God?

I ASKED GORDON IF, AFTER ALL HE'D BEEN THROUGH IN POLAND AND GERMANY, HE STILL BELIEVES IN GOD, AND IF THERE IS A GOD, HOW GOD COULD ALLOW SUCH AN ATROCITY TO HAPPEN. THESE ARE QUESTIONS THAT MANY JEWS ASK AS THEY COME TO TERMS WITH THE HOLOCAUST.

. . .

We were taught that we were good people, religious people, the chosen people, but we didn't think we were chosen to die. I was just a little kid. I did nothing wrong to anybody: I went to school, I had good grades, and I minded my mother and father. I could not think of a reason why I should be murdered.

Of course there is no explanation. It is a question that millions of Jews asked. I cannot answer. Many Jewish people felt that there wasn't a God—how could a merciful and loving God allow this to happen? Certainly there isn't a God if He lets His chosen people be murdered, gassed, and burned. Many Jewish people gave up believing in God.

I never gave up on God. I feel God is not one that can be concerned with each individual. He sets things in motion, and when things get a certain way—good or bad—there is a mechanism to adjust itself. Look at how complicated and intricate life is from the smallest bacteria to the largest mammal—there must be a power, whatever it is, that we call God.

My will to live was a constant prayer that made God a promise: "God, my brother and my mother are already gone. If I die, there will be nobody left." I was the youngest person in the camps. I said, "God, I'll tell you what: if you let me live, I will take revenge. I'll promise you that the blood will not have been spilt for nothing. Just let me live, and I'll prove myself." And He let me live.

. . .

Hitler came to power in 1933. The German people were demoralized and depressed. Inflation was running in thousands and thousands of percent annually. A loaf of bread was something like 50,000 marks and rising daily. Hitler came and gave the country hope.

Hitler needed a scapegoat to blame the current conditions on, and the Jews were a people without a country and without representation. So were the Gypsies. He thought we would be a good place to start. Then, when he saw that the Nazis united around him and there was no opposition, he thought he could get more power. It just went on and on and on.

Dachau was built in 1933 for the purpose of exterminating German people that opposed Hitler's view. There were approximately 80,000 Germans put to death in Dachau. After this was done and Hitler consolidated power, he turned against others.

You get somebody who is fanatic and who plugs a goal long enough over the airwaves with a propaganda campaign, and eventually many people will believe him if things begin to get better. How could Hirohito get all the Japanese people to bow to him like he was a god? Hitler put everybody to work. They started building factories and airplanes and cannons and ammunition. All the German people were employed, and suddenly there was bread. If he was savior, how could he be wrong?

Why Was Gordon Spared?

———

GORDON INITIALLY BELIEVED THAT HE WAS SPARED—ACCORDING TO HIS DEAL WITH GOD—SO THAT HE COULD TAKE REVENGE ON THE NAZIS. OVER TIME, GORDON HAS COME TO BELIEVE THAT HE WASN'T SPARED TO BECOME AN INSTRUMENT OF REVENGE, BUT RATHER SO THAT HE COULD DOCUMENT AND SERVE AS EVIDENCE OF THE HOLOCAUST.

. . .

When I saw the [European] Continent disappear behind me, I said to myself, "Oh, God! Thank God I am leaving. I hope I'll never, never, ever see it again." Then, after five days at sea, we approached the New York harbor, and I saw the Statue of Liberty. I'll never forget that moment. I bent down and kissed the soil of America.

I was on the way to the gas chamber when a Nazi put a cane around my neck and yanked me out of line. My father came with me. Ever since then, I've been asking myself why I was spared. I was no better than my brother. I was no better than any of my friends. Certainly I was not any smarter. I don't know why I was saved, but I did believe there was a special reason for me to be saved.

I was going to kill every German that I could lay my hands on. Then I saw things differently at the end of the war. We did take revenge on some Nazis, but I saw that shedding blood was not the way. There had to be a better way than to be a terrorist for the rest of my life. If I was a terrorist, eventually somebody would get me.

I tried to figure out what God intended for me to do with my life. I thought and I thought, and the only thing that I came up with was to remember and immortalize my ancestors and help people let go of hatred and resentment.

It was much better to tell my story to the world in the form of a book. Then my words and the photographs of my family would be immortalized. People would read about us, and the Holocaust would never be forgotten. I was in the service-station business for about forty years. Now that I am retired, I don't go fishing. I don't get out of bed and ask, What am I going to do today? I have a job to do.

The best thing to do is to realize we are all the same people. We must not judge others on the basis of their philosophy, the way they live, and what they do to each other. I don't hate all the Japanese for bombing Pearl Harbor. And there were some German people who threw us food from the windows.

We are all one people. There is only one world. We must learn to live together, because there is no choice. I came to realize that it is wrong to judge people on the basis of their ethnic beliefs or their customs or traditions. We have to quit looking at people as a group. We must look at them as individuals.

Letting Go

ALTHOUGH GORDON COULD NEVER FORGET HIS HOLOCAUST EXPERIENCE AND WANTS THE WORLD TO REMEMBER IT, HE NEVERTHELESS PUT IT ASIDE SO THAT HE COULD LIVE A PRODUCTIVE LIFE.

. . .

In 1970 I took my wife and both children and purchased a Volkswagen camper bus and toured through Germany and nine other countries. I took them to Dachau. I showed them exactly where the gate was and where the river was, and right by the river is a bunch of trees, and right by the trees is the crematorium. I showed them the gas chamber.

It was the first time I saw this as a free person. I remember there were two rows of barbed-wire fences, and there was barbed wire coiled up in the middle. There was a path for the guards to patrol with German shepherds. I just wanted to walk in between those two fences and then walk back on the outside as a free person. So I did.

When I was in Dachau, I used to see dogs and birds. I used to see the mountains in the distance, not too far away. It was the Alps. I would think, There is freedom. It's not that far away. If I could only go over the fence and not get shot, how many days will it take me to go to the mountains and cross over into Switzerland? Wouldn't it be nice to be a bird that landed on the wire and just fly away? Or a dog—dogs can go anywhere they want. Nobody is stopping them. If I was to try to go outside the gate, they would shoot me, but a dog can go anywhere he wants.

I have not forgiven the Nazis. I will never forgive the Nazis. If I knew where the Nazi was who killed my family, I would pursue him in the worst way that I could—though I would not break the law. All I have done is set my hatred of the Nazis aside and let the law take care of them. I am not forgiving all German people—just the people who are innocent of crimes. I am not saying that I can turn the other cheek and say, "Here, kill my mother, and I'm going to forgive you."

I put the hatred aside for self-preservation. If you go on hating, it only hurts you—not the person that you hate. It prevents you from being all that you can be and from doing all that you want to do. It is a burden that slows you down. My father came to this country with me, but he was never able to let go. He and his friends who were survivors of the Holocaust kept rehashing everything for years and years and years. I could see that I needed to do something different.

Life is really short. When we reach a certain age, it's too late to go back and make the corrections that we should have made years ago. After you've killed the person that you've been pursuing for twenty years, what have you got? Only revenge. Revenge is not sweet.

Postscript

_____

As this book was being completed, I sent a draft of this chapter to Ethel Grodzins Romm, whose family comes from Poland. I learned that her mother's family was from Grodno, and her father (the last of seven generations of rabbis) walked to Bialystok after escaping the Jewish ghetto in Grodno. Gordon and Romm discovered they have the same original last name and may be related.

_____

two hundred forty nine

Making Choices

. . .

Bill Bonanno

. . .

RETIRED GANGSTER

UNDERSTANDING THE MAFIA

. . .

How many different things a family can be—a nest of tenderness, a jail for the heart, a nursery of souls. Families name us and define us, give us strength, give us grief. All our lives we struggle to embrace or escape their influence. They are magnets that both hold us close and drive us away.

GEORGE HOWE COLT

My first contact with Bill Bonanno's (age sixty) family was when his youngest son, Tore, applied for a job in my department at Apple Computer. During our interview, he told me that the Procter & Gamble recruiter, who recognized his name, started out the interview by asking, "Where's your shiny suit?" I liked him from that moment on and gave him a job. Through Tore, I came to know his father.

The label "retired gangster" is Bonanno's idea, not mine. Bonanno is the son of Joseph Bonanno, formerly one of the bosses of the New York underworld. He is also the main character in *Honor Thy Father*, Gay Talese's best-seller about three generations of the Bonanno family. His interview will help you understand the Mafia life-style and making controversial choices.

Bonanno and I met in the restaurant of Courtside, a private tennis club in Los Gatos, California. It's probably because I've seen too many Al Pacino movies, but I swear we got extra-special service. Our interview started this way:

Kawasaki: I hope you don't mind if I tape the interview.

Bonanno: No. I've been on all kinds of tapes—official and unofficial.

The Mafia: A Way of Life

———

MOVIES, TELEVISION, AND THE PRINT MEDIA HAVE SHAPED MOST PEOPLE'S UNDERSTANDING OF THE TERM *MAFIA*. BONANNO CONTENDS THAT MAFIA DESCRIBES A WAY OF LIFE, NOT A SYNDICATE OF CRIMINALS.

. . .

The Mafia is not a thing. It's a philosophy of life and a state of mind. What law enforcement, government, and non-Sicilian people refer to is the Mafia with a big *M*. The Mafia that I know and you know are two different creatures. To me, it's a concept and a philosophy that has been developed for seven or eight hundred years.

Sicilians are a mixture of all races and all cultures. As a result, we're a very strong people, and our nature is such that we've taken the best of all of these races and discarded the worst. At least that's what we like to think. As a result of these various intrusions on our native land, we've become very suspicious of any kind of authority, including the Roman Catholic Church.

Sicilians have this exaggerated concept of ourselves that we can and must handle all problems internally. We don't trust anything that's "organized." As a result, we have the reputation of being very independent and hard to get along with. You don't go to the law, because the law is not to be trusted.

Our relationships are built on kinship and on friendship. A violation on you is a violation that requires a comeback. Whatever that comeback is depends on the degree of the violation. Tradition teaches us what is right and what is wrong, but my tradition may be wrong for you but right for me. Your tradition might be wrong for me, but it's right for you.

Values are handed down through example. They're handed down through word of mouth. You don't know why something is right. You don't know why something is wrong. You just know that this is right and this is wrong. You don't join the Mafia to become a gambler. You don't join the Mafia to become a union organizer. You don't join the Mafia to get into prostitution. That's all a by-product.

Accepting the Consequences

BONANNO HAS SPENT A TOTAL OF ABOUT THIRTEEN YEARS IN PRISON. HE IS

NOT ASHAMED OF HAVING A CRIMINAL RECORD. HE HAS ACCEPTED HIS LIFE-STYLE AND WHAT COMES WITH IT—INCLUDING SERVING TIME IN PRISON.

. . .

I knew when I was young that sometime in my life I was going to go to jail. It was part of the price that you had to pay for leading the life-style that you believed in. I went to prison because it was a matter of honor. I was entrusted with a secret, and I was duty-bound to keep it to myself—regardless of the risk.

As far as I'm concerned, we have the finest criminal-justice system in the world. There are other places in the world where they'll take you out and shoot you. My last trial lasted six months from the day they picked the jury to the day the jury came back— four days a week, every week except for the Fourth of July. I also know that sometimes it's a lot more humane to take you out and shoot you. [*Laughs.*]

In all the years I've been in prison, I never met a guilty person. I was sitting in a Los Angeles County jail one day, and there were eight of us in a four-man cell. One guy said he had been framed, and another guy said the cops just didn't understand. We went around the room—same story.

I was in the top bunk, and they looked up and asked, "What are you in here for?" I said, "I'm in here because I'm guilty. I did what they accused me of doing." They all looked at me as if to say, Where'd this nut come from? I said, "I'm just here doing my time." That's the first way you can live with yourself—accept the responsibility and then the consequences of that responsibility.

―――

MANY PEOPLE BELIEVE THAT PRISONS HAVE FAILED TO REHABILITATE PRISON-ERS. BONANNO DISAGREES—BECAUSE HE DOESN'T THINK REHABILITATION HAS EVER BEEN TRIED.

. . .

The experience I had in state prison I wouldn't wish on my

worst enemy. I consider myself a worse person now than when I went in. Everything is negative, nothing is positive, and you have no chance of making life better for yourself.

When I was at Terminal Island back in the seventies, I was walking down from the cellblock one day, and I heard this splat behind me. I turned around and there's a guy lying on the floor with a knife stuck in his neck.

A few weeks later, the stabbing was still unresolved, and I was sitting in the yard. I saw the guy who did the stabbing, and I said, "What was all that about?" He says, "I don't know. I just wanted to see what it would feel like to stick a nigger."

Think of what the guy's saying: We have degenerated to a point that we kill somebody just to see what it feels like. That guy was ready to be turned loose on society. More importantly—what have we done for him while he was in there locked up in his cell? The system gives him no opportunities to better himself.

Mafia Family Life

BONANNO HAS BEEN MARRIED TO HIS WIFE, ROSALIE, FOR THIRTY-SEVEN YEARS. HE EXPLAINED THAT THEIR RELATIONSHIP HAS LASTED BECAUSE THEY BOTH HAVE A SENSE OF DUTY.

. . .

The fact that we're still together is a tribute to our tradition and to our religion. When we got married thirty-seven years ago in a church on an altar, we made a commitment, and we said those famous words, "I do."

It wasn't something to be taken lightly. We didn't say, "Well, if it doesn't suit me, I'll go do something else next week." It's a lifetime commitment, and you do what you have to do. There is no out.

My wife is a Sicilian girl who went to a convent school. She went away when she was in the first grade and returned when she graduated high school. She was taught by the nuns that men can do no wrong and that once you're married, that's the end of it.

———

ON THE OTHER HAND, TIMES HAVE CHANGED.

• • •

My wife was thirty-five years old before she started asserting herself. When we got married, she was nineteen and I was twenty-two. Now she says, "I'm going to go do this," instead of, "Is it OK if I do this?" My wife and I have a great relationship because we lead separate lives together.

———

WHEN BONANNO'S DAUGHTER AND THREE SONS WERE GROWING UP, THEY HAD TO COPE WITH NEWS STORIES ABOUT THEIR FATHER AND GRANDFATHER. IN RETROSPECT, BONANNO REALIZES THE TROUBLE THIS CAUSED HIS KIDS, BUT HE ALSO BELIEVES THAT IT HELPED HIS FAMILY BOND.

• • •

When I was young, I never gave it a thought. I just said, "Big deal." You do what you have to do, not what you want to do. Something comes along, and it's required that you do this. If the children had a problem, they just had to face it.

My wife was telling me the kids are being teased and that they saw the newspapers. I said they'll learn to live with it. I never gave it any thought until later on in life, when I started hearing some of the stories by talking to Tore, Joe, Charlie, and my daughter, Gigi.

I never realized they had certain problems, but as I look back, I think the training we gave them, that sense of family, that sense of values—one for all and all for one—instilled the sense of togetherness.

I think they're better people for it today. I have no second thoughts about how I handled them growing up, because I see it in them now with their children. We—my wife and I—are an integral part of my grandchildren's lives.

———

. . .

I told all the girls when they were going out with my boys, "Let's go have lunch." I said, "I guess you're serious about marrying my son."

I said, "Let me tell you something. When you marry my son, you're not just marrying him. You're marrying me. You're marrying his mother. You're marrying his brothers. You're marrying his sister and his aunts and his uncles. So you're getting a whole package.

"But conversely," I said, "when he marries you, he's doing the same thing. He's marrying your mother and your father. You're going to have to accept him with all the glory and with all the warts." We all get along very well because they knew going in.

They joke about it today—about this lunch that I had with all of them. Now I'm sixty years old, and my wife is fifty-six. We have nine grandchildren, and we're at the age now where we're past doing things. We have no more mountains to climb and no more worlds to conquer. Our biggest ambition now is to see the grandkids.

The End of the Mafia

. . .

In the sixties, I told a couple of FBI agents, "I don't know what you guys are knocking yourselves out for. It's almost over. The Mafia is a thing of the past."

The ethnic group that's involved in this life-style has risen on the socioeconomic ladder to the point where they're wearing white shirts with silk ties. They don't need to do the kinds of things that people on the lower rung of the socioeconomic ladder have to do.

I equate this with boxing. At the turn of the century, there were Irish fighters and Jewish fighters. After that came Italian fighters, followed by black fighters. After the black fighters came the Cubans. As ethnic groups went higher on the socioeconomic ladder, they became businessmen.

The so-called Mafia element in this country has almost no power per se, and the story of the Mafia is the story of the dispensation of power. There was a time when we would sit around a big table deciding who was going to hold public offices.

Today that can't happen because of the breakdown of the family unit. The degeneration of our institutions has put us in a position where we can't dispense power.

Honor Thy Father — the Rest of the Story

———

THE KIDNAPPING OF BONANNO'S FATHER, JOSEPH, AS HE WAS ON HIS WAY TO TESTIFY BEFORE A GRAND JURY IN NEW YORK, IS AN IMPORTANT PART OF TALESE'S *HONOR THY FATHER*. BUT THE BOOK DOESN'T FULLY EXPLAIN WHAT HAPPENED TO JOSEPH DURING HIS NINETEEN-MONTH DISAPPEARANCE. HERE IS BONANNO'S EXPLANATION.

• • •

When he was kidnapped, there was a period of about two or three months where he was held, and then he was let go. He was free to come in but didn't because we were, for lack of a better word, in a gang war. It would be silly for him to go to jail when he was needed on the outside.

It was never the intention to kill him when he was kidnapped. They didn't want his death. The Commission [a group of ruling heads of Mafia families] gave an order to come in and talk. He sent word back that the Commission had no authority to issue that order, so "to hell with you."

It was decided by the Commission that the easiest way to resolve this thing was to grab him and scare him to death. They didn't go all the way [kill him] because who was going to make that decision? He wasn't just a bit player. If they had, there would have been a lot more bloodshed.

The Commission's purpose was to maintain the peace if heads of families were having an argument. While the Commission had no power to enforce their wishes, the other twenty-six families in the country would make life a little miserable for you because you couldn't get favors done in this city or that city.

People were talking about the Commission as the ruling body — the all-powerful grand council. That's bullshit. The Commission was made of a number of senior people who were respected, who were asked to sit in judgment of problems.

Few Regrets

———

BONANNO HAS SERVED TIME IN PRISON. HE'S BEEN SHOT AT. HIS HOUSE HAS BEEN BOMBED. YOU'D THINK HE'D HAVE SOME REGRETS.

. . .

I've done a lot of things, and I have very few regrets. If I had to do it again, I'd lead the same kind of life that I have. I don't feel I ever had a choice. Our tradition goes back over eight hundred years — I wasn't just a guy coming along. I come from a long tradition — my father, my grandfather, my great-grandfather, and the families in the old country.

I am not ashamed of who I am or what I've done. If one of my sons had come to me and said, "Hey Dad, school's not for me. I want to follow you. I want to be with you," I would tell him the truth. If he chose a life-style that might require him to go to prison, I would help him. Why not? That's his choice. He'd have to be true to his commitments. If you do anything less than that, are you true to yourself?

———

Carole Yamaguchi

. . .

PARENT

$\mathscr{R}$AISING CHILDREN

. . .

I have found the best way to give advice to your children is to find out what they want and then advise them to do it.

Carole Yamaguchi (age forty-eight) has a problem: She is too embarrassed to walk down the cereal aisle of her neighborhood supermarket because her daughter's picture is on boxes of Special K. Carole is the mother of Kristi Yamaguchi, winner of the gold medal for figure skating at the 1992 Winter Olympics.

Yamaguchi is a mom's mom. She has devoted her life to making a home and raising her kids. She drove her three kids to skating, baton-twirling, and basketball practice for years. Her husband, Jim, is a dentist. Her story is about the choices a parent faces when raising children.

I interviewed Yamaguchi in her home in Fremont, a suburb of San Francisco. There are shelves full of trophies in the house, but they are not all Kristi's. Some belong to Lori, her eldest daughter, who was a member of a world-champion baton-twirling team when she was in high school. Others belong to Brett, the youngest in the family, who was a star high-school basketball player.

Pushing Your Kids

IF YOU THINK THAT KRISTI YAMAGUCHI IS A FOURTH GENERATION ICE SKATER AND WAS DESTINED FOR ICE-SKATING SUCCESS, GUESS AGAIN. CAROLE YAMAGUCHI BELIEVES THAT THE STARTING POINT FOR SUCCESS IS A CHILD'S INTEREST AND BELIEF IN HERSELF.

. . .

Kristi first started skating at the age of six because she wanted to do it. She had an affinity for skating after she saw Dorothy Hamill. Then we went shopping at Southland Mall one Saturday afternoon,

two hundred sixty two

and there was an ice show there, and she liked the costumes.

I don't think any parent can look at their children and think, "Wow, this one is going to do this. This one is going to do that." If they do, then it's what *they* want for them. It's not what the child actually wants.

No one else in our family skates. I didn't sit there and say, "Kristi, you are going to be a skater. Lori, you are going to do this. Brett, you are going to excel in basketball." It is something that she wanted to do herself.

I've seen girls who are around fourteen, fifteen, who just don't want to take it anymore and quit. A child will tell you—they'll give you the cue that you are pushing too hard. They'll resent it, or they'll quit when they are old enough to start thinking on their own.

When Kristi was eight years old, a group of us went to the National Championships, and when we got back, she said to me, "I want to be there someday. I want to be as good as they are." And we said, "Yeah, right. Sure."

You don't know what a child sees. They think they can accomplish this. She didn't always win. In her first competition, I think she was twelfth out of thirteen. I felt bad. I told her, "You don't have to do this again. You are not doing this for me." She said, "Oh no, I like it." She was only six at the time.

Working Hard

IN ADDITION TO KRISTI'S INTEREST IN ICE SKATING AND BELIEF IN HER OWN CAPABILITIES, YAMAGUCHI ATTRIBUTES HER DAUGHTER'S SUCCESS TO HARD WORK.

• • •

Kristi kind of struggled with the skating but had this attitude that she really wanted to do it. She has always been extremely small. I thought that was to her disadvantage when she was younger, but skating was something that she wanted to do, so we just continued.

Some of it is luck, some of it is timing, and Kristi does not give up. This is an asset she has over some of the girls who have more talent or are more athletic. Some girls would skate for fifteen minutes; Kristi would stay on the ice for forty-five minutes or until she could master what she wanted to accomplish that day.

I saw a lot of girls who had the natural ability but maybe pushed too hard and would drop out of the sport. Kristi really worked hard for each jump, each stroke, each spin. She has probably had to work harder than someone who was more naturally talented.

As she got older, I didn't have to push her, because it was something that she already had a desire to do. Even in junior high and high school she was never distracted. She knew that in order to skate well the next day, she had to be in bed by a certain time.

––––

THERE ARE ONLY TWO WOMEN IN THE WORLD WHO CAN DO A TRIPLE AXEL: MIDORI ITO AND TONYA HARDING. KRISTI, HOWEVER, HAS TURNED HER INABILITY TO DO THE TRIPLE AXEL INTO A STRENGTH.

• • •

I think it bugs other people more than her. She worked on aspects of her skating that other girls might have ignored, like style, because she wasn't able to get the jump. She compensated by working harder on what she *could* do.

It's not like she gave up, because she continued to work on the triple axel up until the week she left for the Olympics. More important than getting the triple axel, however, was getting a consistent program.

You can only do what you can do. Not that you are limited, but we have to be realistic. You might want to be a scientist, but not everyone is going to be an Einstein, and that doesn't mean you can't contribute in another way.

Realistic Expectations

YAMAGUCHI AND HER HUSBAND HAD TO LEARN TO SET REALISTIC EXPECTATIONS FOR EACH OF THEIR CHILDREN.

. . .

I hoped that Kristi and Lori would do the same thing so I would only have to drive to one place, but they didn't. The only thing they had in common was dance lessons. I tried to encourage them and always be there to make sure costumes were taken care of and they were fed and rested and prepared, but I tried not to push them beyond their physical limitations.

I tried to be realistic. I couldn't expect Brett, who is only five-feet-nine-inches, to slam-dunk a basketball. People used to compare Kristi to Midori Ito because she hasn't done the triple axel. She tried. She worked hard—I don't think there's anyone else who works as hard as she does—so she, obviously, physically cannot do it.

It wouldn't do me any good to stand there and yell at her, but it's hard not to get involved. My husband always used to tell me, "I don't want you pushing those girls. Let them do what they want." Then we'd go to a basketball game, and he'd be yelling at Brett.

STILL, AT TIMES, PARENTS CROSS THE LINE BETWEEN ENCOURAGEMENT AND PUSHING.

. . .

It's really a fine line. Maybe there were moments in Kristi's career where I appeared to be forcing more. It's difficult when you are involved and preparing for a competition. You want to remain as calm as possible and logical, but a lot of times you are not. You don't know why you act like that or why you get nervous.

In 1990 her pairs coach passed away. Five days later my dad passed away. This is all in the month of December. It broke up her training regimen because she was flying back and forth between Los Angeles and Canada [for the funerals]. Then that year at the U.S. Nationals, she just did not skate well. She must have fallen two or three times during her routine.

I made this big mistake by asking her what happened — "Why did you fall so much?" By then she just kind of fell apart. What I meant was, "Is something wrong with your blades?" But I guess she took it like I was criticizing her. Sometimes mothers tend to say things that they shouldn't.

When she left for Canada [to be with her coach who had moved from California], I wasn't involved anymore, so it had to become her thing. I wasn't in Canada to tell her it was time to get up, go to bed, eat, or whatever. Those were decisions she had to make herself. She was up there for three years before the Olympic Games. You don't know what makes an athlete carry on like that.

Maybe I was crossing the line a little bit when I used to ask her, "Did you do ten triple axels today? Did you land any?" I don't know if that is encouragement or pushing, because there was such a big thing made out of that triple axel. Maybe I wanted it more than she did.

Making Sacrifices

LUCRATIVE PRODUCT ENDORSEMENTS ARE A RECENT DEVELOPMENT FOR KRISTI. UNTIL THESE ENDORSEMENTS WERE OBTAINED, IT COST THE YAMAGUCHIS $10,000 TO $20,000 PER YEAR FOR TEN YEARS TO SUPPORT KRISTI'S ICE SKATING.

• • •

We've had to take out a loan to keep Kristi in this. My husband's never had a new car — well, maybe one. We need new furniture — everything is over twenty-five years old. We expanded our house, and maybe we wouldn't have done that if we had known what was in our future. My husband kept saying she has to cut back, but the higher Kristi got, the more expensive it became.

Maybe my husband wouldn't have encouraged Kristi to keep skating, but I would have. He is the one who has to work and balance the books. Maybe we would have budgeted better. We didn't realize that skating would become such a financial burden, because when you start, your child only takes a lesson once a week. Then you start going twice a week. Then it's three times.

It just builds, and meanwhile your family is growing, and your expenses are growing as your children get older. We've known families who have gone into debt, mortgaged their home, and then the kids quit skating.

———

KRISTI'S SUCCESS HAS BROUGHT FAMOUS PEOPLE INTO THE YAMAGUCHIS' LIVES. THE WEEKEND BEFORE OUR INTERVIEW, FOR EXAMPLE, YAMAGUCHI AND HER HUSBAND WERE INVITED TO WATCH THE SAN FRANCISCO 49ERS GAME FROM THE OWNER'S BOX. STILL, LOOKING BACK, YAMAGUCHI WISHES SHE AND HER HUSBAND HAD MAINTAINED THEIR EARLY FRIENDSHIPS.

. . .

There has been a big gap [in our lives] because we got so involved with our kids' activities. We were not able to attend our friends' gatherings, so after a while we weren't invited. My husband had a group of friends that he graduated dental school with, and we used to all have dinner together and go to the Civic Light Opera. We lost all of that.

Parents have to try to maintain their own identities although you get so busy with your kids. All parents lose that for a while: you go to soccer games or whatever with your son, so this group becomes your social group. You tend to forget about your own friends.

Now that things are slowing down a little bit, we are kind of lost socially. We've lost touch. We heard from a lot of them after the Olympics—nice cards and greetings and things—but when I look back, we should have tried a little harder to maintain our friendships rather than letting all of that go because our kids and/or we were too tired.

Simple Rewards

———

YAMAGUCHI TAKES GREAT PRIDE IN ALL HER CHILDREN'S ACCOMPLISHMENTS. IN KRISTI'S CASE, IT'S NOT THE WORLDWIDE FAME OR LUCRATIVE ENDORSEMENTS SHE'S EARNED. IT'S SOMETHING SIMPLER.

· · ·

One of the biggest gifts is that I see my daughter as a role model—the younger kids look up to her. That's really special—more than anything else. The money is nice, but it is not comparable to seeing a bunch of kids' faces light up when she comes into a room. That's the biggest reward.

———

Rene Russo

. . .

SUPERMODEL

$\mathcal{B}$UILDING SELF-ESTEEM

. . .

Beauty comes in all sizes — not just size five.

ROSEANNE ARNOLD

Of all the people in this book, it was the most difficult to schedule an interview with Rene Russo (age thirty-eight). We traded telephone messages and didn't even talk person-to-person for almost six months. At one point I had given up, but when a friend's wife said she'd be very interested in reading Russo's hindsights, I started calling again.

Russo's career as an actress keeps her extremely busy. You would probably recognize her from the movies *In the Line of Fire* with Clint Eastwood, *Lethal Weapon 3* with Mel Gibson and Danny Glover, and *Freejack* with Mick Jagger. In spite of her high profile, Russo has chosen not to be blinded by the illusion of happiness created by Hollywood glitz. Instead she leads a quiet existence that allows her to appreciate life's simple pleasures.

Before she became an actress, Russo was one of a handful of models who commanded fees of thousands of dollars per day and posed for world-renowned photographers such as Richard Avedon and Francesco Scavullo. She appeared frequently on the covers of *Cosmopolitan* and *Vogue*. Other models of Russo's era include Beverly Johnson, Kelly LeBrock, Cheryl Tiegs, and Christie Brinkley.

Unfortunately, Russo's calendar was so full that we could not schedule a meeting in person. Still, she cared too much about how her hindsights might help young people to decline my request, so she agreed to be interviewed by phone. (This is the only interview in the book that I did not conduct face-to-face.)

Being Discovered

RUSSO WAS DISCOVERED WHEN SHE WAS SEVENTEEN YEARS OLD, AND SHE BECAME AN INSTANT SUCCESS. FROM HER HOME IN LOS ANGELES, HER FIRST STOP WAS

. . .

I had been approached to be a model several times, but I felt that a lot of young women were approached. I never thought I was even remotely attractive, so I never pursued it until this gentleman saw me at a Rolling Stones concert. He got out of his car, came up to me with his wife, and asked me to bring my mother with me and to come to his office.

He set me up with a local agent, Nina Blanchard, in Los Angeles. She signed me right away and sent my book to the Ford Modeling Agency. They sent it to Richard Avedon. He liked my photos, so he immediately told me to come to New York to do some Revlon commercials and ads. It was one of those things that really did happen overnight.

I had no idea who Avedon was and what it meant to do a Revlon ad. Three months later, I was on the cover of *Vogue*. Then I met Francesco Scavullo, who did all the *Cosmopolitan* covers, and he took a liking to me, so I was on more covers. It was fast for me and, needless to say, very scary. I was not prepared for going to New York suddenly and being thrown into all of this. It was a do-or-die situation because I didn't have any self-esteem.

It took me a long time to adjust to it. I don't know how I coped, but somehow I believe our spiritual side drives us when our physical and emotional sides are unable to. At the time, I didn't have a relationship with God, but in hindsight, I realize there was a greater power at work helping me [*laughs*], because left to my own devices, I would have just...who knows?

I never enjoyed modeling, but I am not sure I would have enjoyed anything in my twenties. I really can't blame it on the modeling—there was an interesting paradox: here I am with no self-esteem and thinking I'm ugly, put in a business where I have to be confronted with my looks all the time.

On one hand, I liked the attention because I'd never had it before. On the other hand, I realized the attention was going to be short-lived because the same people who were saying, "Oh, my God, you are the most beautiful thing since…" were also saying, "Oh, have you seen so-and-so? She's thirty now, and she's really not looking good."

I was smart enough to think, "I'm twenty now; let me count on my fingers—how many years do I have left?" So it was a very awkward time because people were giving me attention and reinforcement, which I desperately needed, and yet at the same time I knew it wasn't real reinforcement. I knew it wasn't lasting. What this did was reinforce my wanting to look good when that's not the thing I should have been working on.

———

PART OF THE NEW YORK MODELING SCENE IN THE SEVENTIES WAS HANGING AROUND WITH "BEAUTIFUL PEOPLE" AT PLACES LIKE STUDIO 54, DRINKING, AND TAKING DRUGS. NOT FOR RUSSO.

. . .

I was kind of a loner. When I went to New York, I did my work and then I flew back to Los Angeles as quickly as possible because I was afraid of everything. Maybe this protected me, oddly enough. I went to Studio 54 twice, but I didn't do drugs. That scene wasn't interesting to me.

I know this sounds crazy, but if I smoked pot, it would have made me 25,000 times more paranoid than I already was! Somehow, alcohol just put me to sleep. I think my drug of choice was to stay in my room and not really enjoy life. It was just to be still and quiet and hide—in a way, that was an "abuse."

If there is anything I could do over, it would have been to finish school. There wasn't anything after modeling, so the transition was difficult. There was a period when I wasn't doing anything at all. That was hard. For me, there weren't too many options because I dropped out of high school, so I didn't know what the hell I was going to do.

Building Self-Esteem

———

MOST PEOPLE WOULD THINK RUSSO HAD IT MADE. AFTER ALL, SHE WAS A HIGHLY PAID AND FAMOUS MODEL. SHE EXPLAINS, HOWEVER, THAT BEAUTY AND SELF-ESTEEM ARE NOT AS CLOSELY RELATED AS YOU MIGHT THINK.

· · ·

I never thought I was beautiful, so I needed constant reassurance. I know it sounds strange—you hear about models who are on covers saying, "Oh, I hate the way I look." It was exactly that way for me. I had a body cast on from the age of ten through fourteen, so I was a geeky, skinny kid with scoliosis who had to wear her shoes backwards.

Your image of yourself as a child stays with you long after—even after you're on the cover of *Vogue* magazine. I don't care how many people tell you that you're beautiful or how many covers you're on. If you don't believe it—if you don't have any belief in yourself—it doesn't matter. The only real self-confidence I got was through other people helping me along this very painful process, but ultimately I had to feel it myself. You can't be told you're beautiful and believe it.

For me, it has taken years of therapy. It's taken a lot of time. My mother was basically abandoned with two kids and no money. It was very hard for her because it was a day and age when pay for women was terrible. I saw her struggle. I don't know how she did it. She gave up her life. She didn't pass down a lot of self-esteem because she didn't have much herself.

———

AS A MODEL, RUSSO RECEIVED FAN MAIL FROM WOMEN AND GIRLS WHO WANTED TO LOOK LIKE HER. TO THEM, OUTSIDE APPEARANCE WAS WHAT MATTERED, BUT THEY HAD BEEN MANIPULATED BY MEDIA IMAGES.

. . .

I've had young girls write to me asking how I got my hair a certain way and which products they should use. Advertising can be very destructive. I won't say that about all advertising, but a large percentage of it says, "You need to look like this, and if you don't, then it's not OK." It puts young women and men in these horrible little boxes.

As I grew older and understood the complexities of it, it was harder and harder for me do certain kinds of advertising. It's just sad, because beauty to me is individual. Advertising focuses on just the outside, ignoring what's inside. Some advertising and fashion is evil, frankly, because it robs people of who they are, their individuality, and, ultimately, their self-esteem.

I've worked with what the business considers the most beautiful women and men in the world, and I can tell you that on the inside, they were insecure, lacking in self-esteem, and unhappy—I include myself in this group. Whether you have large breasts, small breasts, or big lips, God put you together in a way that works. You can take this and use it and make the most of it. To me, self-confidence is what is most attractive, no matter what outside appearances are.

Women are thrown back and forth. The sad thing is that women will be taking the collagen back out of their lips when big Twiggy eyes and thin lips are back in vogue or be wishing they'd never gotten huge breasts when the waif look returns. I know people may read this interview and say, "Well, that's easy for her to say—she was on the cover of *Vogue*." I understand that, but there were plenty of things I would have liked to have changed about my body. I'm not saying that cosmetic surgery is bad—just that it's important not to be influenced by every wind of fashion that blows through.

The Modeling Industry

THOUSANDS OF YOUNG MEN AND WOMEN ASPIRE TO BE MODELS. THEY, AND OFTEN THEIR PARENTS, ARE ATTRACTED BY THE MONEY, GLAMOUR, AND FAME THEY THINK A MODELING CAREER WOULD BRING THEM.

• • •

A lot of mothers and fathers, for good reasons, think their daughter is very, very beautiful. They spend a lot of money getting pictures and doing these modeling schools because the daughter wants to model. You don't need to spend one dime on photos until you are signed with an agency, and at that point they will set you up with the proper people.

These modeling schools that you go to and these photographers who want to take your picture and promise you things—it's complete bullshit. The best thing that you can do is go to a reputable agency, and they'll be honest with you. There are many, many, many beautiful women, but they may just not have the height, may not have what it takes at that time, or there may be too many women like them at the agency.

A lot of it has to do with how you photograph. I have worked with a lot of women who would walk into a room, and you would not even know that they were models, but when they're in front of the camera and the make-up is on and the light hits their face in a certain way, it just works. I have also met women who are extraordinarily beautiful in person, and they just don't photograph well.

Fashion is always changing. In the fifties, you had big-breasted, bigger-boned women. I was very waiflike, and in the seventies that happened to be the style. Thank God, because they wouldn't have looked at me twice in the fifties. In the eighties, a bigger, more athletic kind of fresh, healthy look came into play. At the end of the eighties, it was back to the fifties—bigger-breasted. That's why half of the nation went out and got breast implants. Unfortunately, in the nineties we're now going back to the waif look. You can't win.

The chances of becoming a Cindy Crawford or a Paulina are so slim that you really have to think about what you're going to do after modeling or if you don't succeed. Believe me, you're lucky if you get a five-year ride from modeling. Even if you model until you're twenty-seven, you've got your whole life ahead of you, so I would strongly suggest that you make what you're going to do after you're twenty-five, twenty-six, or twenty-seven your number one priority.

———

AT THE TIME OF OUR INTERVIEW, RUSSO WAS FIVE MONTHS PREGNANT WITH HER FIRST CHILD, SO I ASKED HER IF SHE HAD A DAUGHTER, WOULD SHE WANT HER TO BE A MODEL.

• • •

I've thought of that. If I had a daughter, and if she wanted to model, and if she were able, I would help her to understand that modeling is a way to make a lot of money in a short time, it's a way to see the world, and it can have a lot of positives, but the pitfalls can be deadly.

I would not send a fourteen-year-old girl over to Europe, because a lot of them are going over there and being completely abused sexually, emotionally, and every other way you can imagine. I would probably want my daughter to wait until she was older — seventeen or eighteen, at least — and I'd hope that she would have sense enough to see through the bullshit.

Fame, Fortune, and Joy

———

RUSSO, BY MOST PEOPLE'S MEASURE EXCEPT HER OWN, IS FAMOUS.

• • •

It's funny, but I don't feel that most people are relating to me as a model or actress. Most of the people I know and work with just know me. I've never thought of myself as Rene Russo, movie star, or Rene Russo, model. I don't think I come off that way, so when I meet people, they are immediately confronted with who I am, not what I do.

I wouldn't even know who the Hollywood crowd is, to tell you the truth. I have friends in the industry and outside the industry. I would just as soon be inside my house, make a nice meal, and have a couple friends over. I don't go out a lot. I don't go to too many parties because I find that I really like more of a one-on-one or an intimate group.

———

THEN HOW DOES RENE RUSSO, ACTRESS, WIFE, FORMER MODEL, AND SOON-TO-BE-MOM DEFINE JOY?

• • •

Joy for me is finally being able to define boundaries for myself—which I had never done before. In other words, letting your yes be yes and your no be no, and not feeling guilty or bad about any of it. There is a wonderful scripture that resonates within me that says that any door the Lord opens, no man can shut, and any door the Lord shuts, no man can open.

I love that I don't feel at the mercy of people. I don't feel at the mercy of a producer to guide my career or to say no or to say yes— or at the mercy of ratings. It's a partnership with me and God. I'm not saying I can sit back and God will just pour favors down on me. You've got to work hard. You've got to cast your bread. You've got to get up every day and plan your steps and be a partner with God, but I know I'll always be taken care of.

At this point in my life, wisdom is the most important thing. Joy is not always in tremendous amounts of fame or money. Along the way I think, Well, hell, I wanted that part, or I wanted that car, or I wanted that house, yet I know deep down in my spirit that I'll be getting wisdom. There is another beautiful scripture that says that wisdom is better than rubies or anything you could wish for.

Finally, I've always been the type of person who focused on negative things. It's possibly just part of my melancholy nature — maybe it's part of my old programming from childhood. I have to — and it's a daily battle — focus on my blessings. Before I go to bed, I have a good-news report.

I say out loud, "What happened today that was wonderful?" And I answer, "I had a beautiful lunch with a girlfriend out on my patio," or "Those roses were gorgeous." No matter what it is, I ask myself, What are the little things that were blessings or really beautiful that happened in my day?

———

Toshio Akabori

...

SUSHI CHEF

$\mathscr{M}$AKING A HAPPY HOME

. . .

I'm in favor of liberalized immigration because of the effect it would have on restaurants. I'd let just about everybody in except the English.

CALVIN TRILLIN

Toshio Akabori (age thirty-nine) is the owner and chef of a restaurant called Tokyo Subway in Menlo Park, California. His restaurant is on Santa Cruz Avenue, right off El Camino Real (about fifty yards from Kepler's bookstore). My favorite dish is his ginger chicken—teriyaki chicken is only for tourists.

Akabori is from Tokyo, Japan. He moved to Guam in 1976 to work for the Hilton Hotel. In 1978, at the age of twenty-two, he moved to St. Louis, Missouri, to become a chef at Benihana. Akabori returned to Japan for a brief period to get married. After a year, his wife was able to get a visa and move to the United States. He and his wife moved to northern California in 1980. Five years later they bought Tokyo Subway.

People frequently ask Akabori why he doesn't open another restaurant or franchise Tokyo Subway. He tells them that he's found his happiness and doesn't want any more money—or aggravation. He simply wants to spend time with his wife and two children. His story is about knowing when enough is enough and what really makes a person happy.

Our interview took place in his restaurant between the lunch-hour rush and the dinner rush. Akabori cut vegetables and mixed sauces as he talked. His English may not be good, but his hindsights are, as the British say, spot on. I chose not to introduce each of Akabori's hindsights with a paragraph of explanation—this is the only interview like this in the book—because he says it all.

Small Is Beautiful

I always wish to someday have business because my father had a business. I have one sister and three brothers in Japan—everybody have restaurant business. That's why more easy for me. I'm youngest kid in the family, so always I see what they doing.

When I started, we don't have any money. My wife is pregnant, and my daughter is only two years old. We spend all when I started. I ask my wife because I know she has some own money—*naisho hesokuri* [secret money]. So I ask her, and I got from her some money.

When we started, I'm so afraid. At that time, I don't know business, but just try. We have lots of problems. We argue, and she cries lots, "Why we start business like this?" When I start, it was so hard, but little by little I make it, and I'm getting a lot of regular customers. I feel very much confidence later.

My business grow, grow, grow. Now I don't worry too much about my business. I never, ever expect a big business, but I like to keep going this way. Some people don't care about food—just want to make business grow. But I cannot do that because I've been too long chef.

I was never thinking of a big restaurant because I know how many people I can handle. I don't plan to use another chef, and I don't want to do that way. I know U.S.—not only U.S.—is people problem, employee problem. If I want to do quality food, then I don't do big restaurant. If I do big restaurant, I have to use other chef. Chefs always quit. If they quit, I have to train another. If too big, I cannot control. But if small, I can control more easy myself.

Defining Success

We already talk what important for us, and of course, business important. Make money important. But more important thing is the family. So what is compatible for the doing business? My restaurant serves five lunches, five dinners. Usually restaurant seven day open. Now Sunday all day and Saturday lunch and Monday dinner I can enjoy with my kids.

This much big I can do whatever I want to. Like national holiday, I close for four, five days. And then Christmastime I close. And when I go Japan every other year, two weeks I close. I like to keep my family important to me. I saw many people after business they divorce because too much work and then getting no communication with the family.

I cannot do: "If I can make money, I don't care whatever kind of business." I care about my food, and I care what I'm doing so much. I care very much for the satisfaction for my job, because I don't get satisfaction only for making money from my job.

Money of course important, but more important thing is how much you enjoy what you're doing in life because, especially for men, we have to work forever, because one-third our life we sleeping, one-third our life we working, and one-third our life just our time. If I don't enjoy my work, it means I don't enjoy my life.

For me these days, success is important, but when we become successful, there's many things we have to think. Especially some people have successful business, but don't have successful home— divorce or whatever. I don't want to be that kind of successful.

For me, successful means happiness life—means not money. Of course if I make money a lot and then buy more big house or become rich, then we comfortable, then I don't have to work here. But if successful like that, still I want to work here.

Family Life

If I don't have a good family life, I cannot make successful business, because I'm always worry about my kids, my home. I cannot concentrate for my job, I cannot smile in the front of customers. It's no good. 'Specially like my restaurant is an open kitchen, so mostly people want to see my face and me cooking. If I don't say hello or nothing, no one come here again.

It means it's important people wake up always try to be smile face. It's hard to do it, but I want to try that way every day. Hard to do, but we have to try. Means after, when I retire or seventy, I can say I had a very good life. I try every day smile my face. Means I cannot smile only face—I have to smile from my inside, from my heart. Means I have to have a good life.

If I cannot control my life this way, I cannot be successful in many things. That's why for my mind, family especially important for me—for us. Always we talk about it, and then my wife very much understand my mind, so that's why we can go together.

If my wife push me to make more bigger restaurant or whatever, I have stuck. But she agree with me. Means we always talk what is important for our life. When I was young, I saw one picture like older-people picture—like ninety years or like eighty years old. Picture is very, very interesting: very much good face—like smiling. I don't know what kind of lives they had, but I can tell smiles on face—very, very nice face. Always I wish to be that kind of face when I was old.

I see that kind of face a lot in the country of Japan and in many *nisei, sansei* [second- and third-generation Japanese-Americans]. I know they have lots of hard time, but face is a very, very nice face. I enjoy to talk to them. I don't have to say many things, but they understand because maybe their life hard life or whatever, but I can feel very many warm things from them. That's way I want to be when I am going to be old, I want to be that kind of people. I want to be very warm person. Means important how to live my life.

Understanding Your Spouse

I think if I going to understand my wife, then I need forever. That much. Life is not easy. People is not easy for each other. Almost we divorce, many times. And at that time, I think lots because I'm not this kind person before. More "I want to be myself this way," and she don't like me that way.

We talk and argue and then she understand my mind, my real mind. When people marry, they are like a square. After they are married, they get round, round, round and then fit together. No way from start everybody get together very good. No way. Argue, fight, whatever, then they find out what is good, what is bad. But I feel once you decided to marry to someone, why don't you try your best? Try your best forever. Too easy to give up.

I'm so happy life because of my wife. She know better than I do what is life. She opened my eyes. Before my wife, I not this kind of people. More young because always young guy want to show to how good I am. Always I tell her my dreams: I want to do this, I want to become rich, or I come here U.S. because I want to be franchise restaurant.

I talk to my wife about some dream and then she know. She listen. She tell me, "Tell me...show me more what's your inside. Inside you, I want to see more." Always like I show her outside. I meet many women before her, but nobody tell me that. Young people always want to show how good they are, my dream like that. My wife tell me one time, "You show me just only outside. Why you don't tell me more your weak things?" Because I want to show her how I am strong or whatever, I never want to show her what a weak person I am, but she know it. She tell me one time, and God, I'm so shocked.

After that, I can tell her everything. My bad things, good things, ugly things. I have that kind person in my wife. I'm lucky because she understands lot—my good things, my bad things. We can talk many things for many ways, and I don't have to hide in my mind to her. It's not easy sometimes even wife and husband.

That's always my mind: I don't hide, I try to not hide. I open my heart and then sometimes she angry, but I thought that better way because if we do each other that way, later we know more than before and understand each other more deeply.

———

Index

. . .

$\mathcal{I}$NDEX

. . .

The author most nearly approaches the ideal as indexer.... At the same time, authors are sometimes so subjective about their own work that they are tempted to include in an index even references to milieu-establishing peripheral statements and, as a result, prepare a concordance rather than an efficient index.

CHICAGO MANUAL OF STYLE